Dirt

GADFLY

First published 11 November 2015
by Gadfly Editions

© 2015
Martyn Clark
Mary F McDonough

British Library Cataloguing in Publication Data
A CIP catalogue record for this book is
available from the British Library

ISBN 978-0-9928060-5-7 Hardback
ISBN 978-0-9928060-6-4 Paperback

Design and typesetting
by Martyn Clark
Adobe Garamond Pro 11.5pt
and Helvetica Neue

Additional photography credits:
Benjamin Clark
Daniel McDonough
Stephen Smith (Shiva Sadhu)
Vasilis Tentomas (Syrian refugees in car)
Villy Tentoma Zervou (neon installations)

Artworks reproduced:
Alleluia, *Fingers In Ze Nose*, and *Smile, idiot!* by Zabou
Floor installation by Yiru Feng
Untitled by Konstantinos Gioris
The Rolling People on Hassard Street

www.gadflyeditions.com
www.maryfmcdonough.com
www.martynclark.com

Dirt is a collection of fragments: writing, text messages, emails, poetry, prose, diary entries, iPhone photos and colour. In it, we tell the story of what it means to us to have been ideological refugees; people who have escaped "-isms".

We've woven together fragments of many stories: things we've seen, people we've met, the paradoxical story of us as a couple, and our individual stories—the daughter of a Catholic seminarian who didn't quite make it as a priest, and the son of a Presbyterian minister turned evangelical missionary.

In sharing our stories, we have tried to balance the shame and pain of our experiences with the joy, freedom, and aliveness that we found through embracing our own ways of being, and the insight we've gained into the world around us, and what drives much of the destructive behaviour in it.

To Jonny
and
to refugees
everywhere

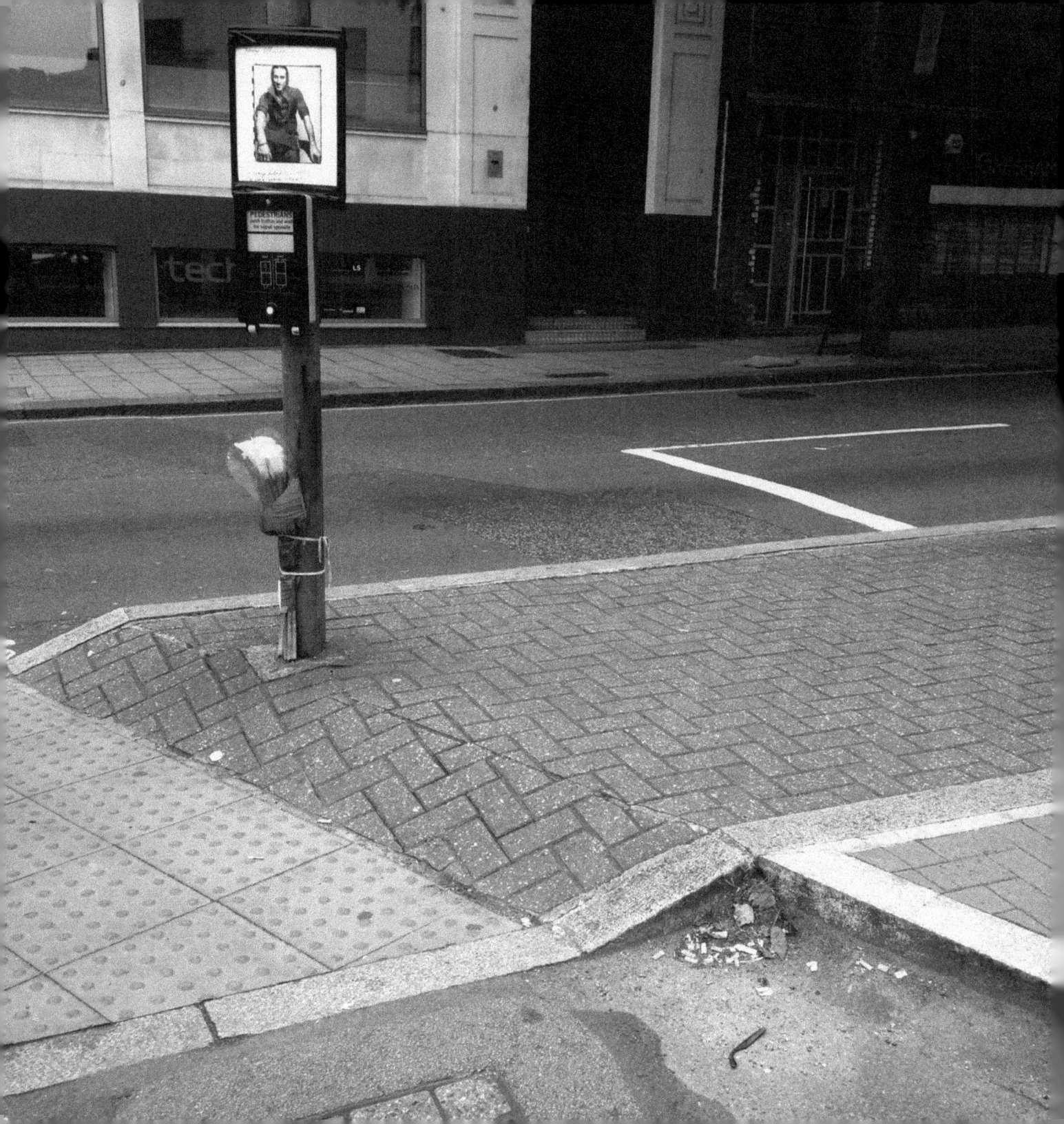

I punish the children for the
shame of their fathers.

                —God

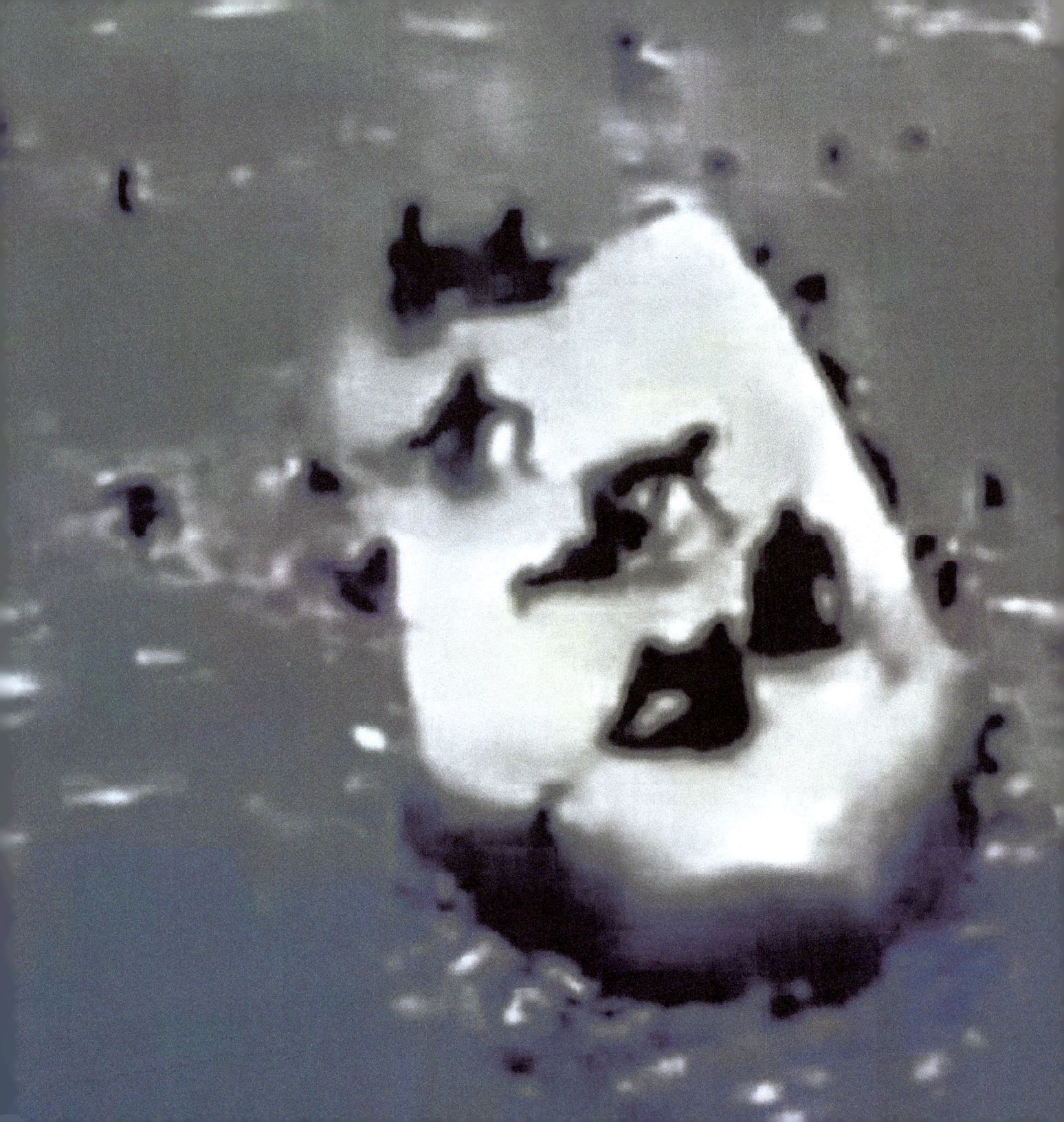

We were all floating, once.
Floating in
cramped twilight, once.

None of us could survive
without others,
once,
without warmth,
food from an other.

No one puts their children in
a boat unless the water is safer
than the land.

— Warsan Shire

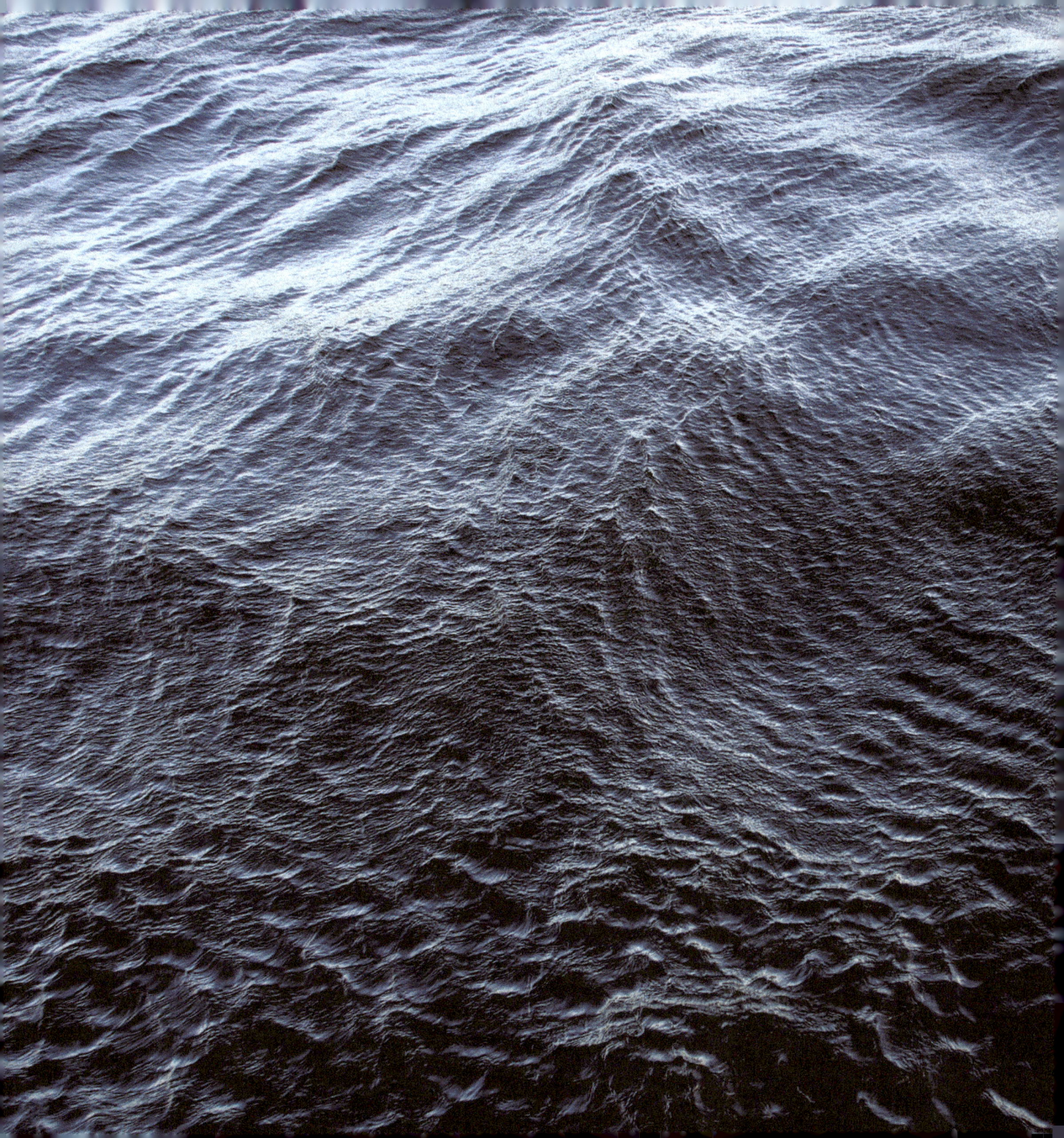

William says she was a princess,
and she's a great lady still—
she doesn't talk,
but I can hear her voice
in my head
all the same.

Mind your manners.
Answer her questions.
Don't cry—
you'll smear your eyes if you do.

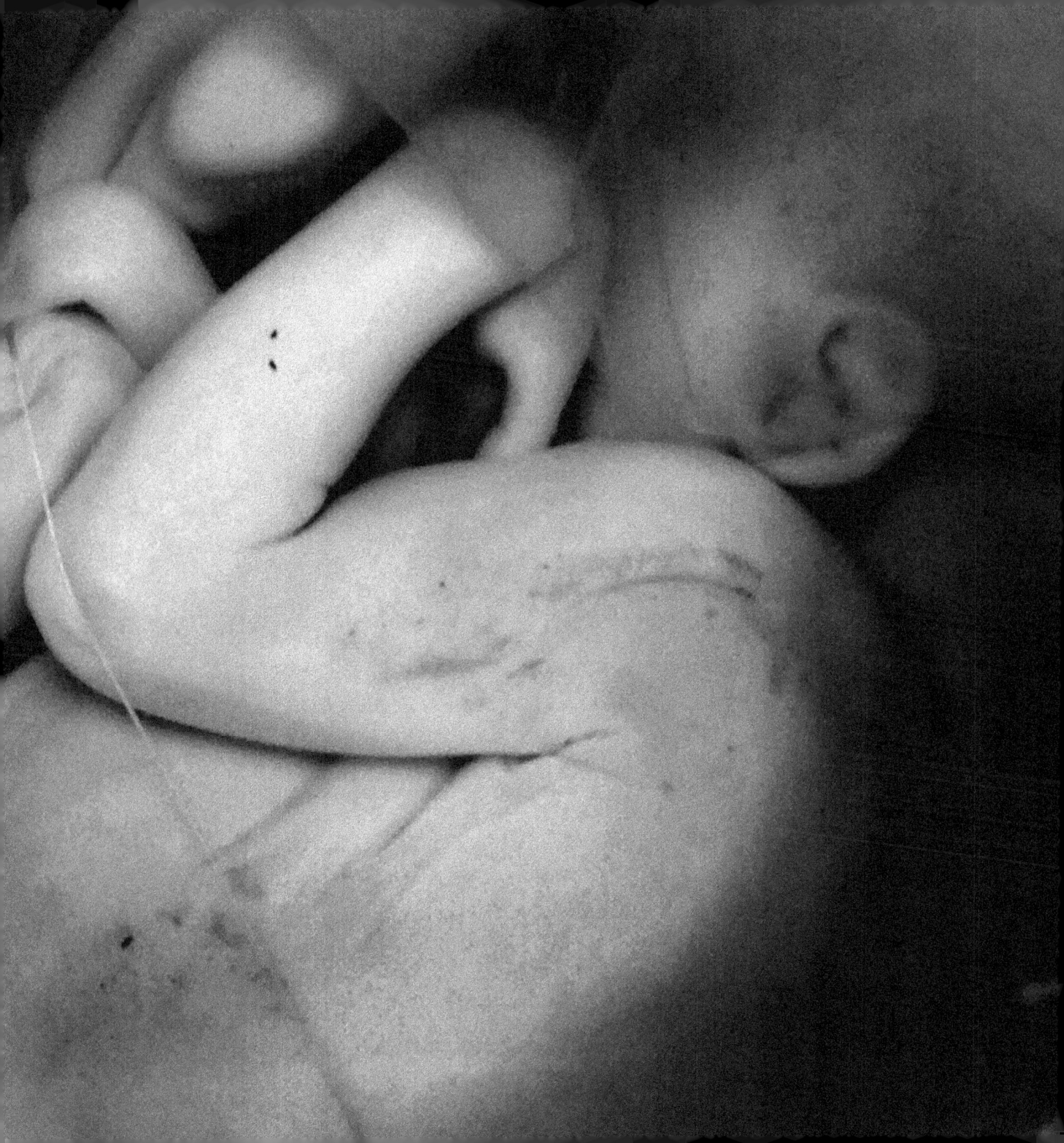

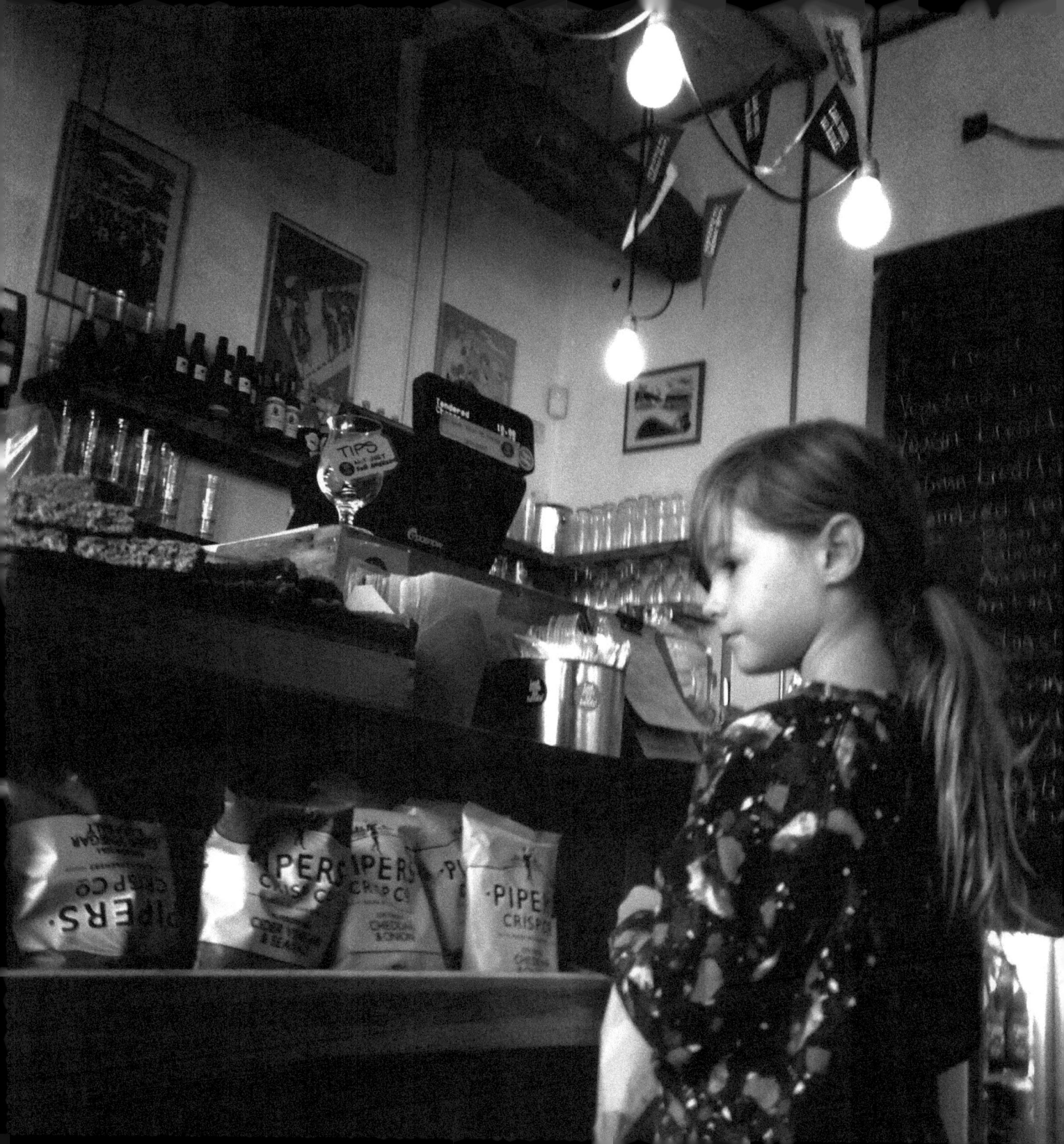

The line of irritable boys swells
outside the church door,
9:25am on Sundays.

Anxious mothers
spitting into Kleenex.
Hovering.
Jabbing hands, hair, faces.

Dirt is the real sin.

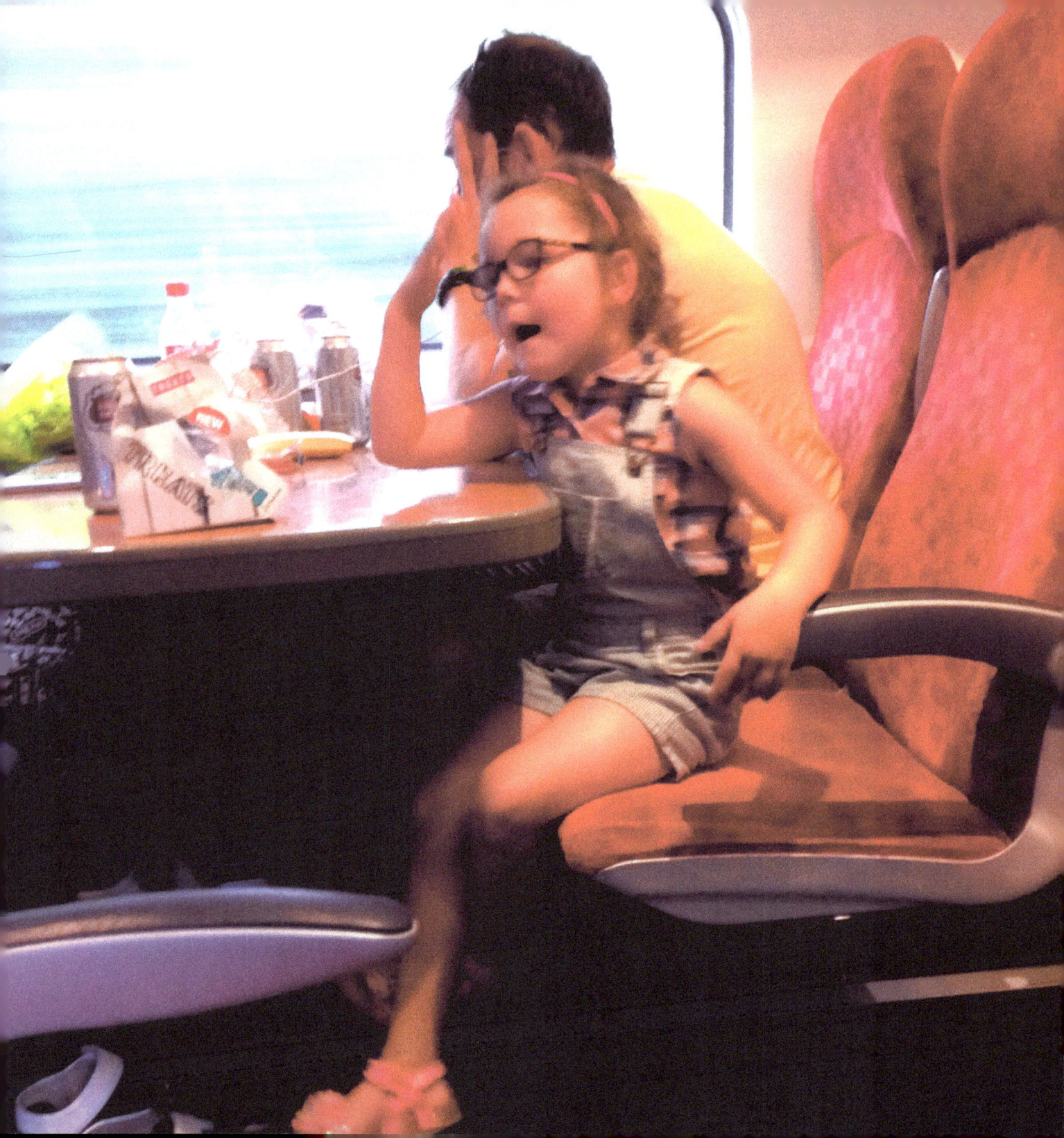

Wriggling. Squirming. Whining. Bouncing.

Are we there yet?

Shhhh! Just sit still!!

But I want another Coke!!!

*I told you. You've had
enough. Put that bottle
down!!*

Give your Dad's phone back!!!

Get back in your seat!!!!

Sit still!!!!!!!!!

Her mother nags her, without effect. She dances
along the aisle, Coke in hand. Shame there's no
adult in her family.

hell if ya
sleep with
anyone.

If you enjoy sex,
you're evil.

Sexy w...
are just...
have your...
It's a ...

Sending
it's a si...

a sensual

Don't
go ...
go

Dab your fingers in.

Don't leave them there for a long time,
or the font will get as dirty as a bird bath.

Remember to use your right hand,
or Sister will hit you.

    Father.

        Son.

            Holy Spirit.

Up and down, then left to right.

Leave Mary out of it altogether.

Au musée

Plaster figures
crumble.
Bones, too.
Time weathers all.

Wood cracks.
Wrinkles deepen
in saints' faces,
as they suffer
asymmetrically.

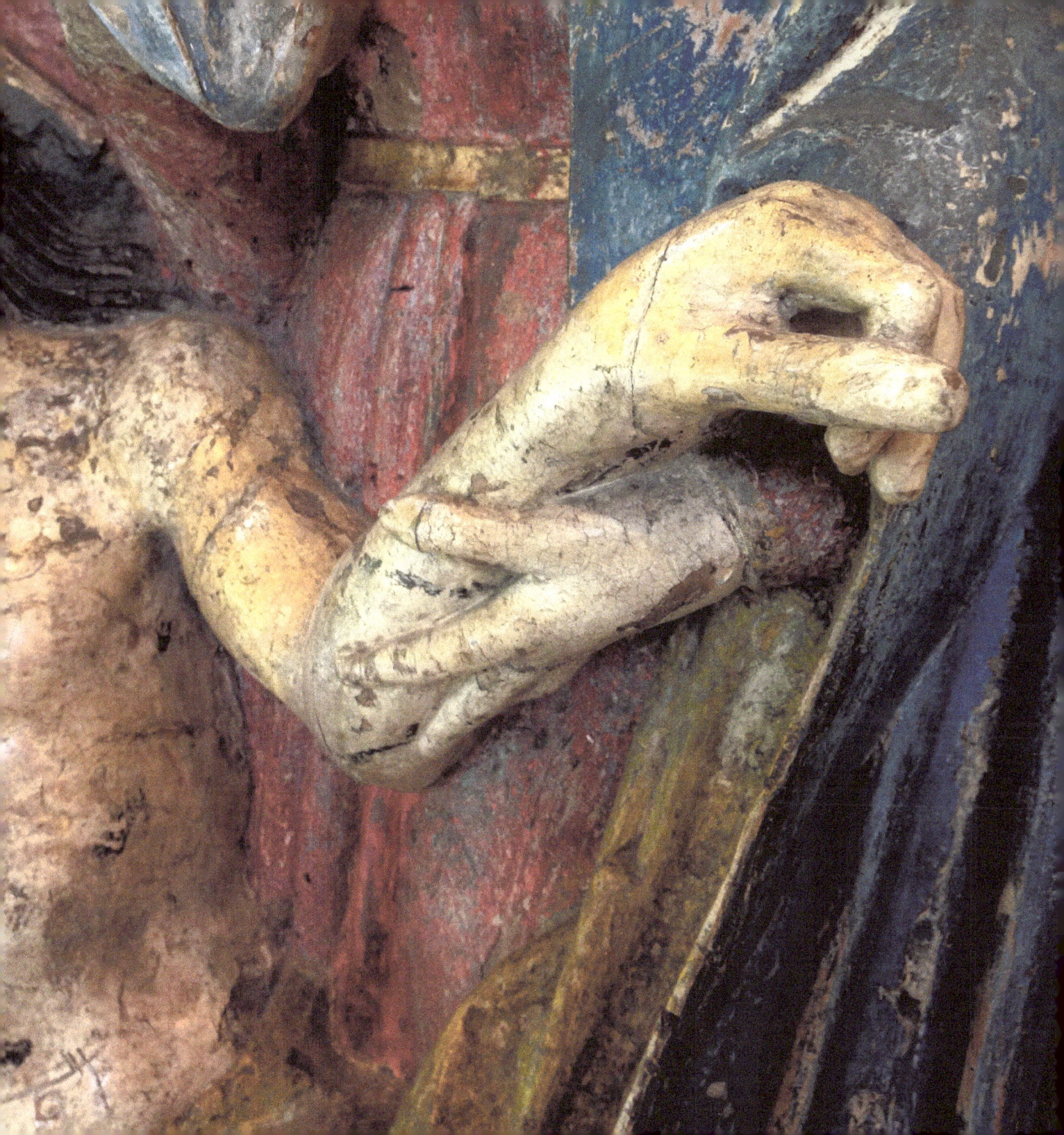

A psych ward, preaching Christ.
United in delusion. Feeling safe,
hiding from the truths of life.

A cosy little bubble.

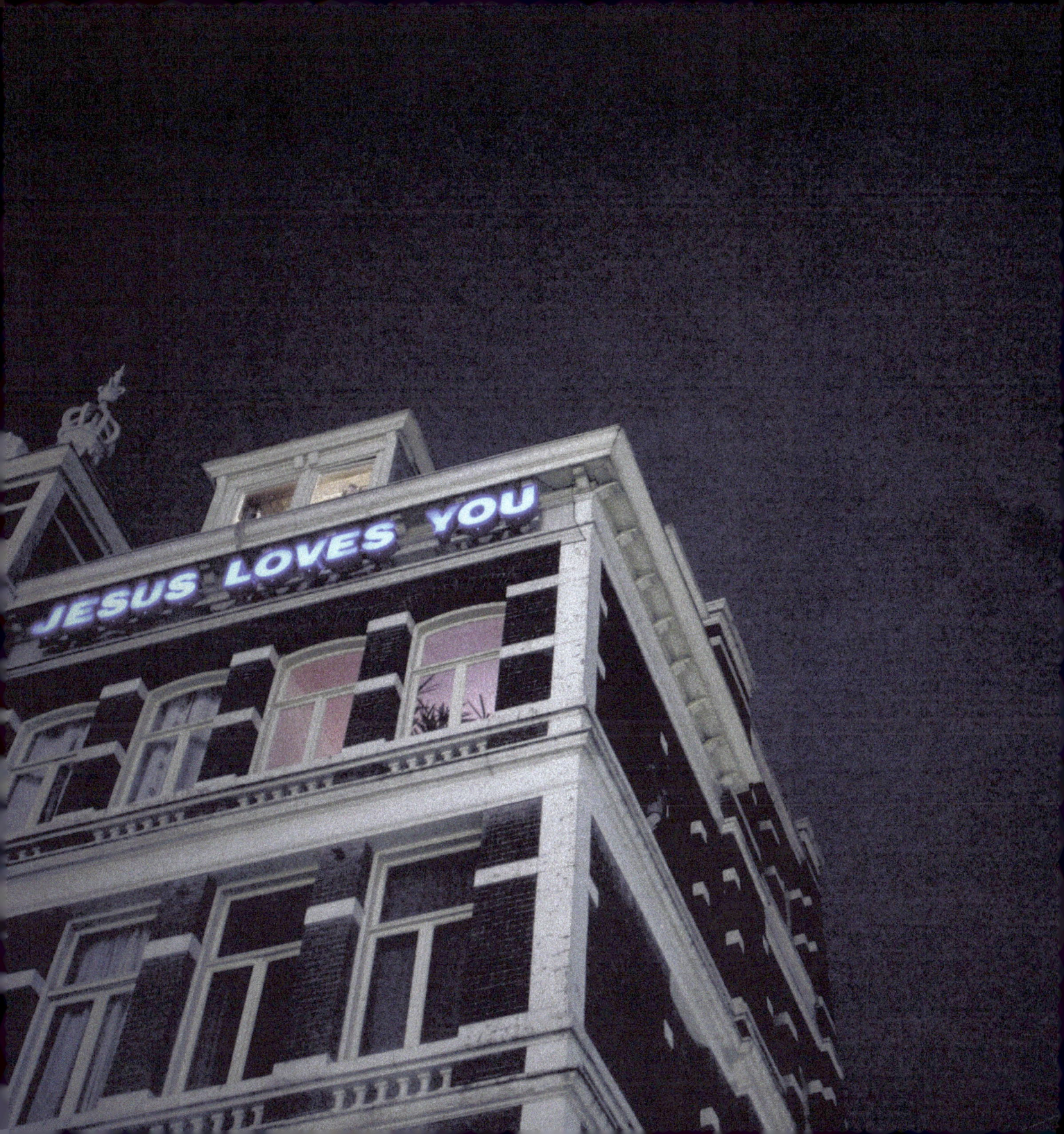

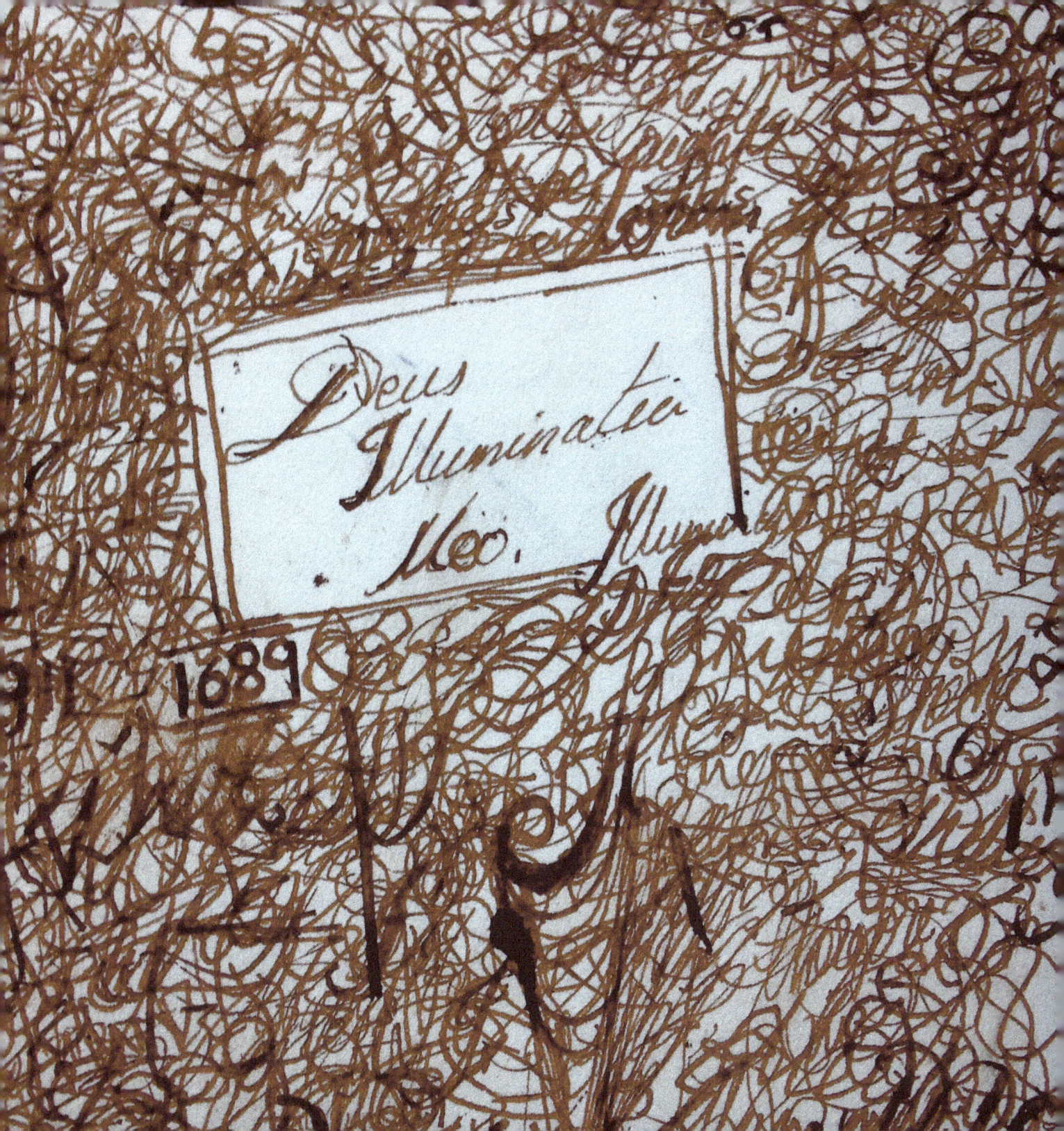

Deus
Illuminatio
Mea.

1689

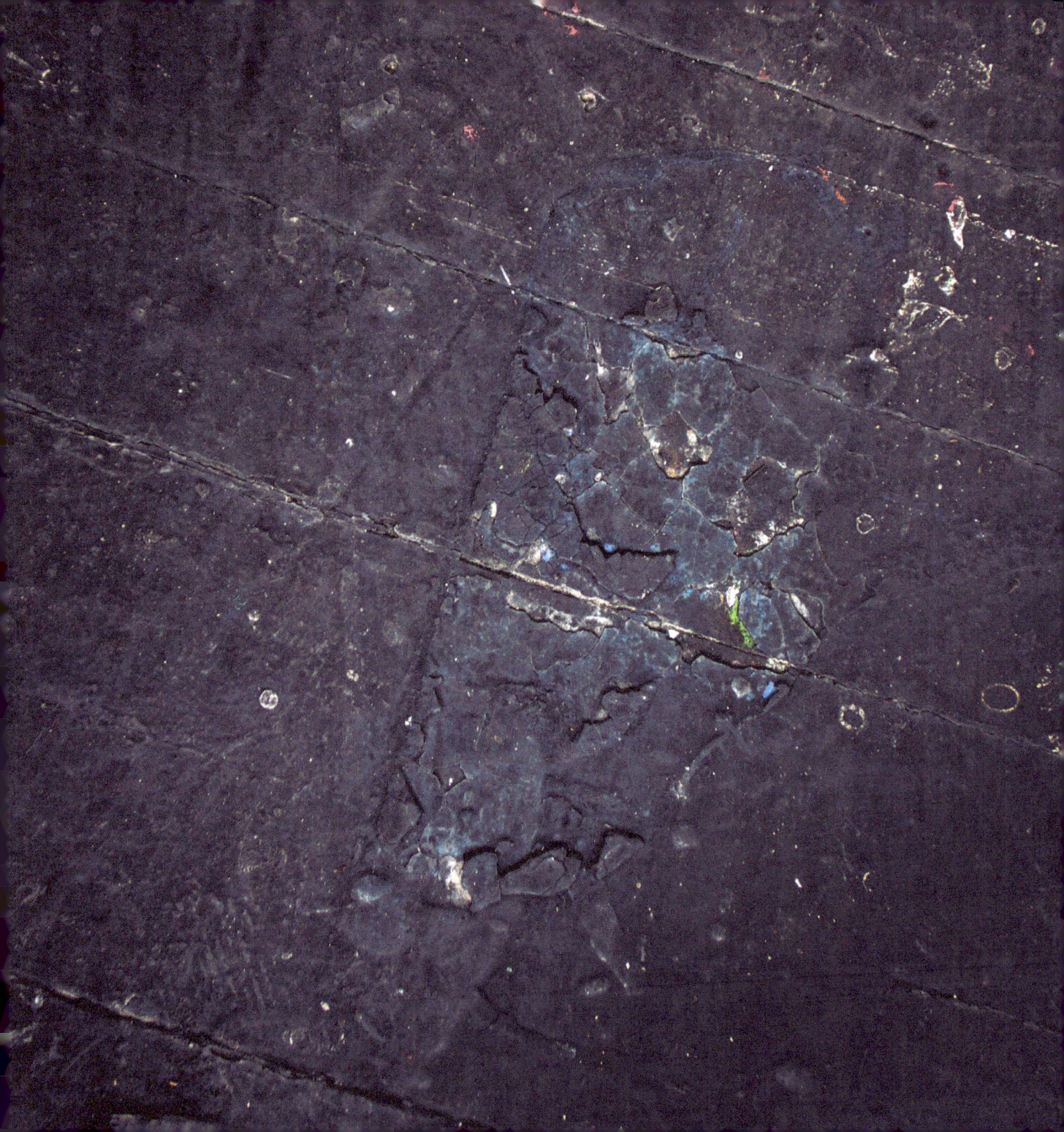

The dirt on me—
I clean up the truth.

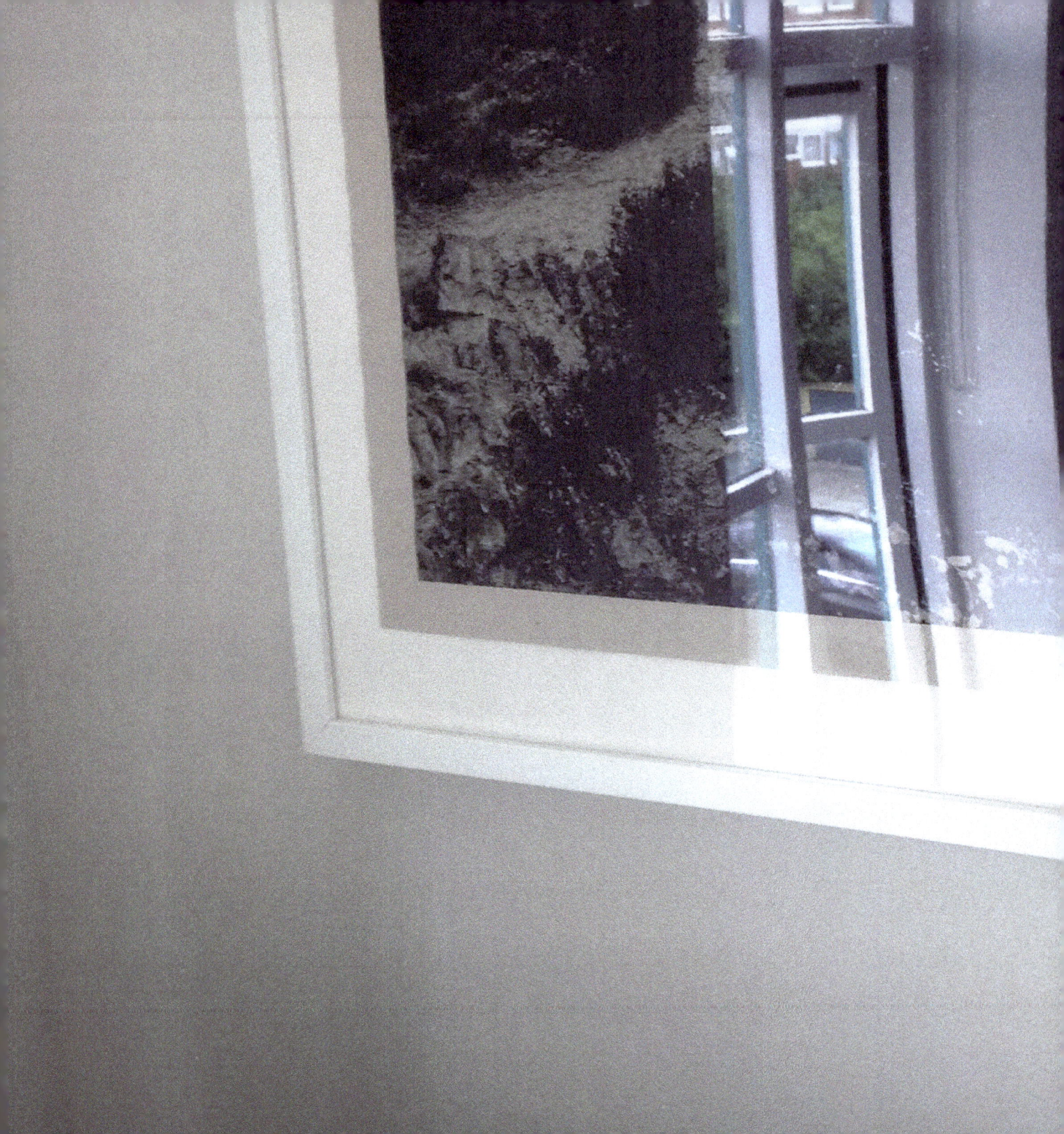

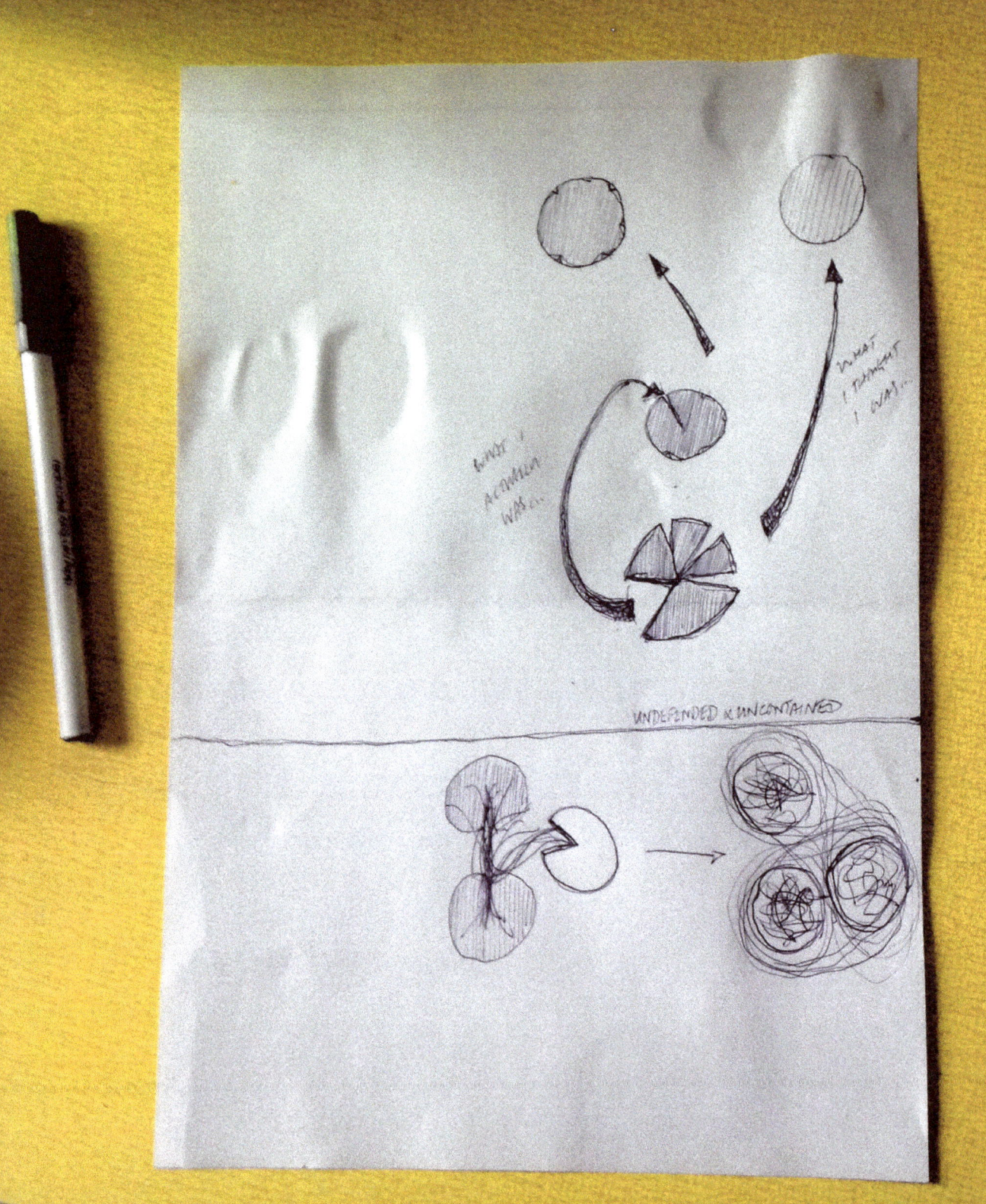

Archaeology in marriage.
Scraps and intentions.
Who can interpret honestly?

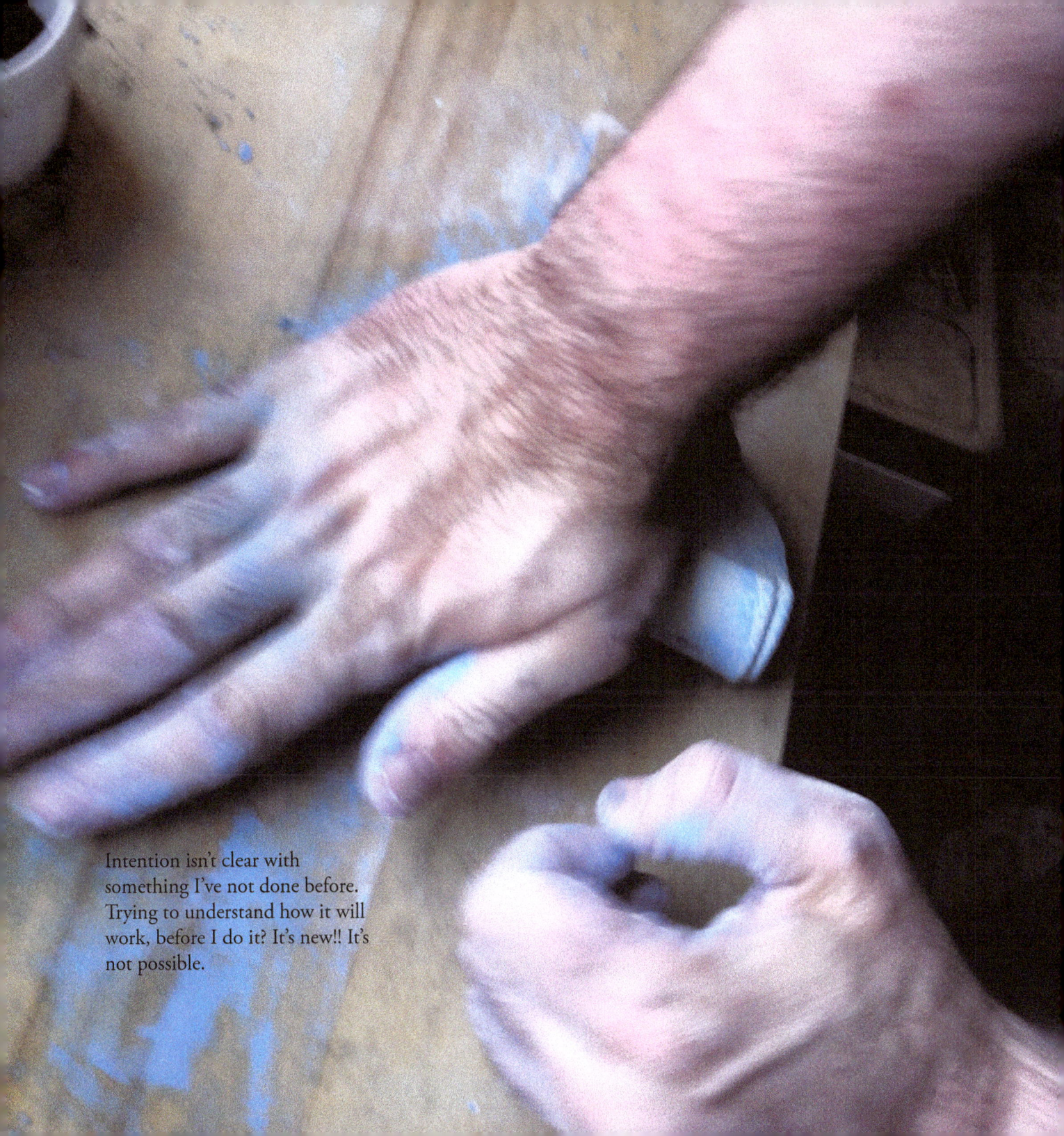

Intention isn't clear with
something I've not done before.
Trying to understand how it will
work, before I do it? It's new!! It's
not possible.

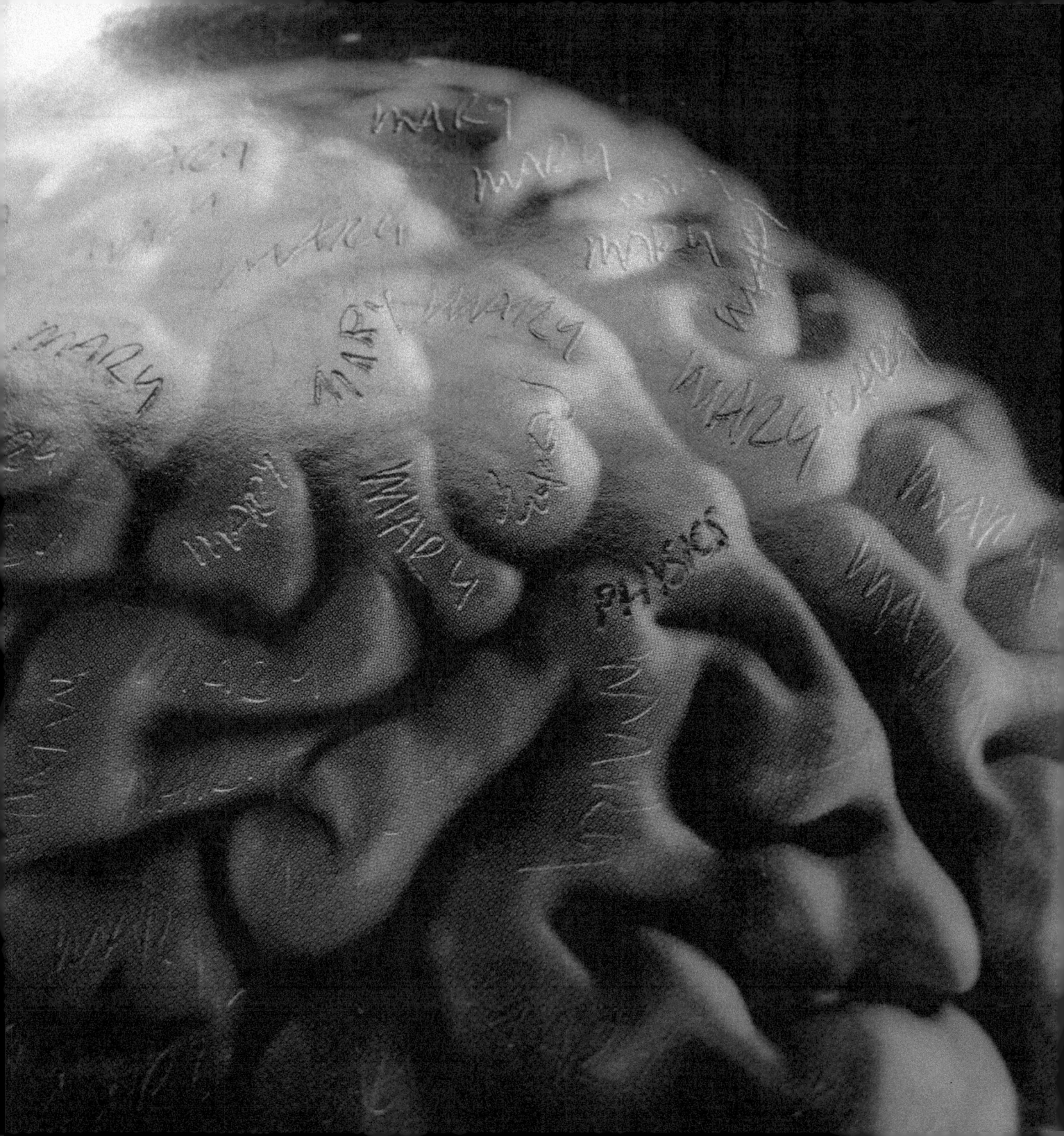

Not for me
the hiss, the flare of the match—
lust is for other women, other
loves.

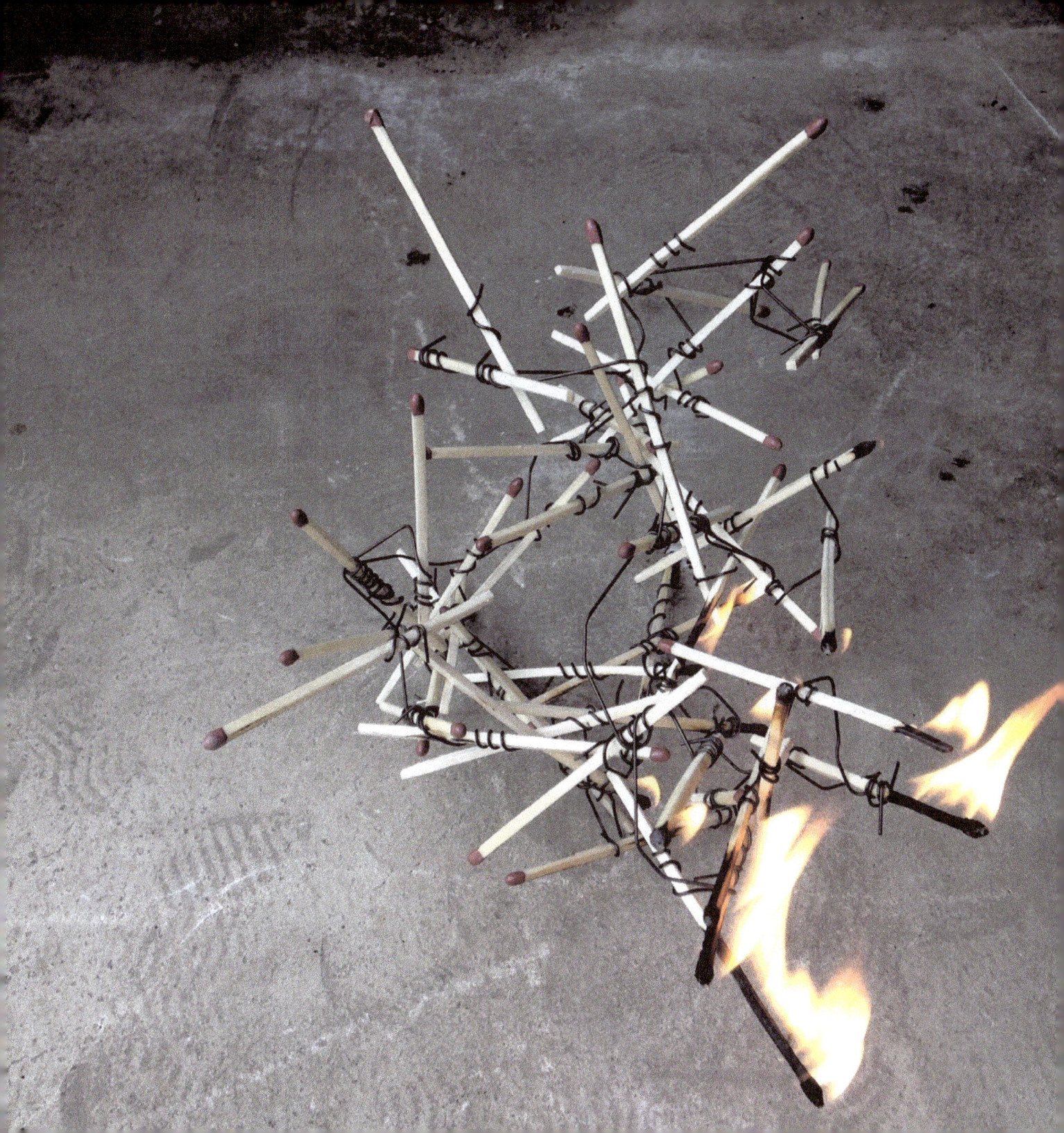

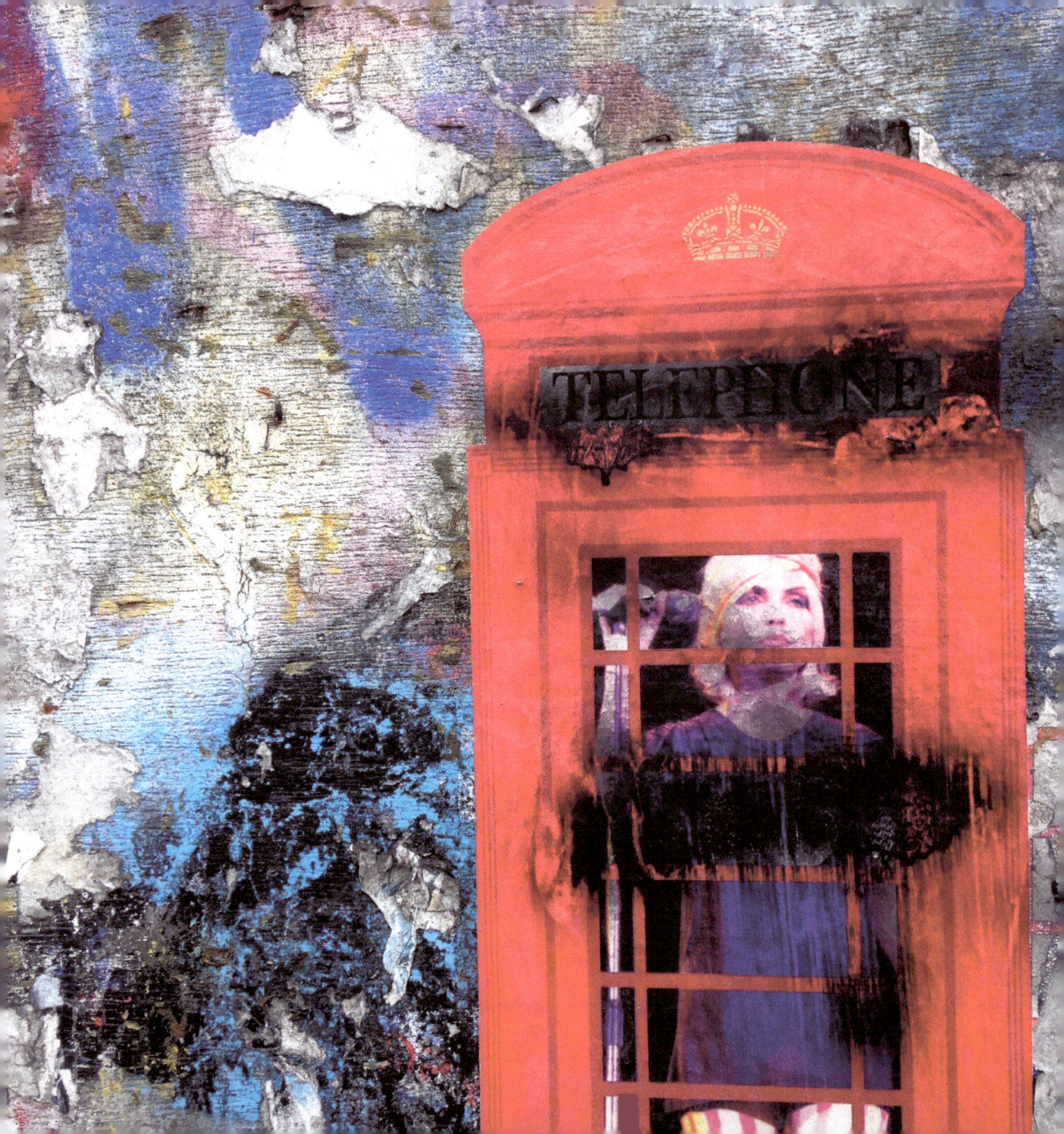

Run with me.
Howl with me.
Feed with me.
Love me.

Or leave.

Perfect kitchen,
broken life.
Perfect house,
girlfriend gone.
Riddled with doubt,
mirror behind the stove.

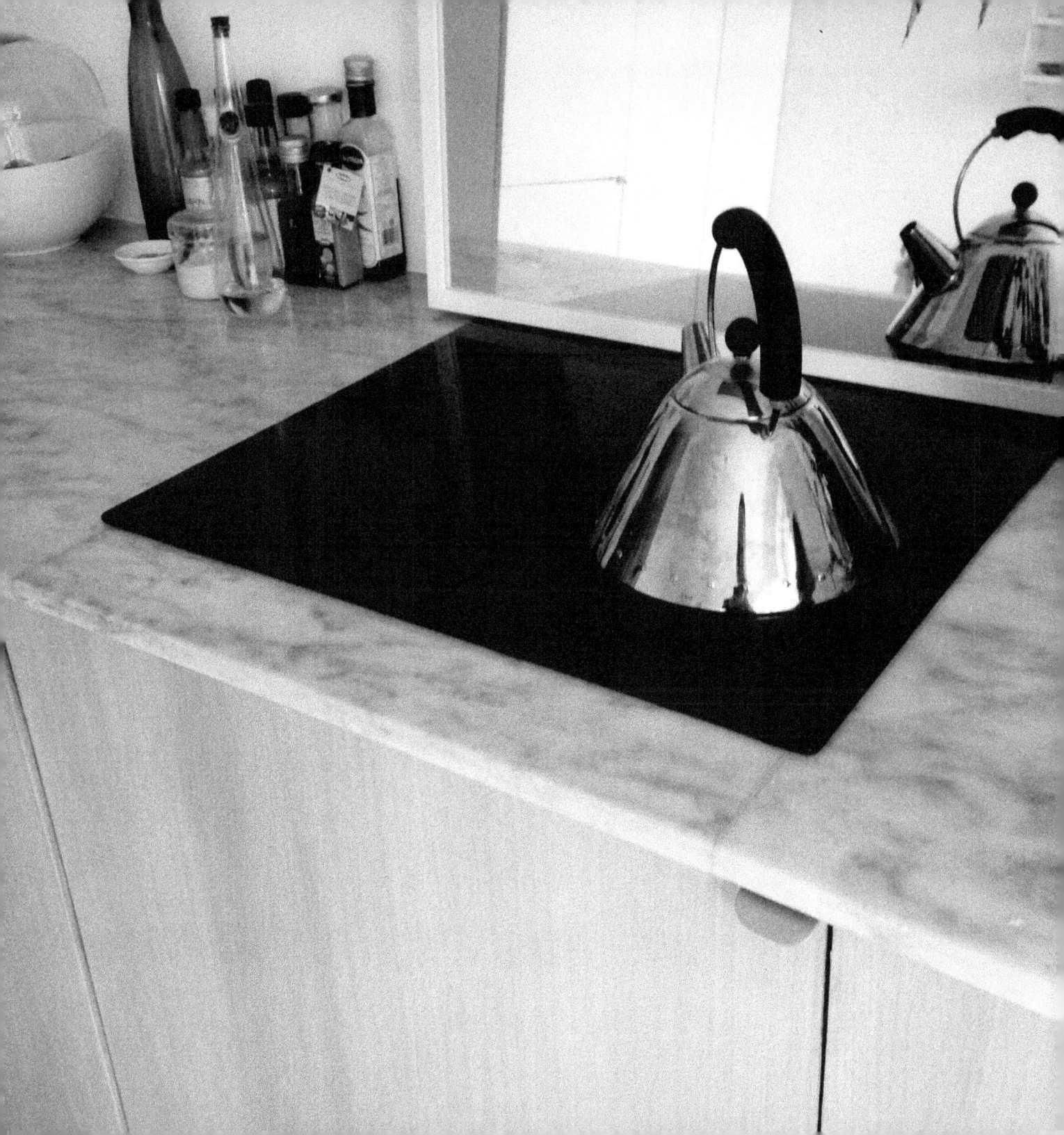

our shame,

your prurience

Bingo.

Two fat ladies.

Day-glo tan.

Lycra is a privilege, not a right.

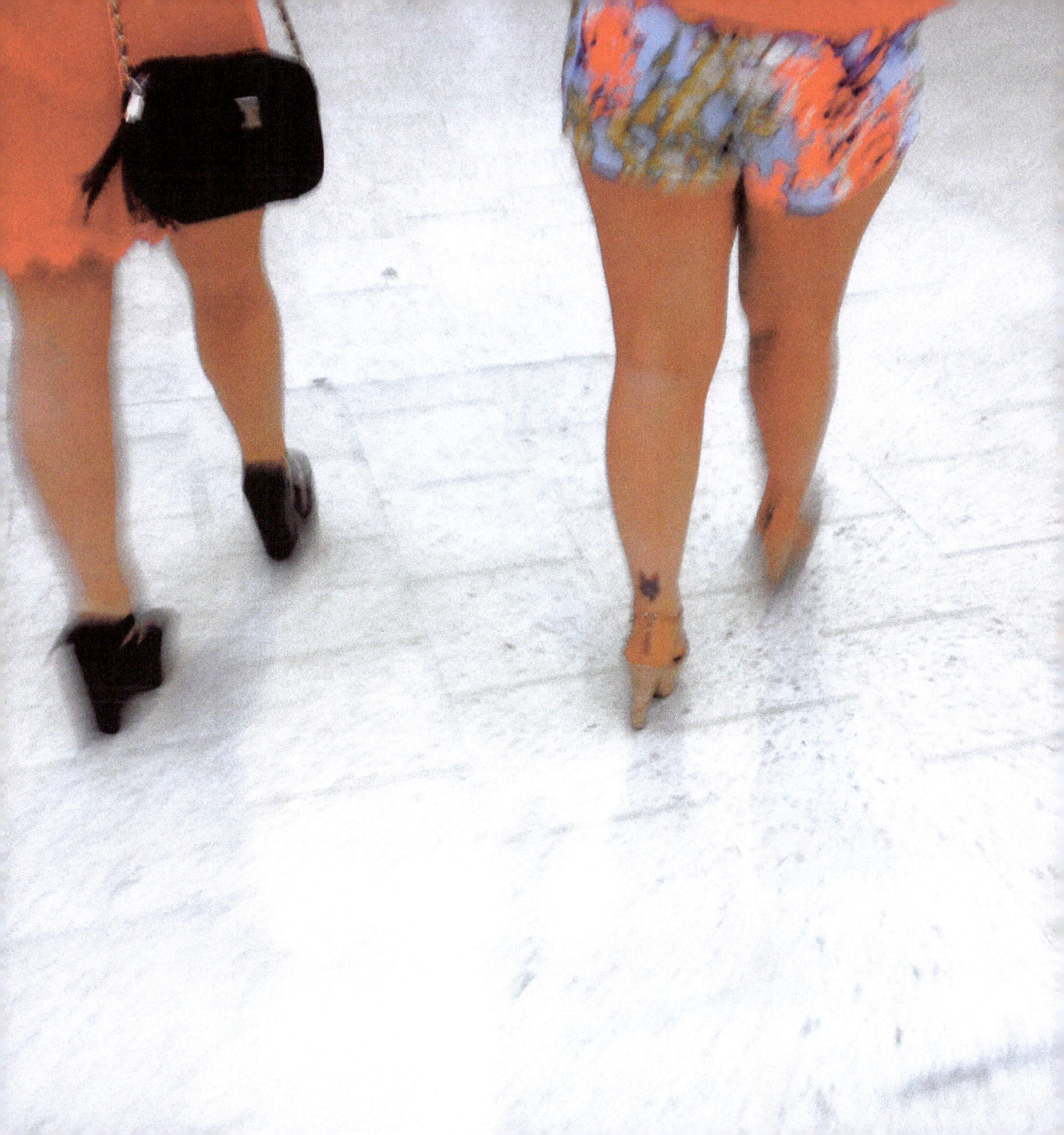

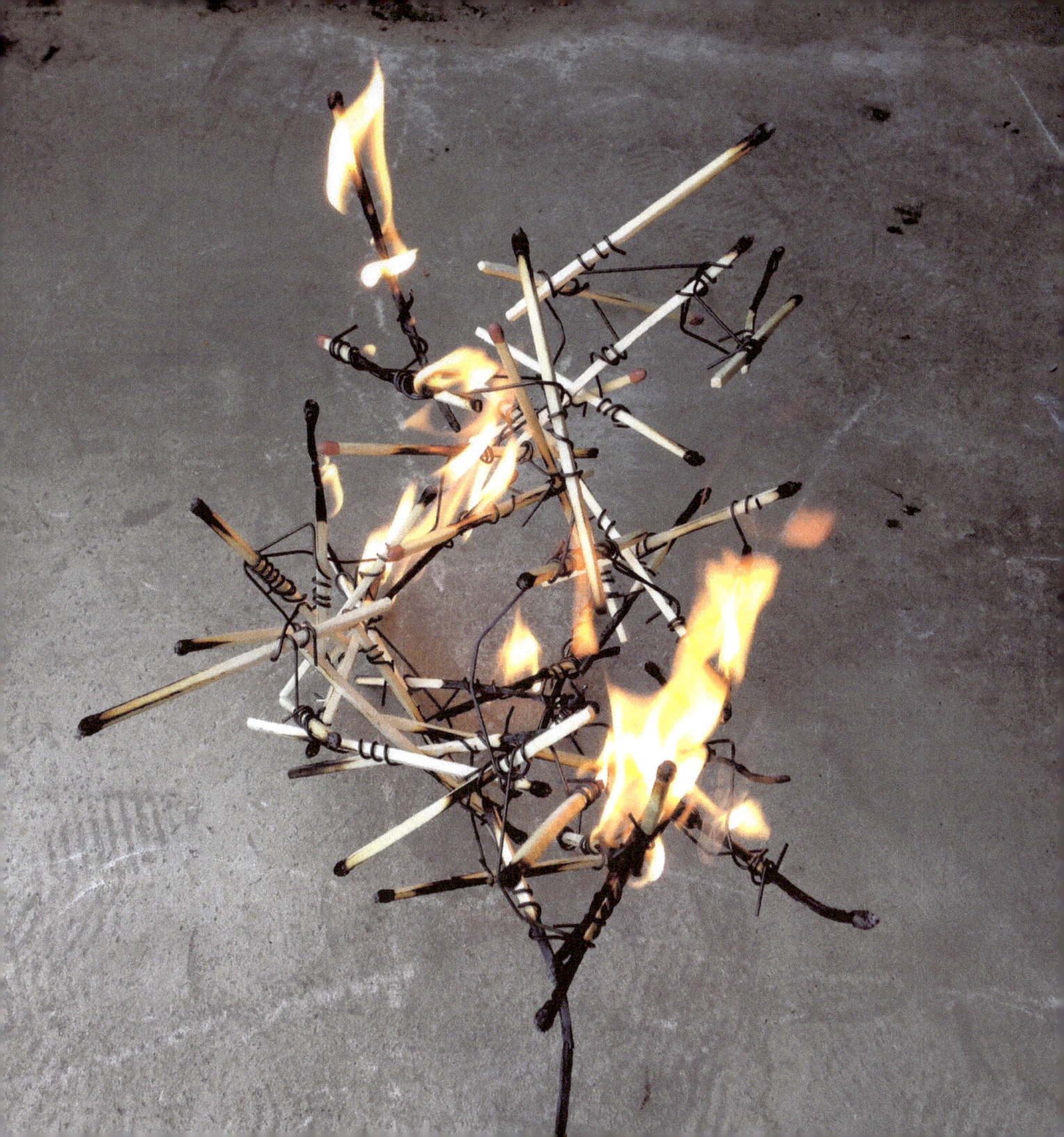

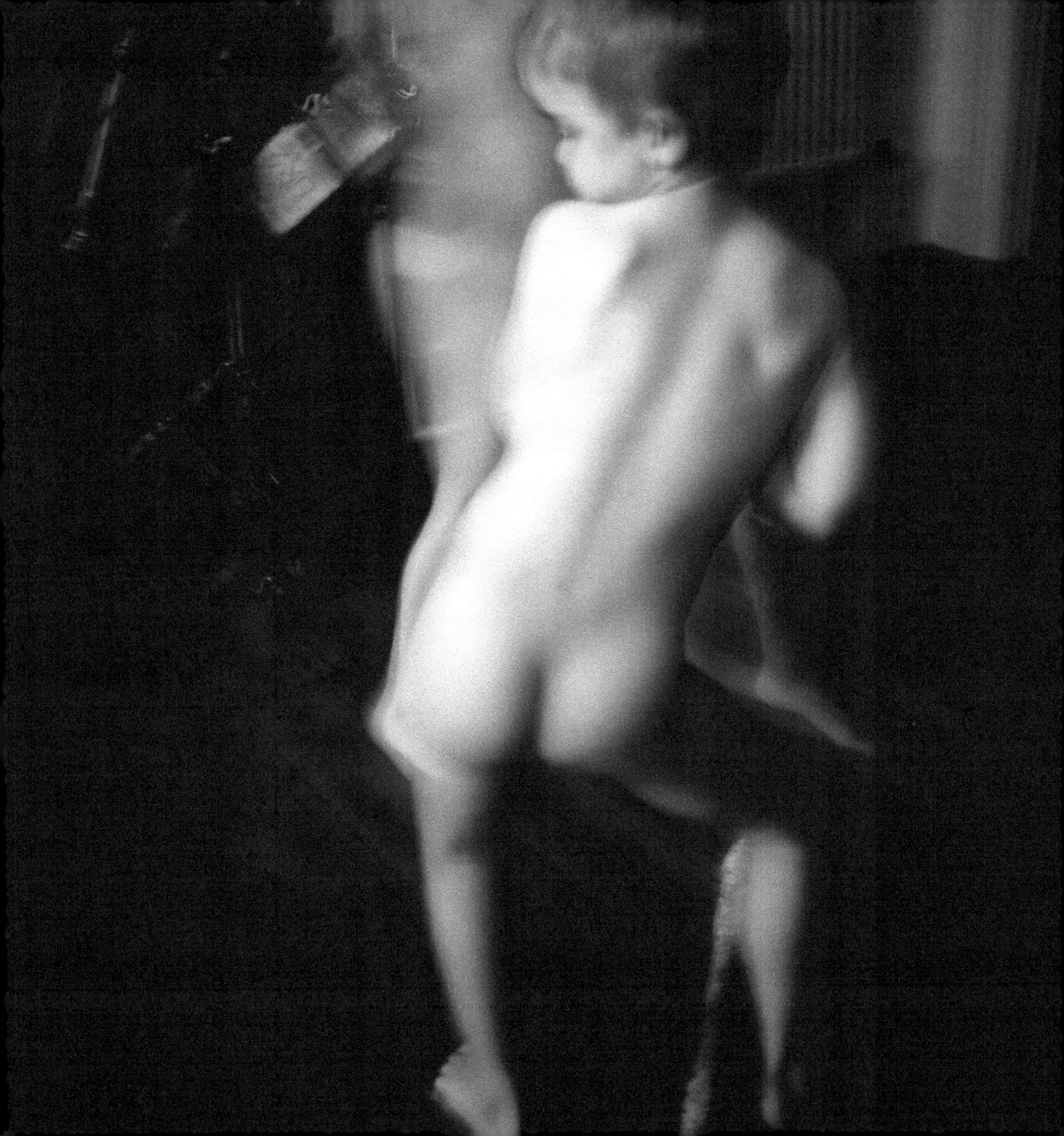

I was feral.
Naked as often as I was allowed—
oftener, really.

No shoes. No shirt.
Climbing,
hanging upside down from branches,
feeling my hair swirl in the wind.

He's always licking his fingers instead of using water, or soap, or a towel. He sometimes just dries his hands on the towel after. I tell him it isn't the same. He says he likes to be *unhygienic*—but what does that even mean? Is that the same as *disgusting*?

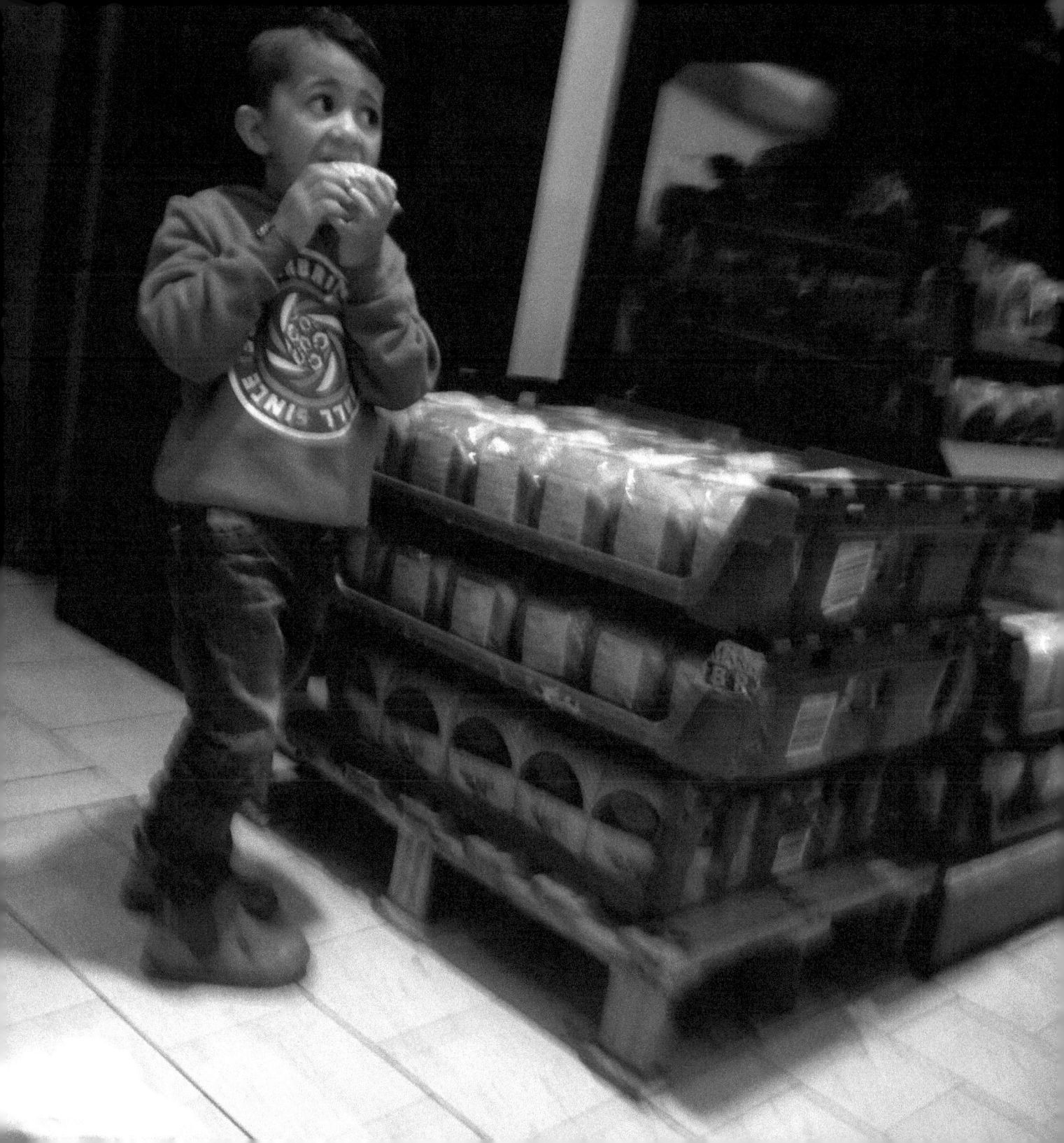

Shame is just shame. Everyone carries some for past generations. The more we avoid it, the bigger it grows.

I'm dancing naked in a stream in the Alps, kicking the water—shrieking when it hits my spine. I stayed outside too long today. My skin is bubbling from too much sun.

Now I'm back inside.

> *Sit still!*
>
> *Don't fidget!!*
>
> *Keep your back straight!!!*
>
> *GOOD people don't move when they're told to sit still!!!!*
>
> *Martyn!!!!!!!*

I freeze, knowing that's what people want. Act like a frightened rabbit. Act like a frightened rabbit. I clench my buttocks, my spine rigid.

> *Oh, that's better!!!*

I remember dancing in the sunshine, the water spray on my face, and I desperately try to not let it show. I shut down my body. Cold. Detached.

> *Oh, You're being such a good boy, now!!*

I want to run, naked, through the woods, screaming, pounding my chest, jumping, twirling, bounding off branches, roaming, marking my territory with claws on trees, playing, fighting with anyone I come across. I sit as still as I can manage. Playing their game. Frightened rabbit. Frightened rabbit.

> > *He has ants in his pants. He never practises.*

My piano teacher. I just wanted to dance the piano to life. Beethoven didn't like dancing, apparently. I don't like Beethoven. Or scales.

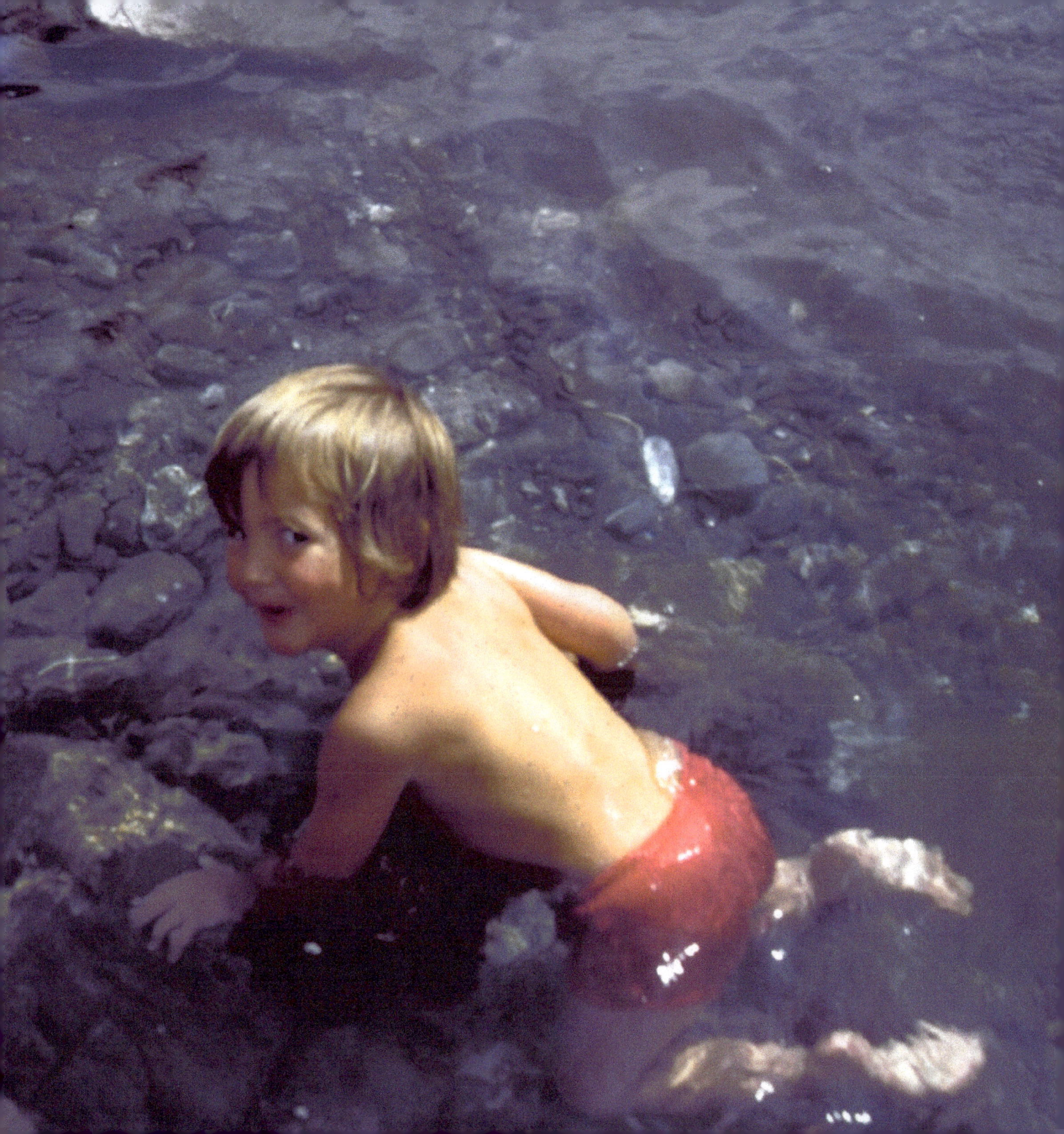

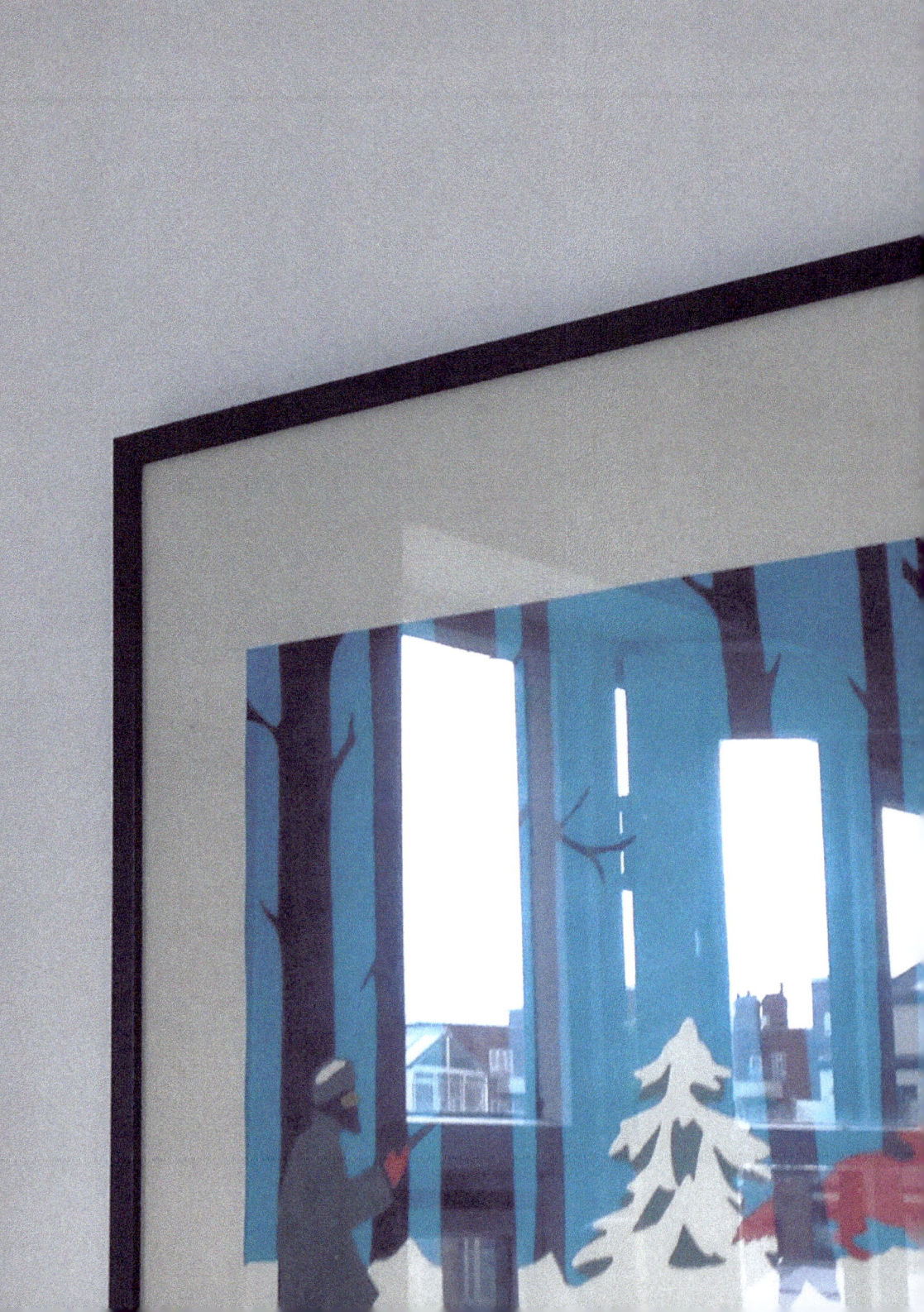

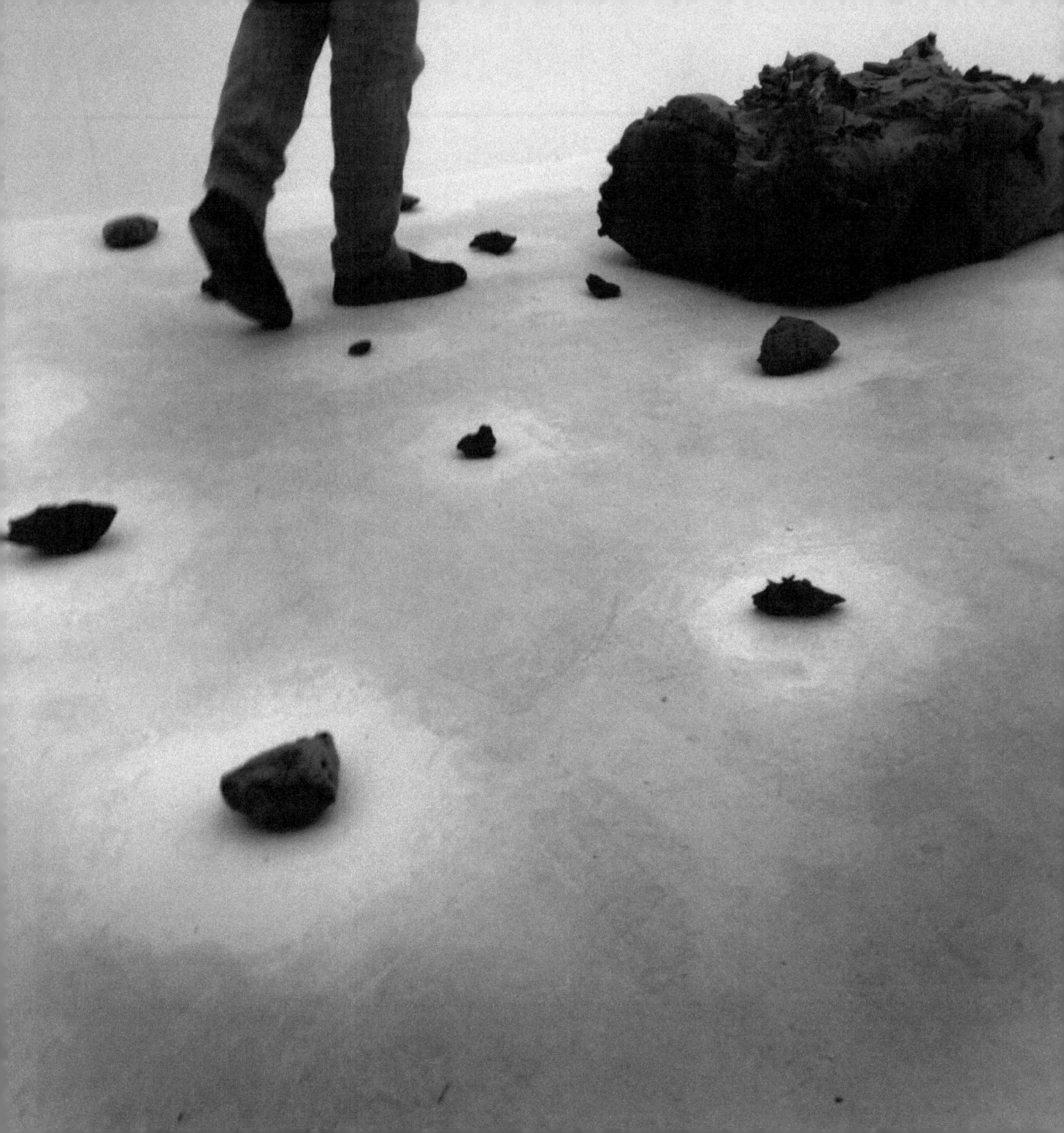

You are speckled.
Every freckle, every
blot of ink on paper, or on your hand,
is a sin.

Do you understand?

Like stepping on lines,
stepping on cracks,
breaking your Mother's back,
sins are things you do on purpose,
leaving marks
you can't erase.

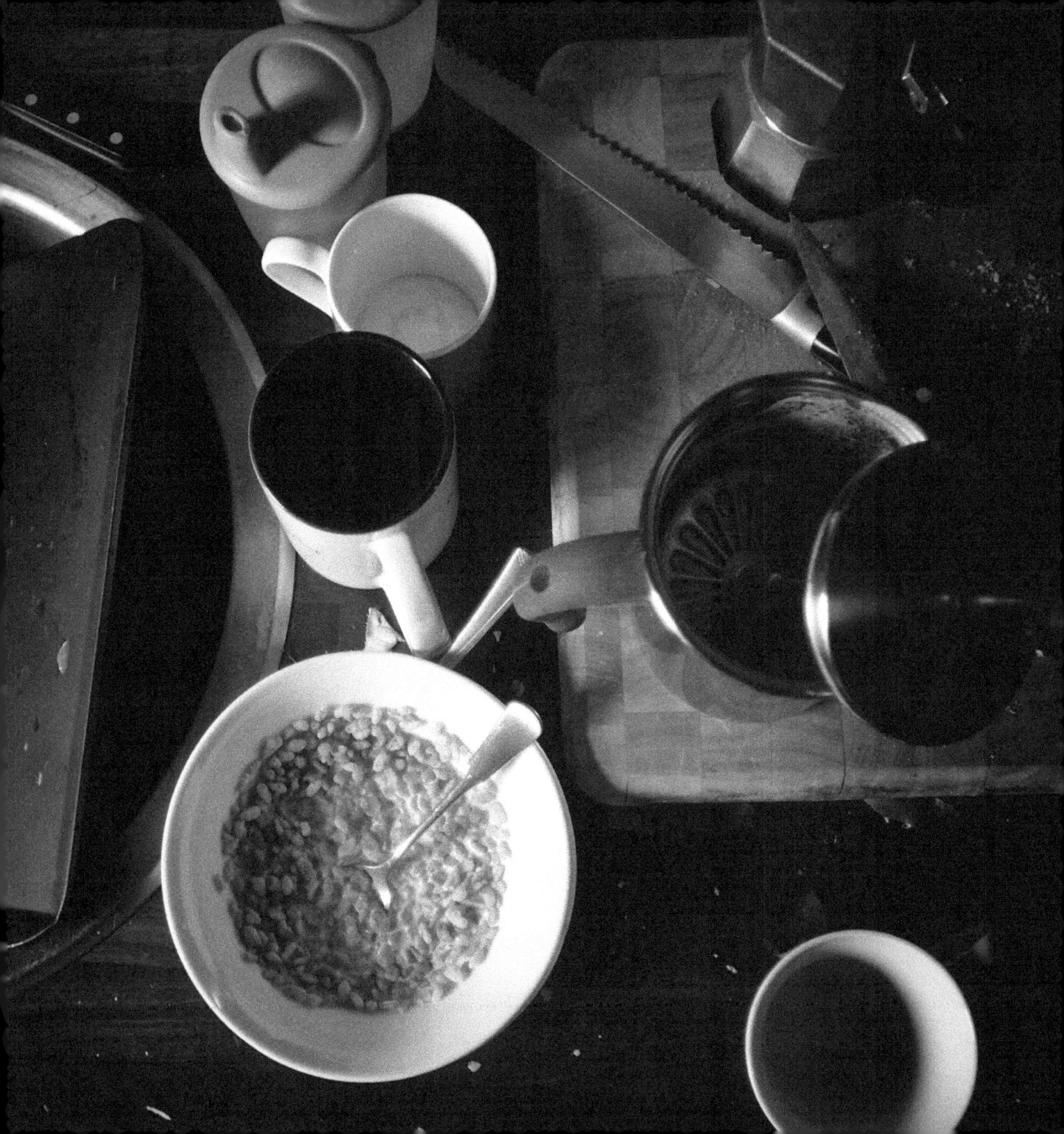

I watch as he slices the skin
from the ginger root.
Meticulous.
Focussed,

I imagine his hands,
but not the knife,
moving down my body
with the same care and precision.

Fuck it. I'll just imagine the knife, tracing
an indentation down my body, never sliding
in. I take a sip of the infusion, and feel the
warmth seep into me, as his eyes devour my
face.

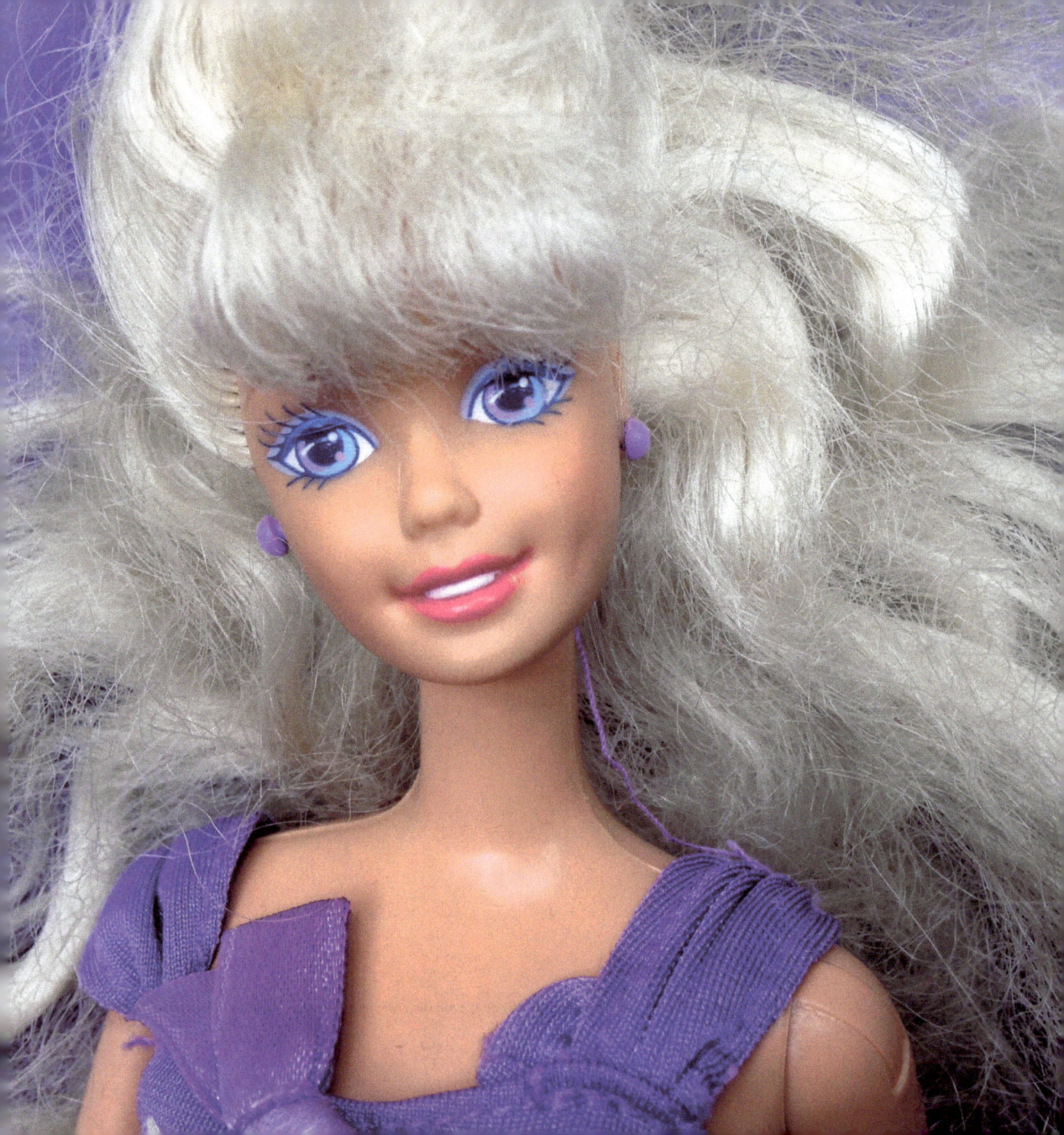

My research?! It focuses on sexual habits and experience in
Scotland after WW2?

Oh. Eem. Eeeeereeem...

Tucks hair behind her ears, removes & resettles her glasses.

Twice.

Shame is a major component of the difficulty of conducting
research about...
            ...se-se-sexual attitudes and behaviours.

Fidgets. Avoids eye contact. Shuffles papers.

I've found euphemisms are very useful in ensuring research
participants don't feel forced to discuss humiliating topics,
like the withdrawal method and eee-eee-ejaculation
outside the female's body cavity.

But who is it, really, who needs the euphemisms?

Naturally enough, none wanted to discuss um
umm
eeem
mastur—
self-stimulation, though.

I'm hopeful men will eventually tell me a lot more about this,
but...ooh. That's not quite what I meant. The thing of it is,
I've not interviewed any men yet.

She buttons and unbuttons the top of her dress,
pulling her cardigan tightly around her.

As for the various methodologies used in preventing
conception, the most popular, prior to widespread availability of
contraception, which most young people seem to have done
without, was withdrawal.

She is pleased. An almost orgasmic flush colours her cheeks,
because she didn't stutter saying 'withdrawal'.

One interviewee referred to it as the 'Haymarket method'
because it was the last... stop, not quite the end of the line,
you understand.

She twists her bracelets around her arm;
her skin is soon as red
as the skirt
which covers her legs
(almost) completely.

Another informant mentioned her mother suggested
that she should keep both of her legs in one stocking,
metaphorically locking boys out.

Which isn't really PRACTICAL, is it?

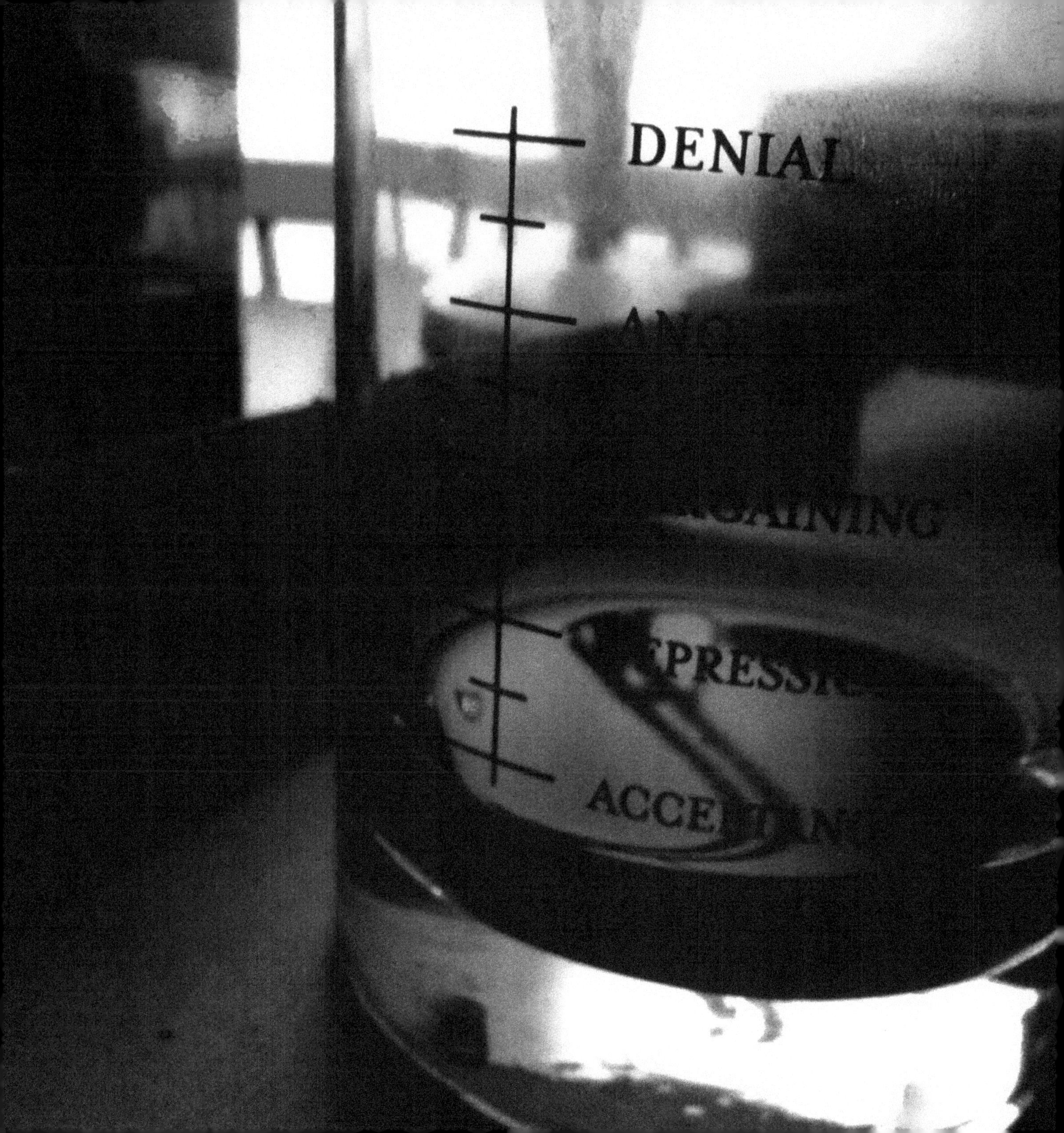
DENIAL

I felt so imperfect, that I couldn't relax and enjoy life. Hollow. Fragile. A rusting statue, crumbling inside.

I didn't let myself feel it. I tried to be perfect, rejecting humanness and animal instinct. I resisted relationship, connection, love— anything to feel better about myself.

In therapy, I became a perfect client. A perfect shell. Nice. Attractive. Elegant. Broken.

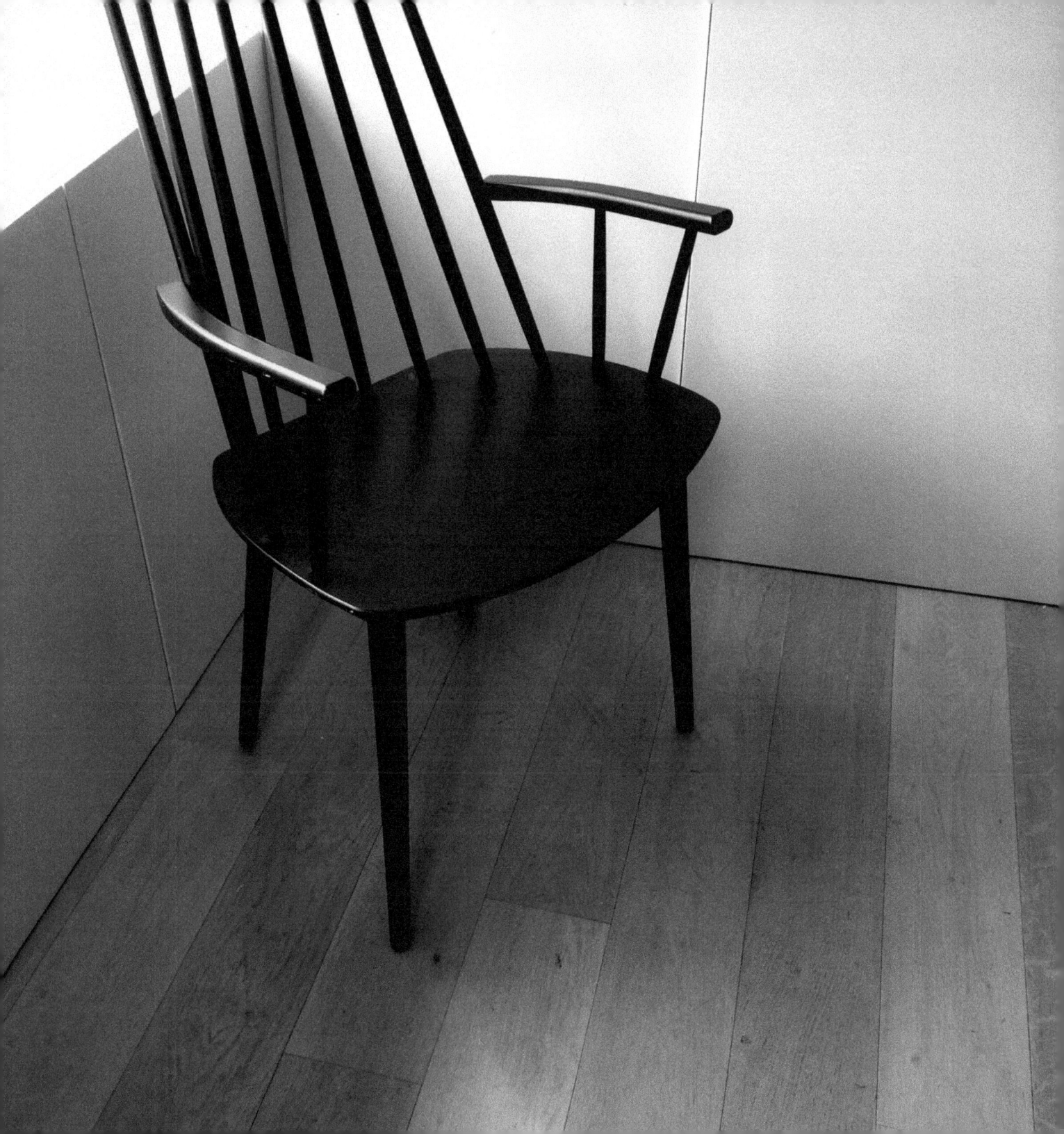

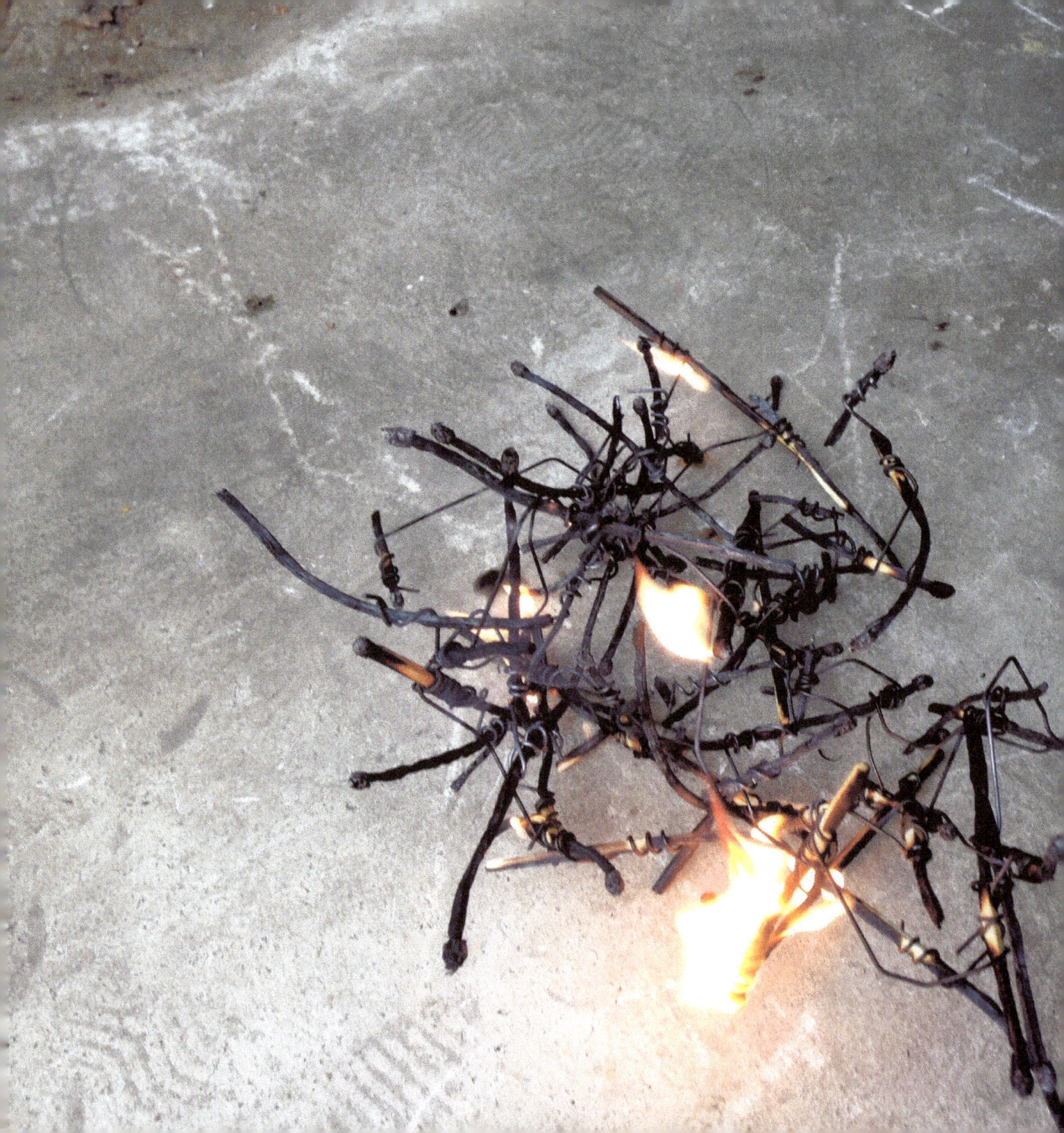

requiescimus

in lucem

Can I take a photo of you?
Yeah.
You have an amazing face.
Thanks.
Bet you've seen some stuff.
Yep.

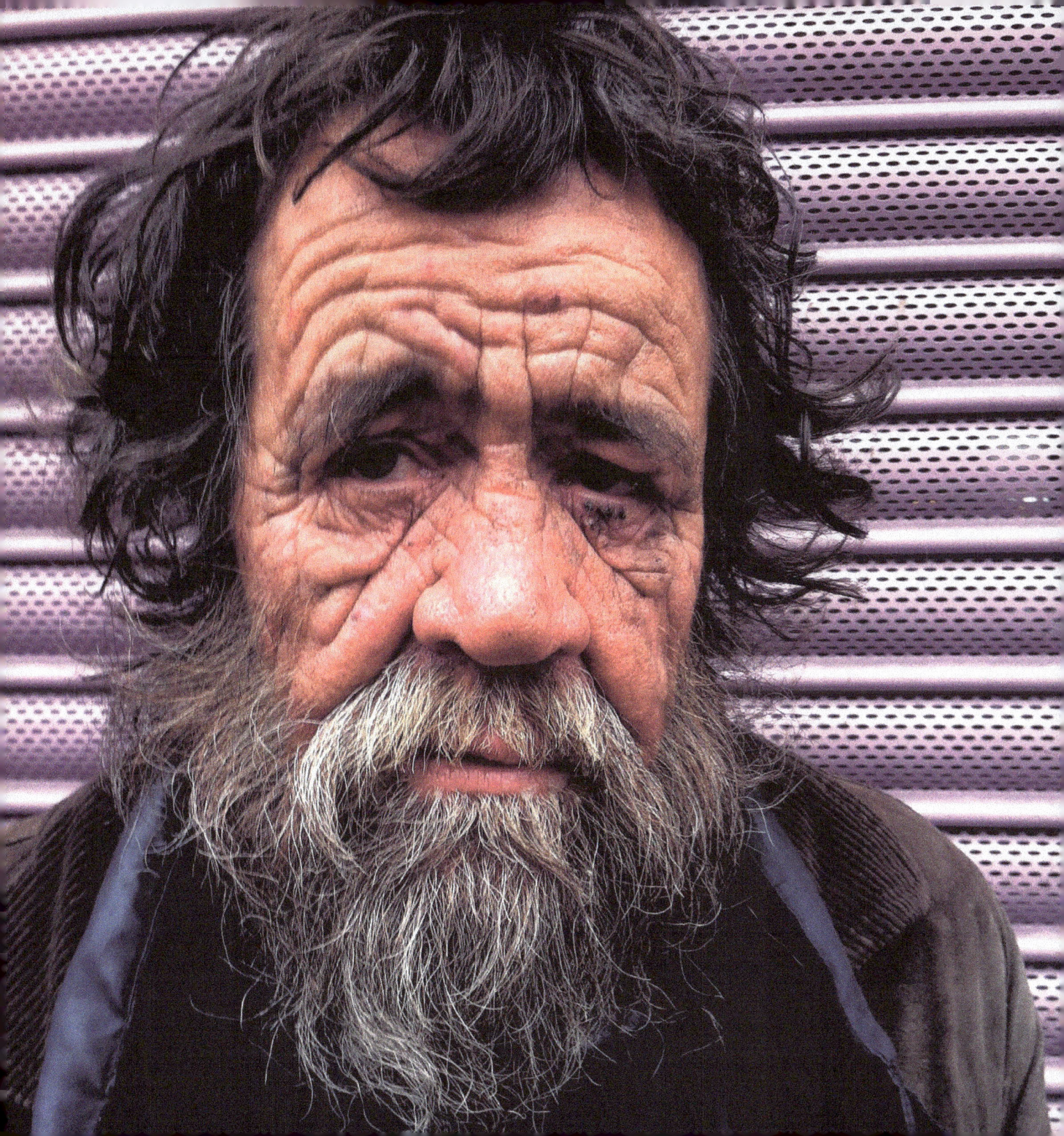

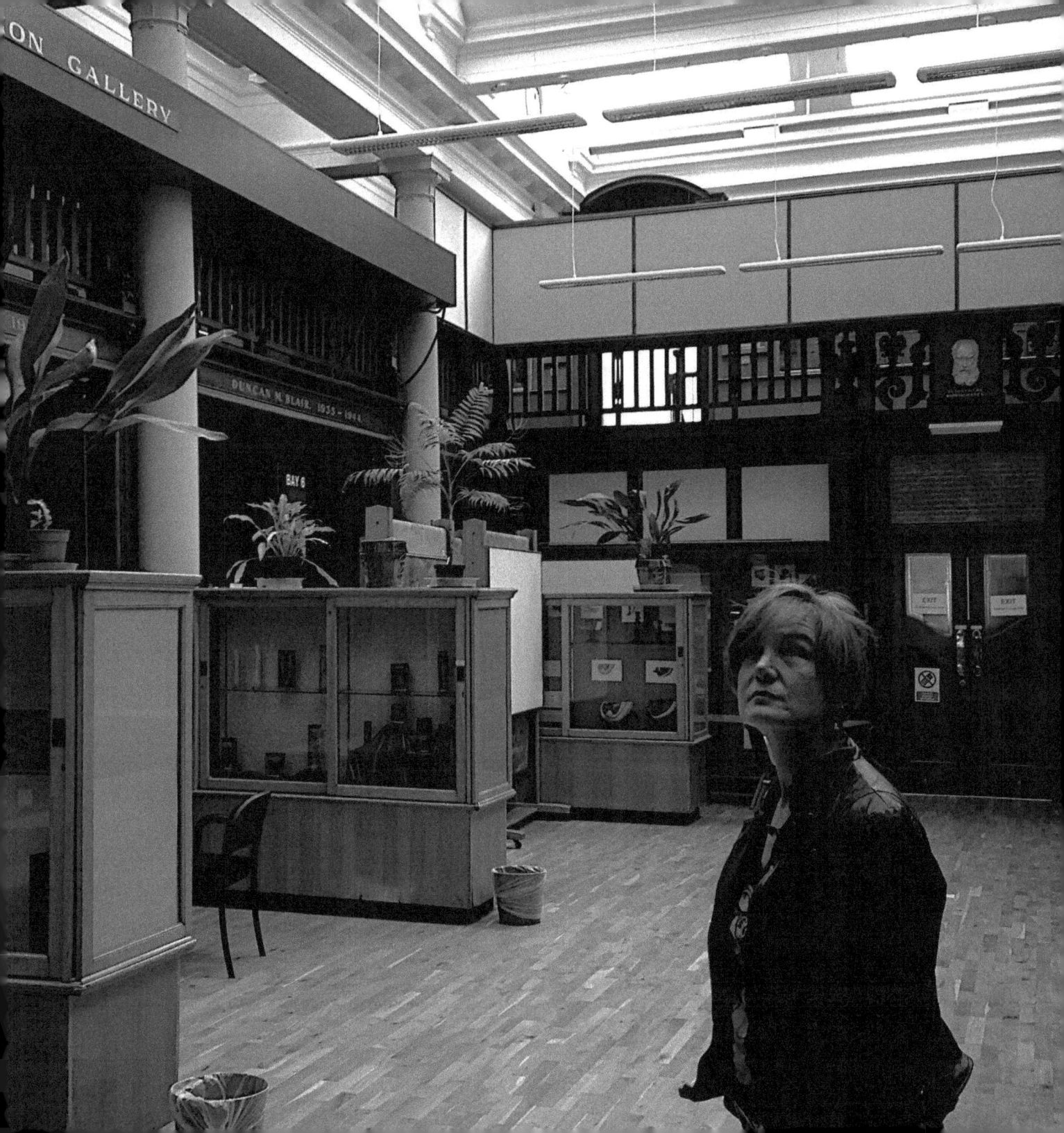

It smells like a library. Wax polish, wood, old paper. We notice the paintings, the card catalogue, the *Ficus Benjamina* someone's forgotten to water. We talk about the other smell, the one hunting memories, tickling the backs of our throats, a basement smell, formaldehyde, a smell for dark places, a smell to be ashamed of, a smell that means something we can't control has happened to someone we don't even know.

We look—then glance away, eyes lighting for a startled second on a 4 centimeter-long spinal column, lurid red, bobbing in a tiny bottle. Then back to rows of squashed faces, parts of bodies we can't even identify without reading the labels. The labels are small, and we don't want to get any closer to the people in the bottles.

We can't.

We can't stop looking. But we have to, overwhelmed by the weight of numbers—evidence of pagan rites, clear canopic jars, sealed with pitch and fat wooden corks.

We are all bystanders. All guilty. And we are the reason this quiet jury has been assembled.

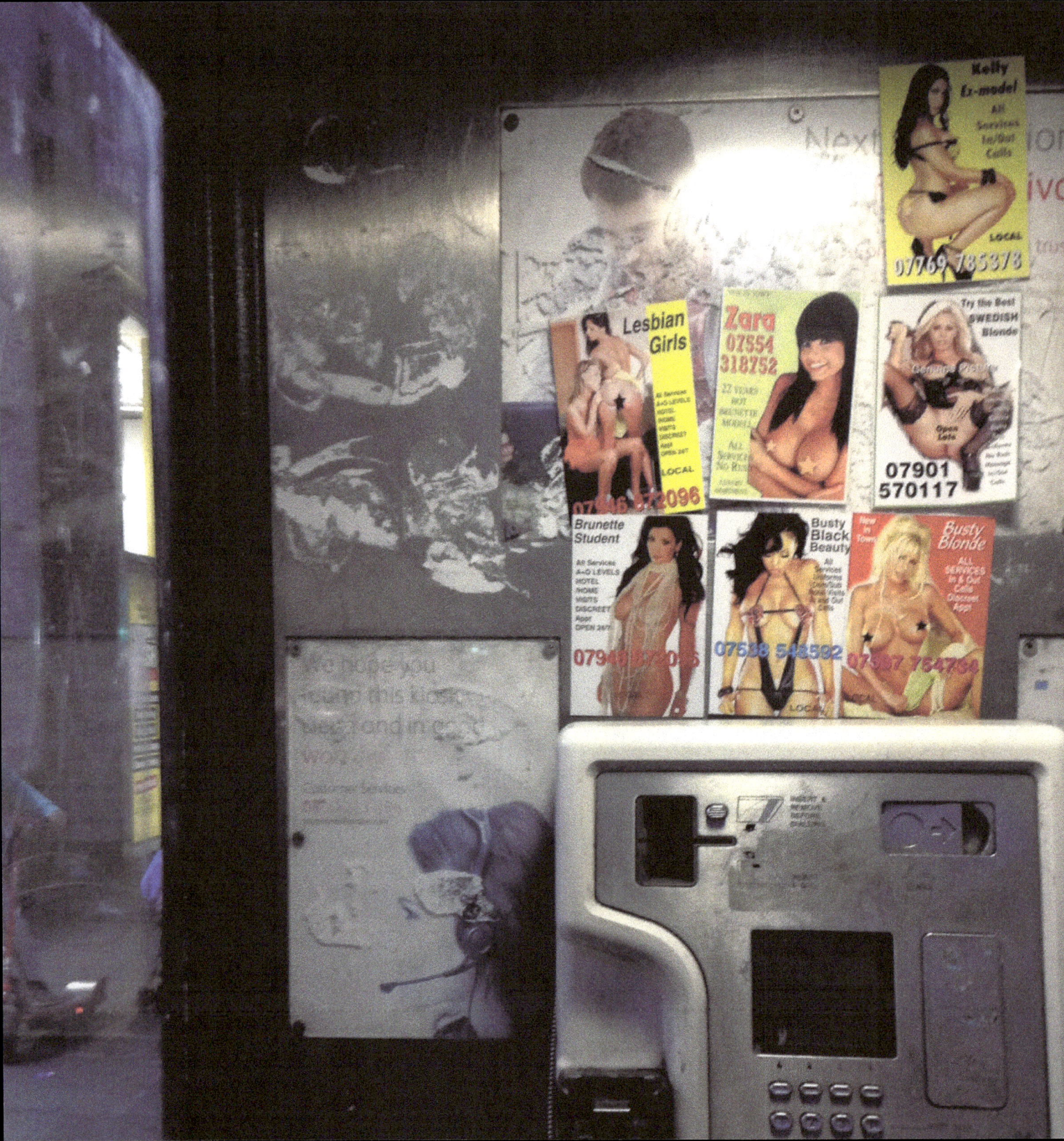

I've been the shape of water,
flowing to fill
whatever container
was offered.

Indiscriminate—

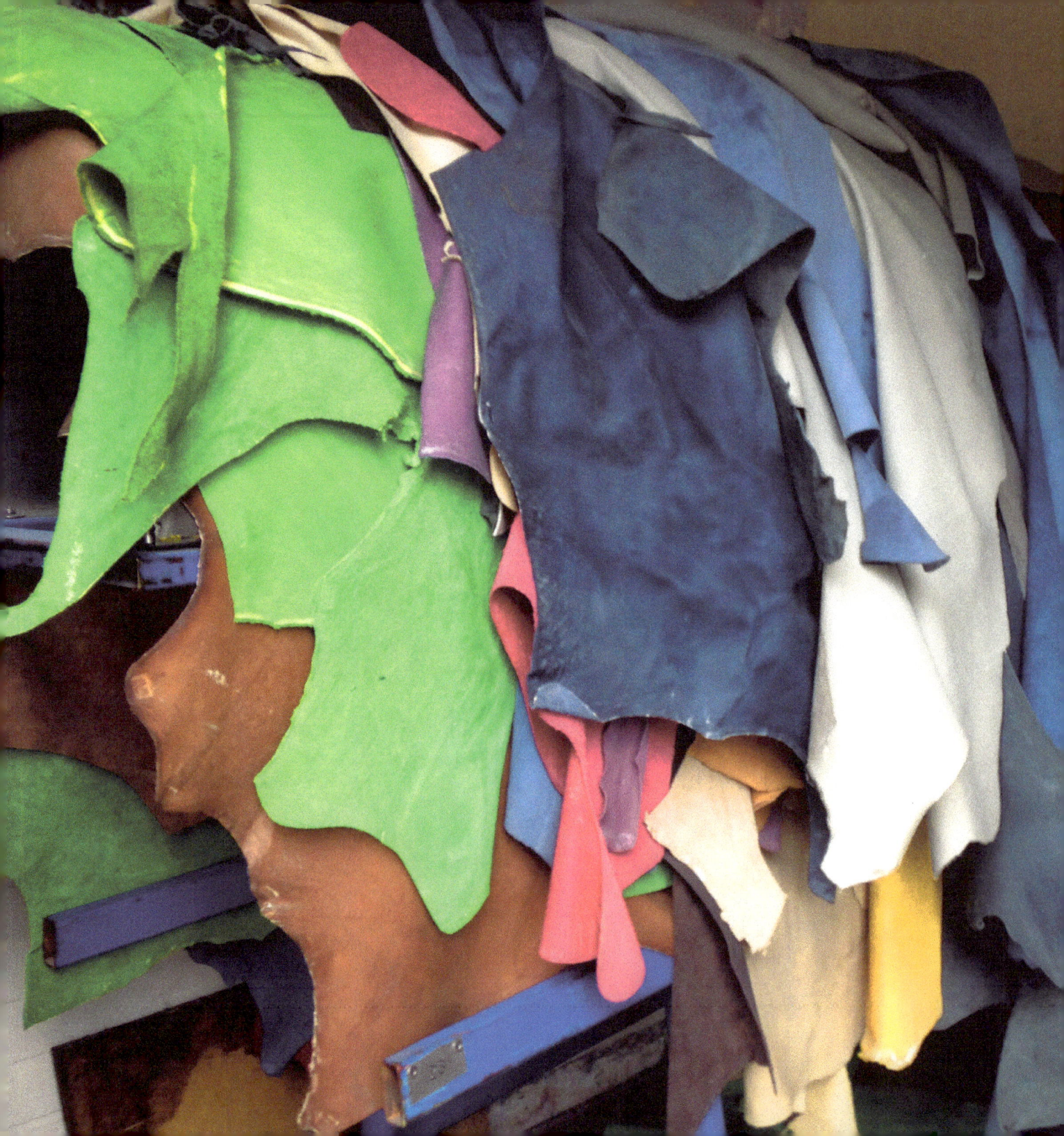

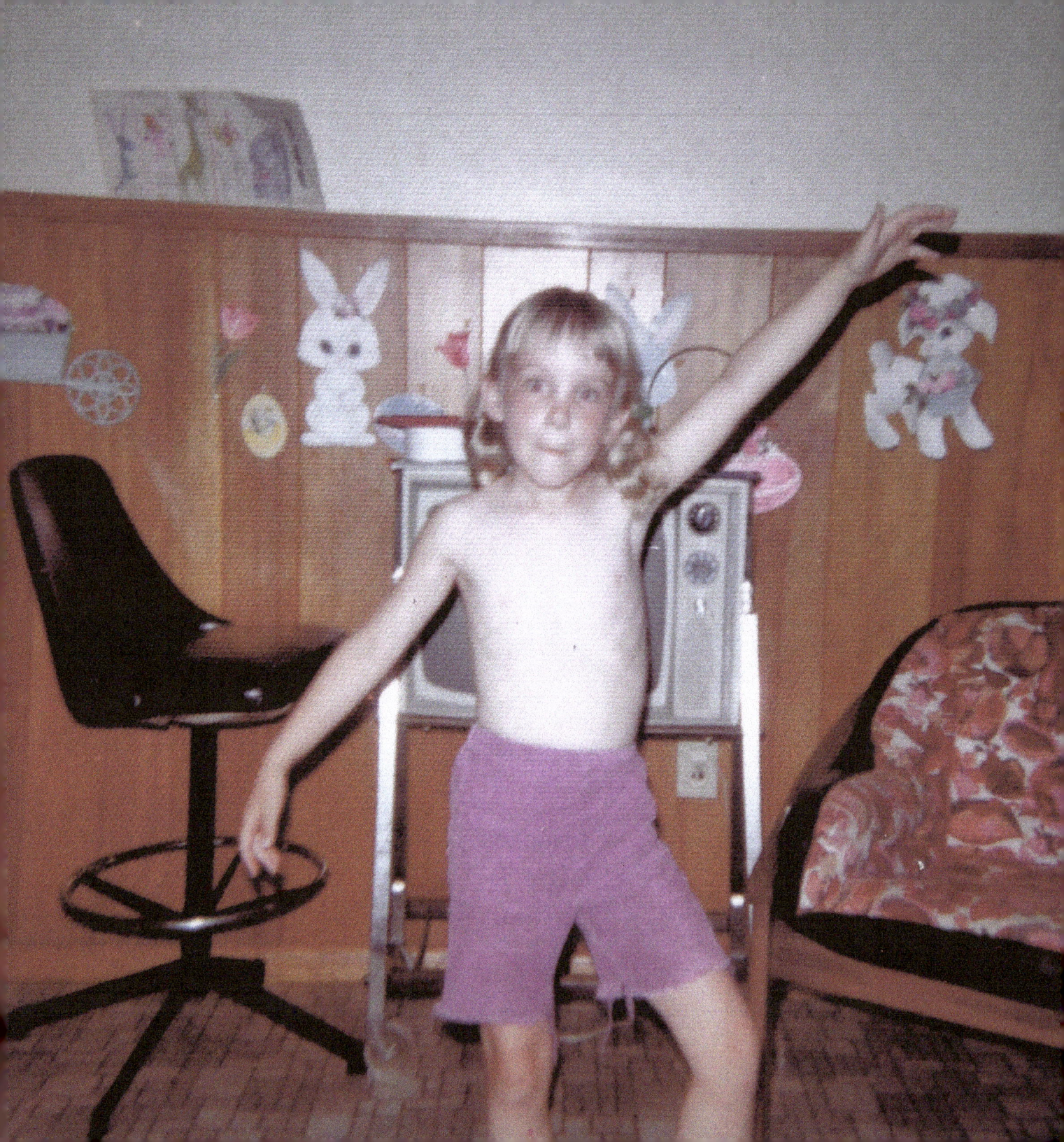

I can see my Mom, a tiny red speck on the beach, flapping the sand from our towels. I'm jumping off Dad's shoulders into yellow-green water. I've never seen the ocean, for real. Just pictures in *National Geographic*. Dad waves me towards the beach; he's talking. I shout *crap crap crap crap CRAP!* over and over in my head, as I dive down to touch the sandy ripples under my toes. I feel wild. I never want to get out of the ocean. Ever.

I'm under the waves, with my eyes open, watching small fish drift past, clumping together, then zooming apart. I fly underwater with them, feeling the waves roar through me. My legs stretch behind me, and I cup the water with my hands. I roll and roll until I'm a selkie. I sprout fur, so I can stay out here forever.

Out of the corner of my eye, I see a something shiny. My brain screams *SHARK!!!* Just like in *National Geographic*. Something nearly as long as me, thin and blue-grey in the water. I don't want to, but I change back; I'm a girl again.

I try to swim faster. I can't keep looking. I don't stop to breathe, until I'm up on the beach, racing across the sand. I don't notice until I sit down that I have lost the top of my bikini. I'm almost naked, in front of loads of grownups and kids and strangers. I can't see it anywhere, so I cover my nipples with my hands. My mother grabs my arm and pulls me up hard; one of my feet is almost off the ground. *You should be ashamed. Running like a wild animal, losing your top. You should be MODEST.*

I know what modest means, sort of: I shouldn't wanna be naked, fast, a selkie being licked by the ocean. Mom pinches me under my hair, pushing my chin up with her other hand. *Thank the boy. Thank the boy who brought you your top. Now, Mary Frances!!* I can't. I'm crying, and my voice doesn't work, and he's a *Teenager*.

He rubs my hair, puts the bikini top in my hand, and walks away.

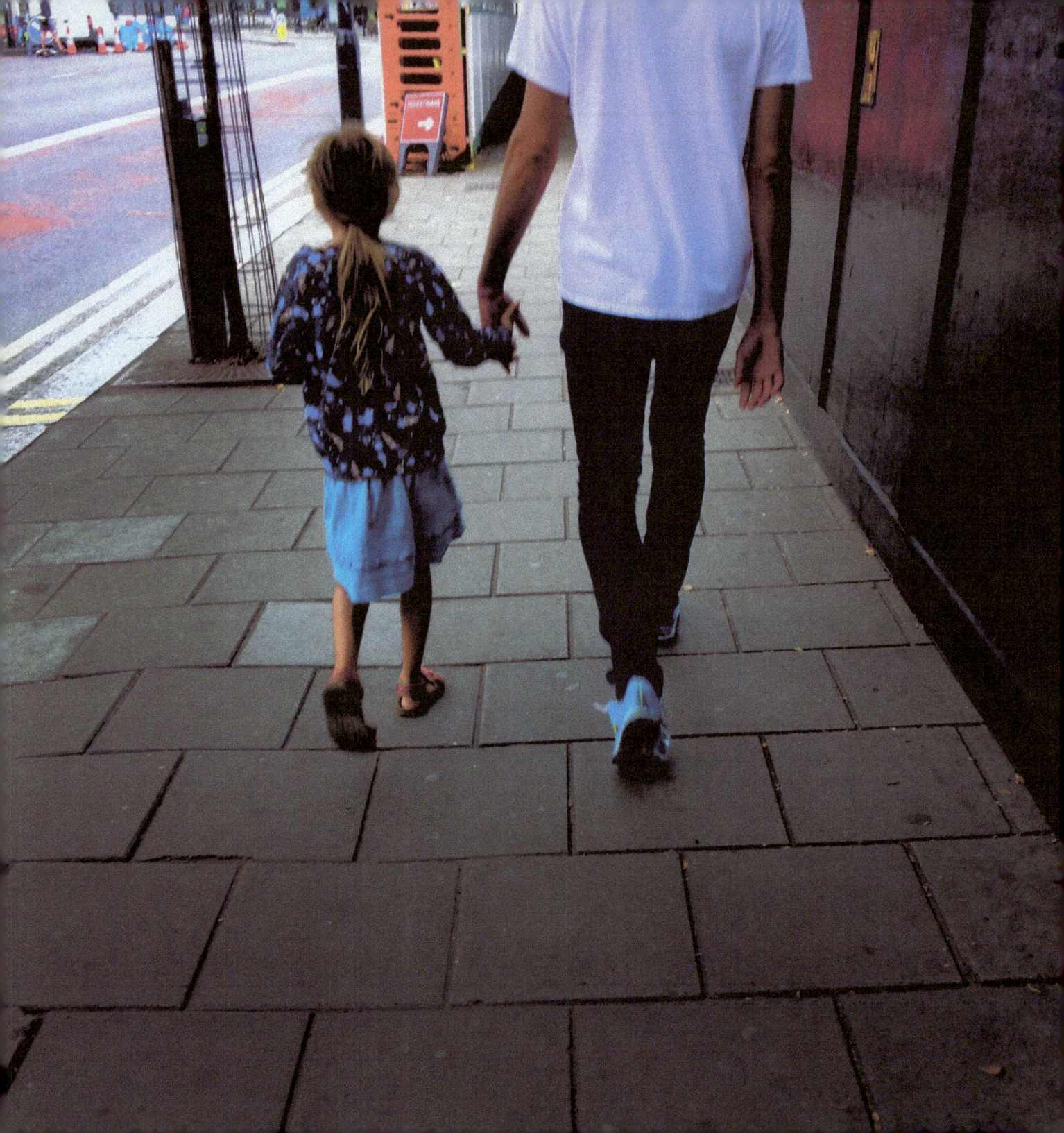

I used to touch everyone
and everything I saw.
My skin sang in water.
My body sang in bed,
sang as I ran,
sang as I knew I would never be a boy called Patrick.

I was wild,
and myself,
even with my fear and shame.

No one could take my light,
but people tried.
People I thought loved me.
I didn't know any better.
They were all I had.

I started polishing off my skin,
my dirt, to appease them.

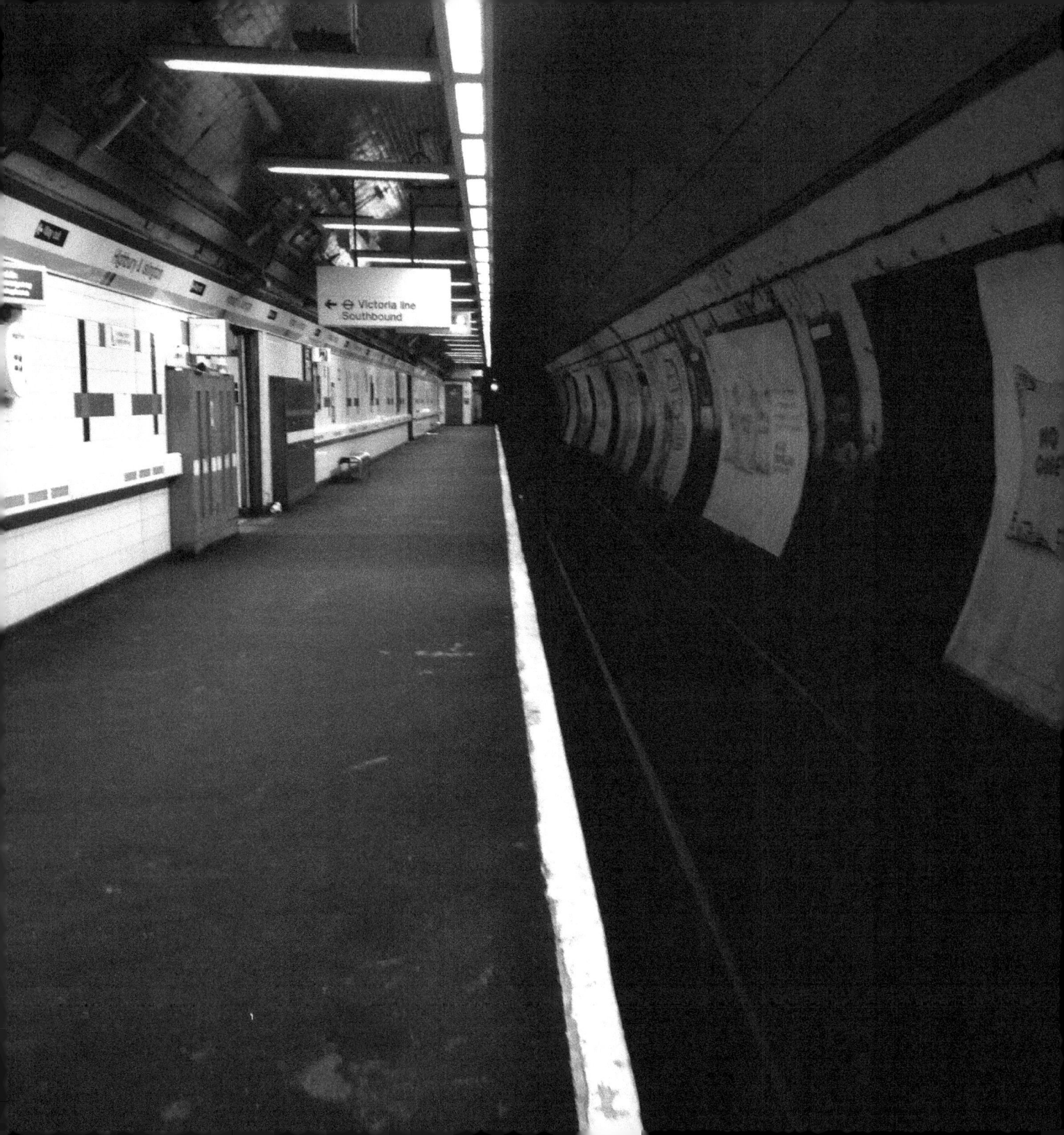

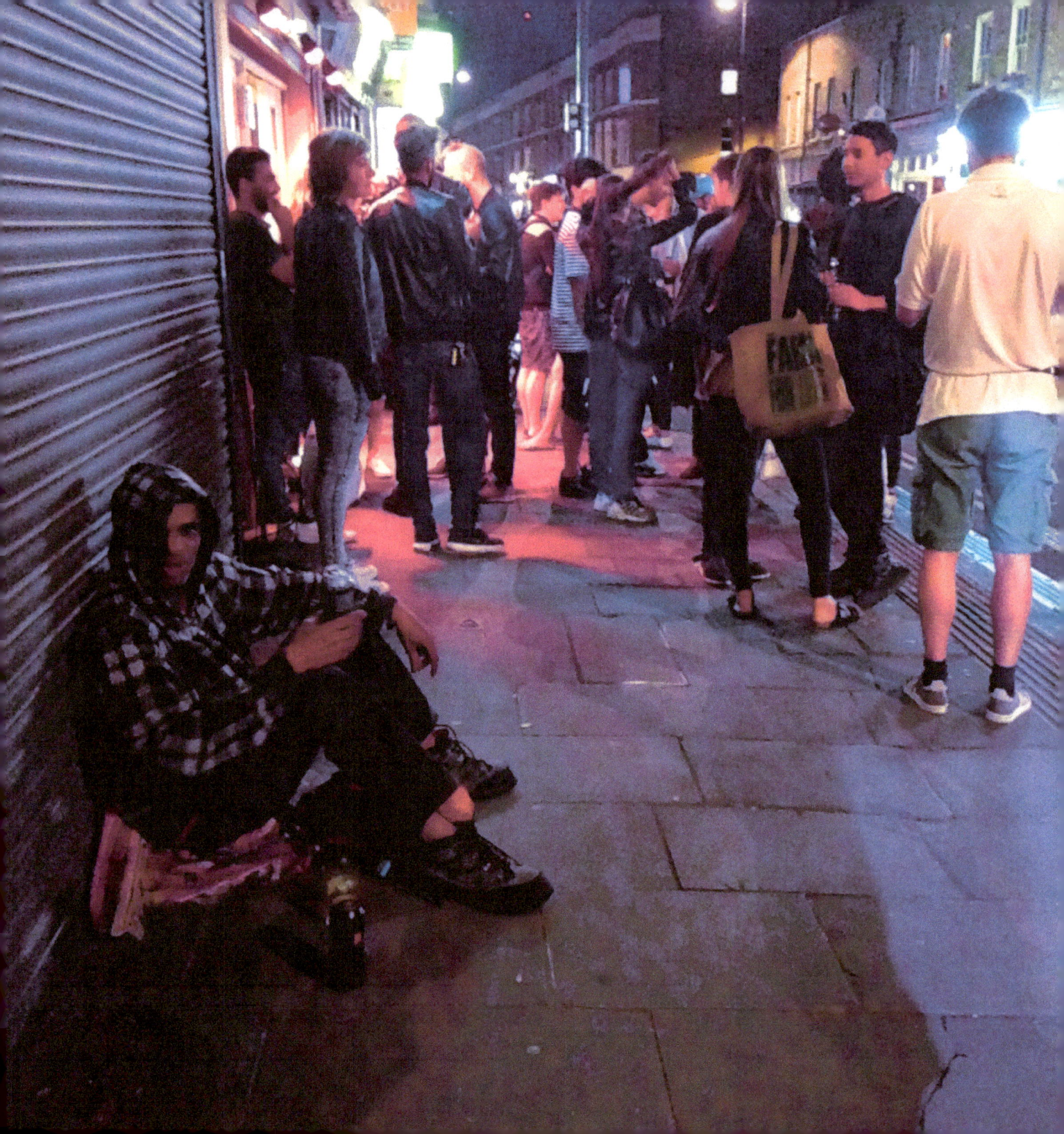

Shame lurks in their eyes, drips out their mouths. Their laughter screeches out of them, sheet metal tearing. They hold themselves open, bodies offering, souls shut, stepping over homeless people like dog shit. They aren't here. But they can tell that I am.

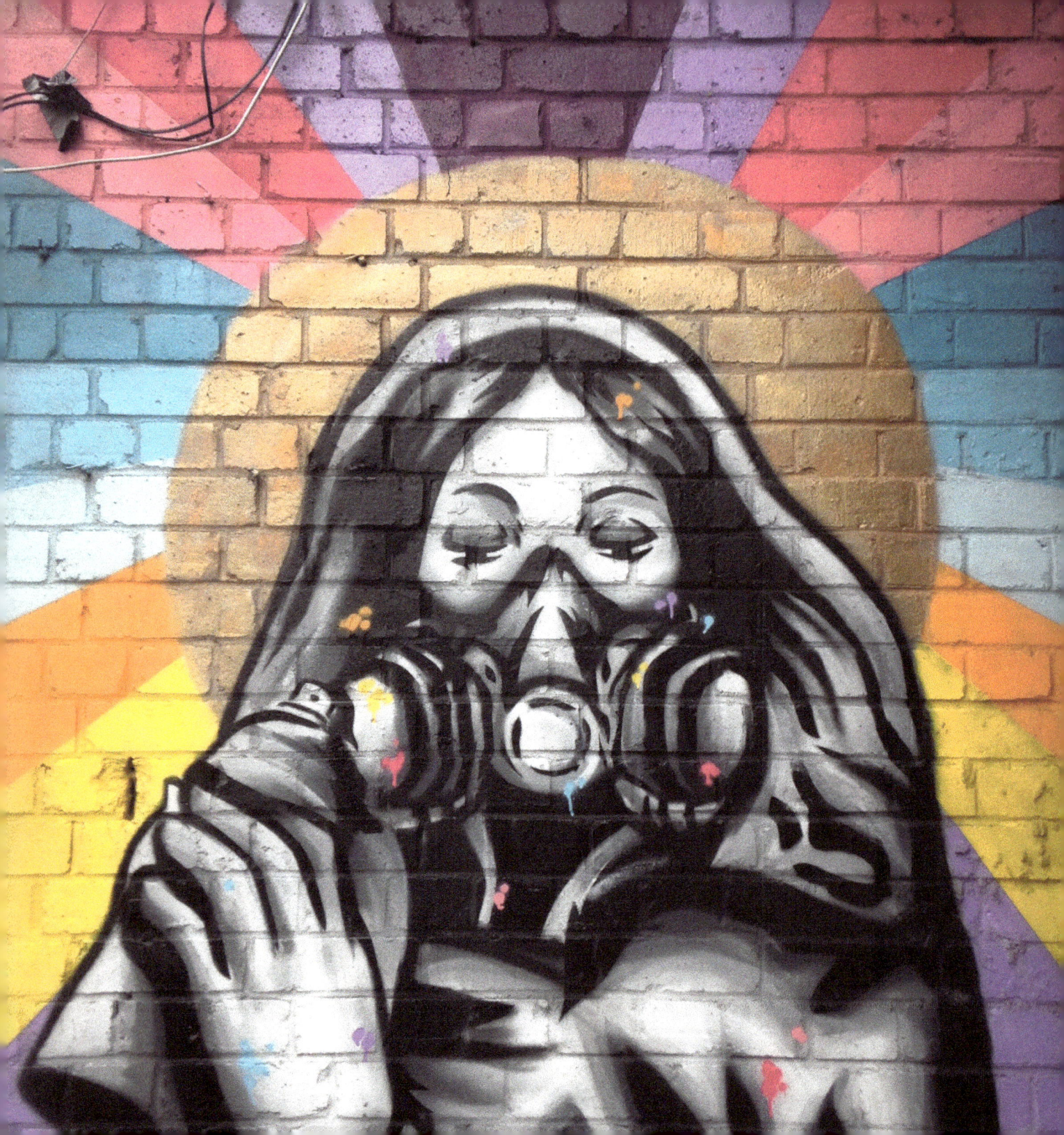

Intellectualised detachment while reading about horrific, painful things, doesn't do anything for me. It's like having crap thrown at me, while being told to be grateful for it. Fuck you. Fuck off. I don't want your crap. Deal with it yourself. Dig a hole. Bury it. Better yet, start looking at what it's about. Turn it over. Feel it YOURSELF before you force me to feel it FOR you. Fuck you and your projections. Since when has it been trendy to be a user, sucking an audience dry, indulging your unprocessed emotion? In your detachment, you push me away, denying me the possibility of relating, of giving a shit about you. I feel sad, not because of anything you've said or done, but because you don't seem to have found a way to be present. To yourself, never mind to anyone else. Use me. Dump on me. I'll just take it, because I don't give a fuck about you, you little user. Maybe I use people in a different way? I expect connection. Want people to be present, open to their experience, to growth, to learning. Maybe I'm using people to gratify my desire to feel alive, to enjoy my life, to feel love and connection. If that's being a user, that's ok with me. At least my using brings people to life, with light in their eyes, a bounce in their step, a sense of being part of something bigger than themselves and their perfect little personas. I dump love on people, cruelly cracking them open, showing them that I care. It's forceful, brutal, unrelenting—can't be stopped, interrupted, contained. Maybe it feels like crap to you. Maybe it is. Pearls before swine.

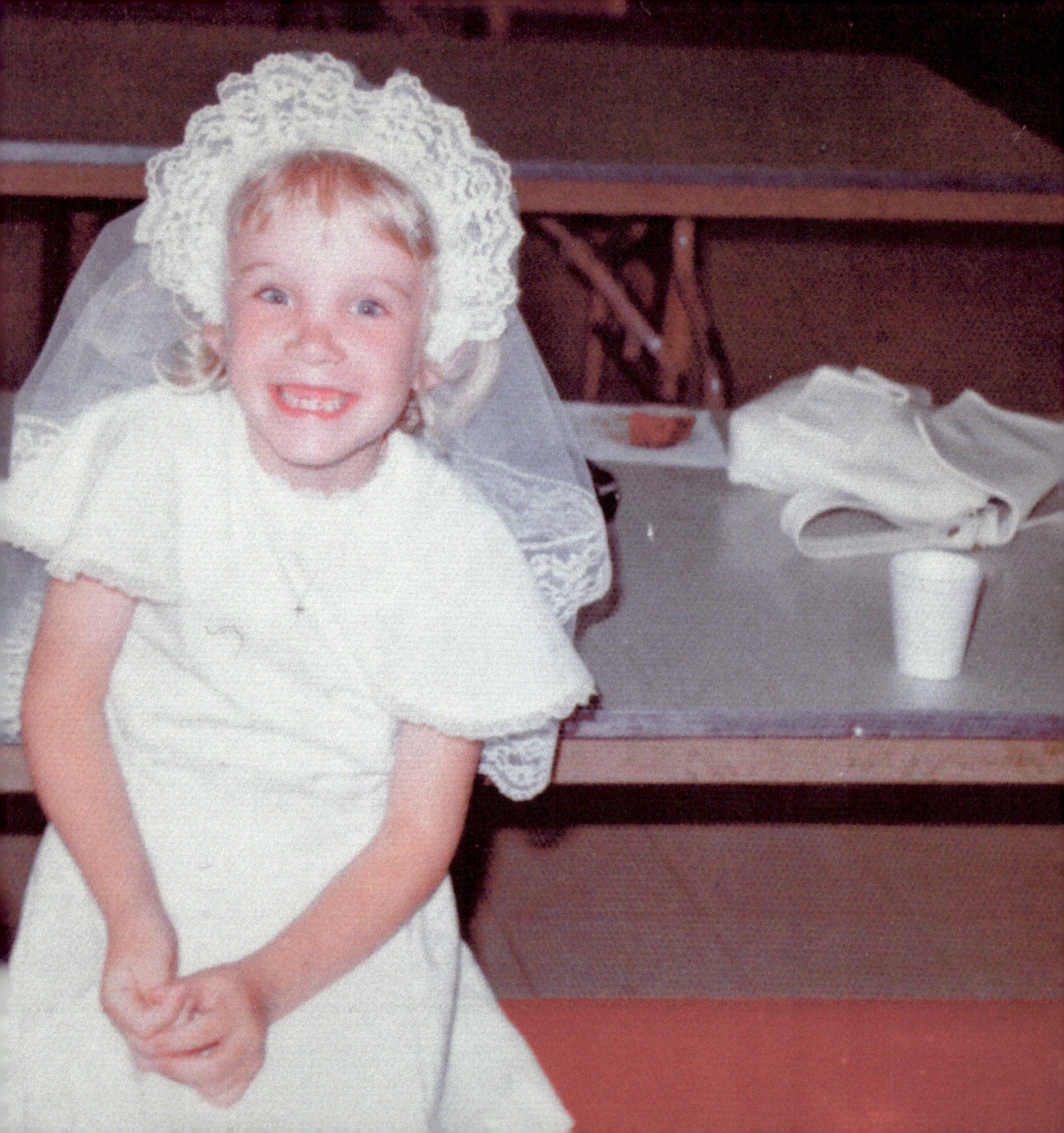

No one can climb as high as me. I can shin two stories up the roof-pole, and reach up to throw down chalky rocks for everyone. We can draw and play Hopscotch right now if I get to the top. I'm a monkey, pushing up hard with my knees and heels. I'm taller than JJ at the top of the slide. He's waving and shouting but I can't hear him. I'm laughing and laughing.

CLANG.

Someone is banging hard on the roof-pole! Sister screeches:

Dirty girl!

Get DOWN!!!

Now!!!

Everyone can see your underwear!

I've already called your mother.

I almost fall. I slide down, burning my legs and my hands on the paint.

My mom is angry, when she comes to pick me up, because I've covered my uniform skirt in chalk and she'll have to wash it.

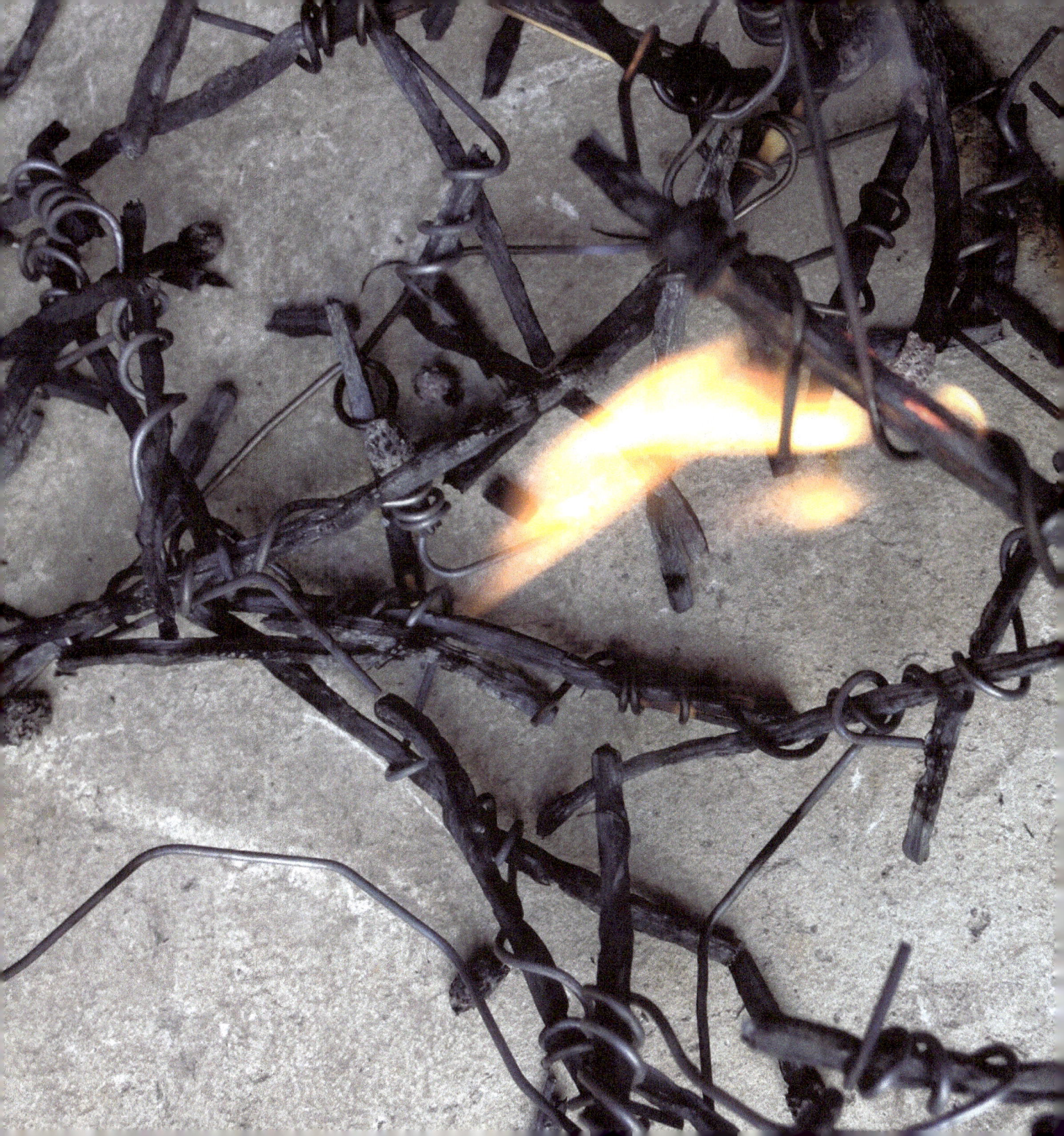

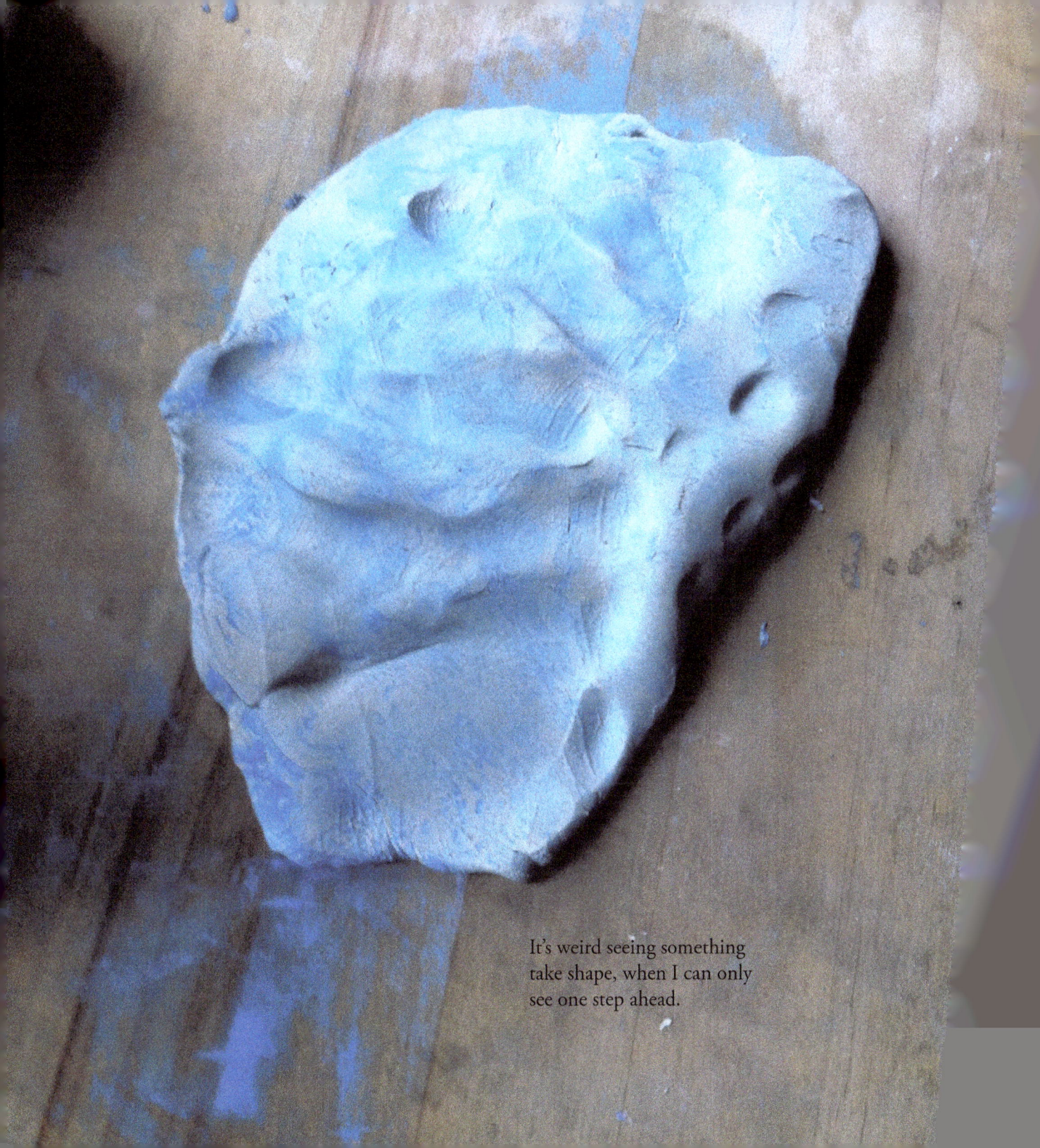

It's weird seeing something
take shape, when I can only
see one step ahead.

et dimitte

nobis

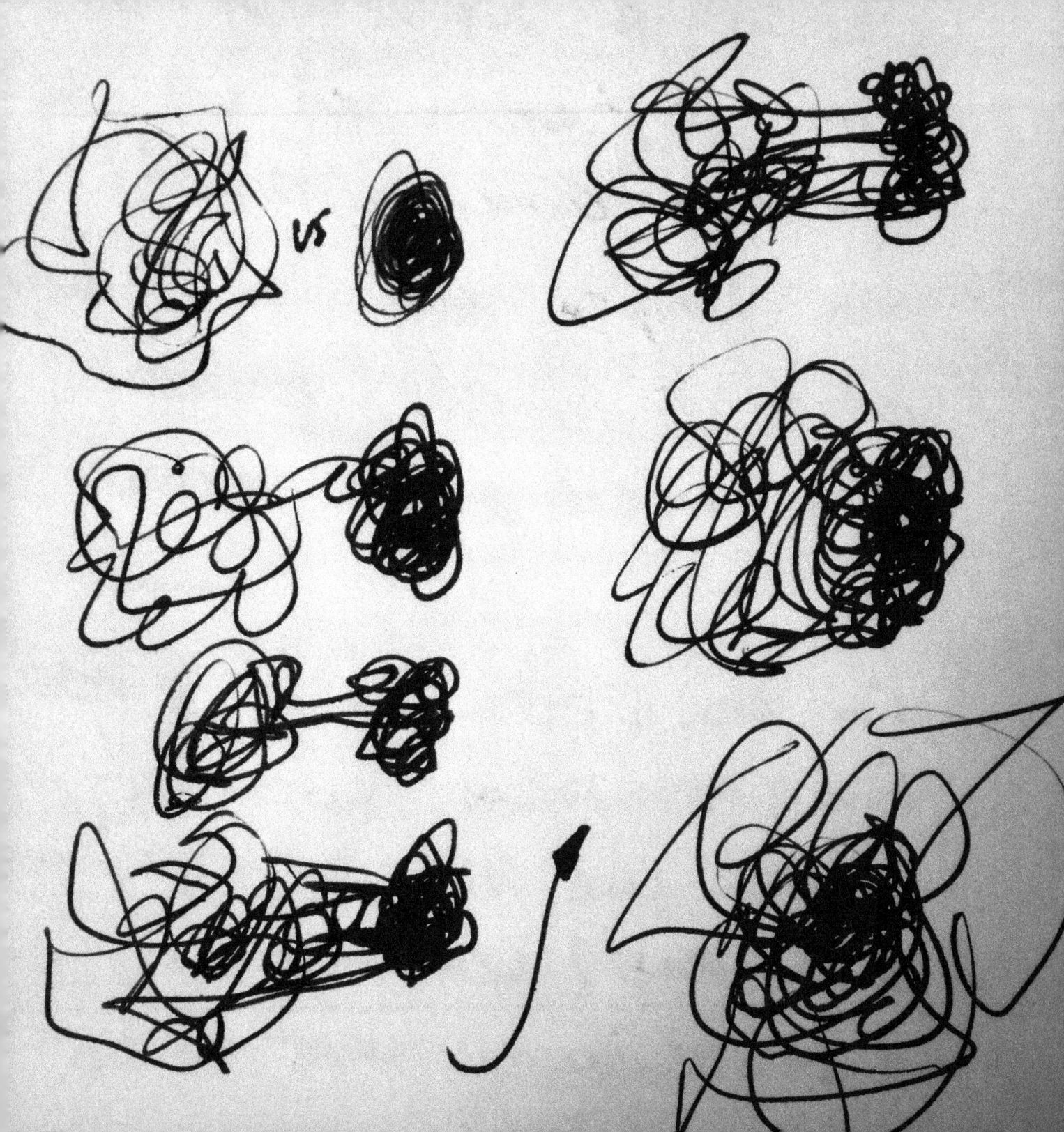

Torn apart, space gapes between us.
Raw mouth of a jagged cut.

We rub torn lips together, stinging,
and know we are alive, if we choose to be.

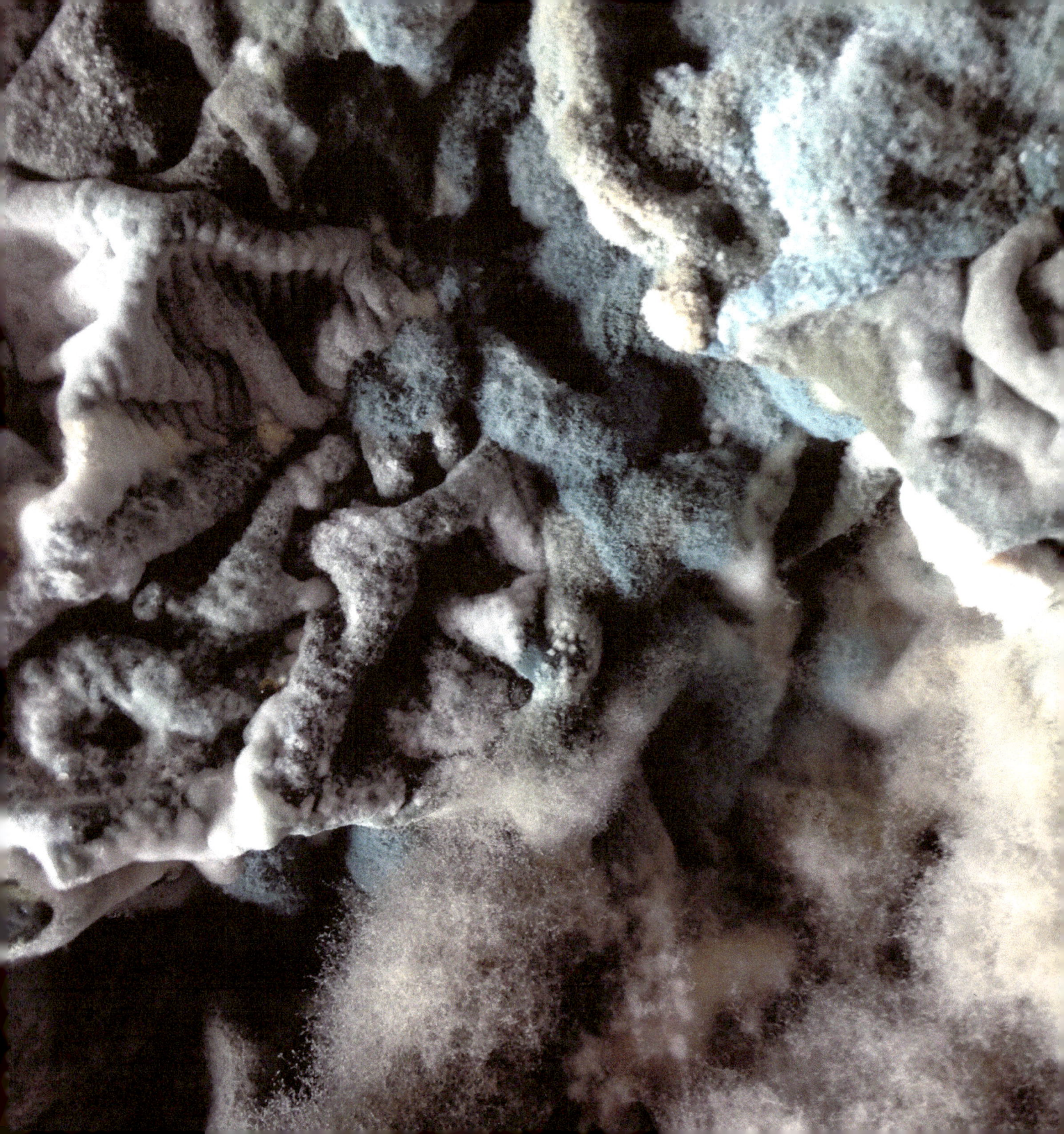

A bag of skin is not an ideal container.
Damp, stretchy, fertile ground
for all the wrong things:
mildew, fungus, slime.

I thought we'd planted a garden—
nothing growing here that I recognise.

Ashamed of our shame.
Feeling guilty about our guilt.
Afraid of our fear.

ARE

ERYWHERE

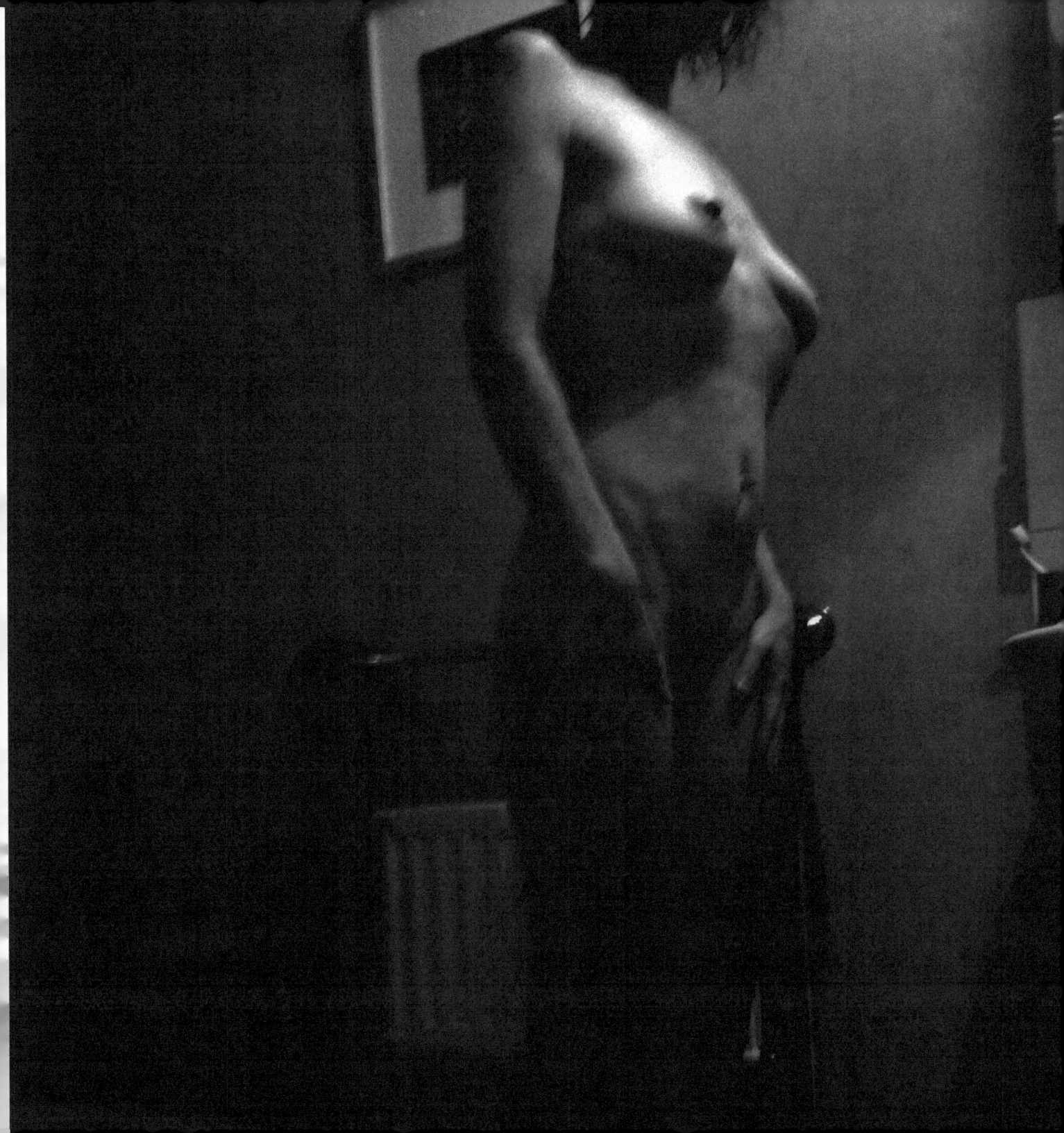

I want you to own my hips,
hold me with both hands.
Pull. Twist. I won't break.

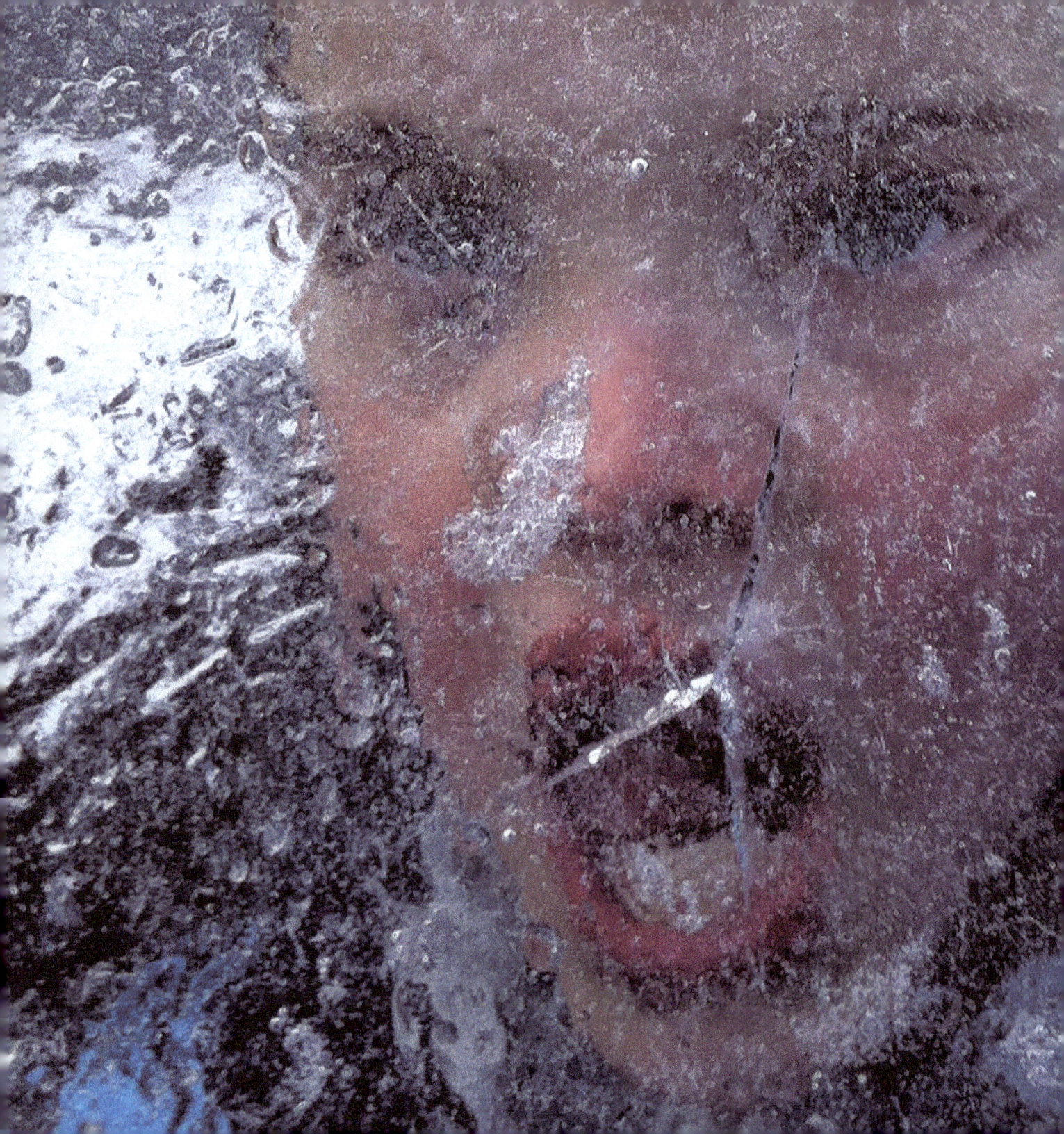

Smother my doubts with kisses

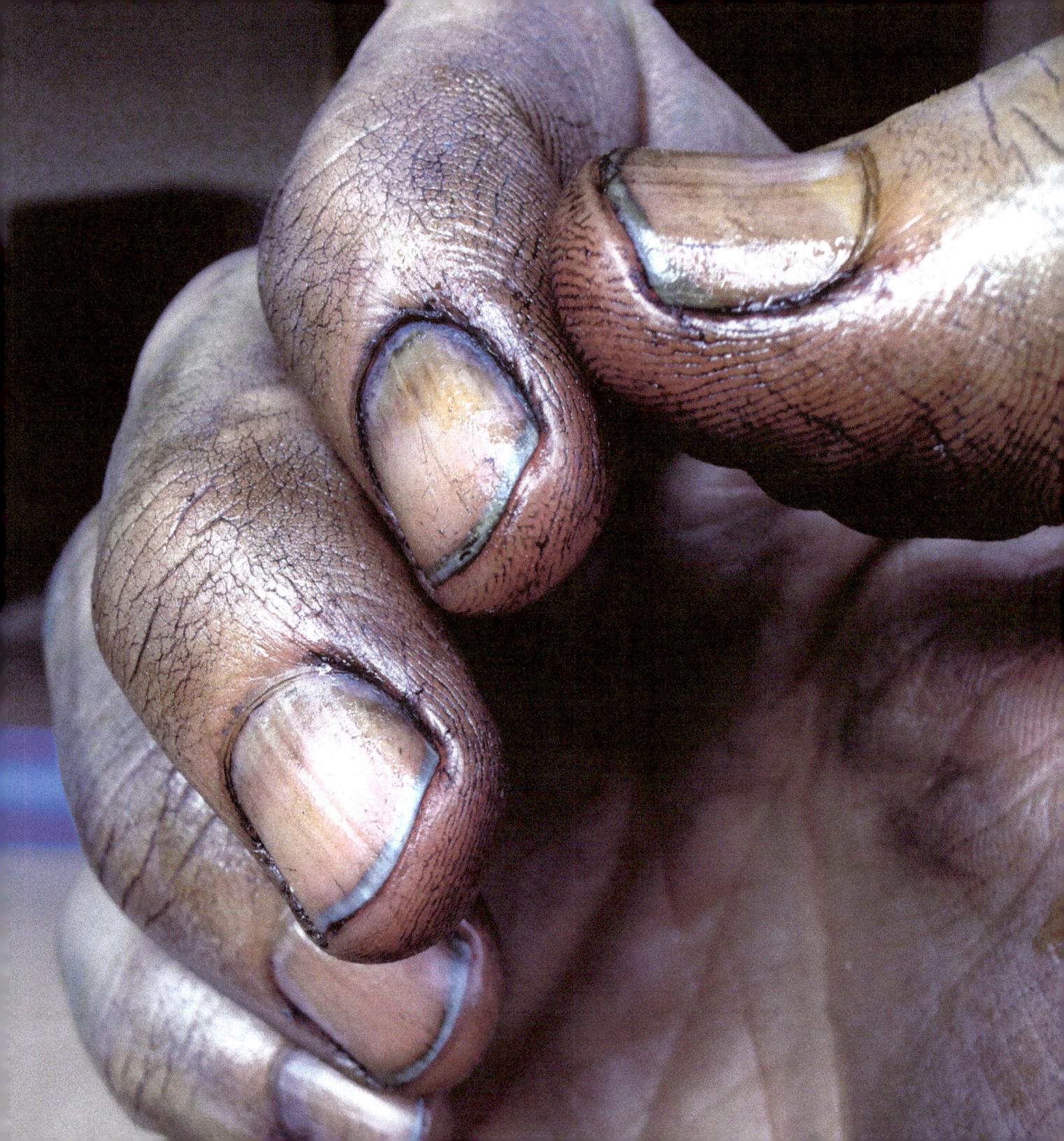

your finger
slides, again
and again

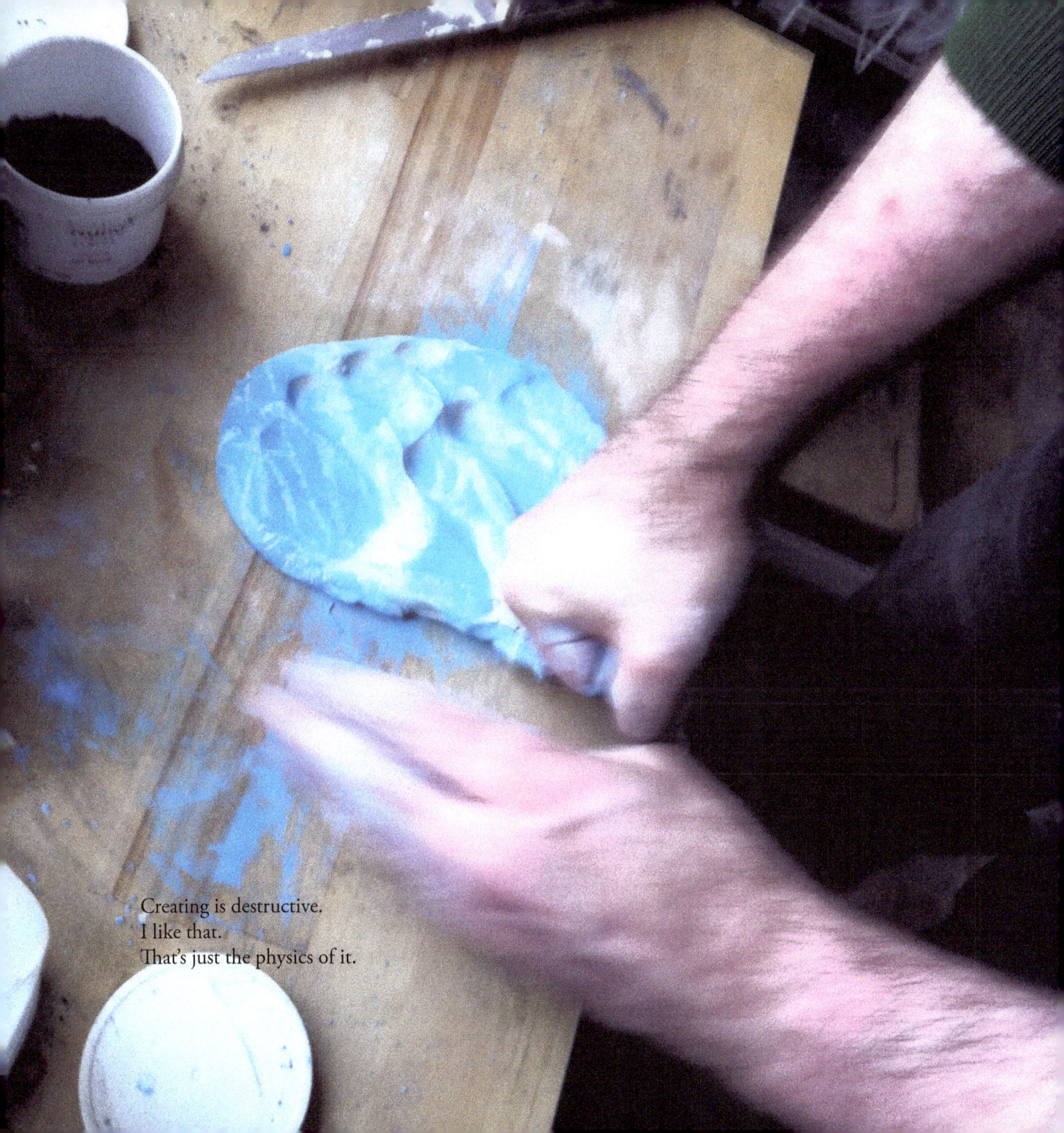

Creating is destructive.
I like that.
That's just the physics of it.

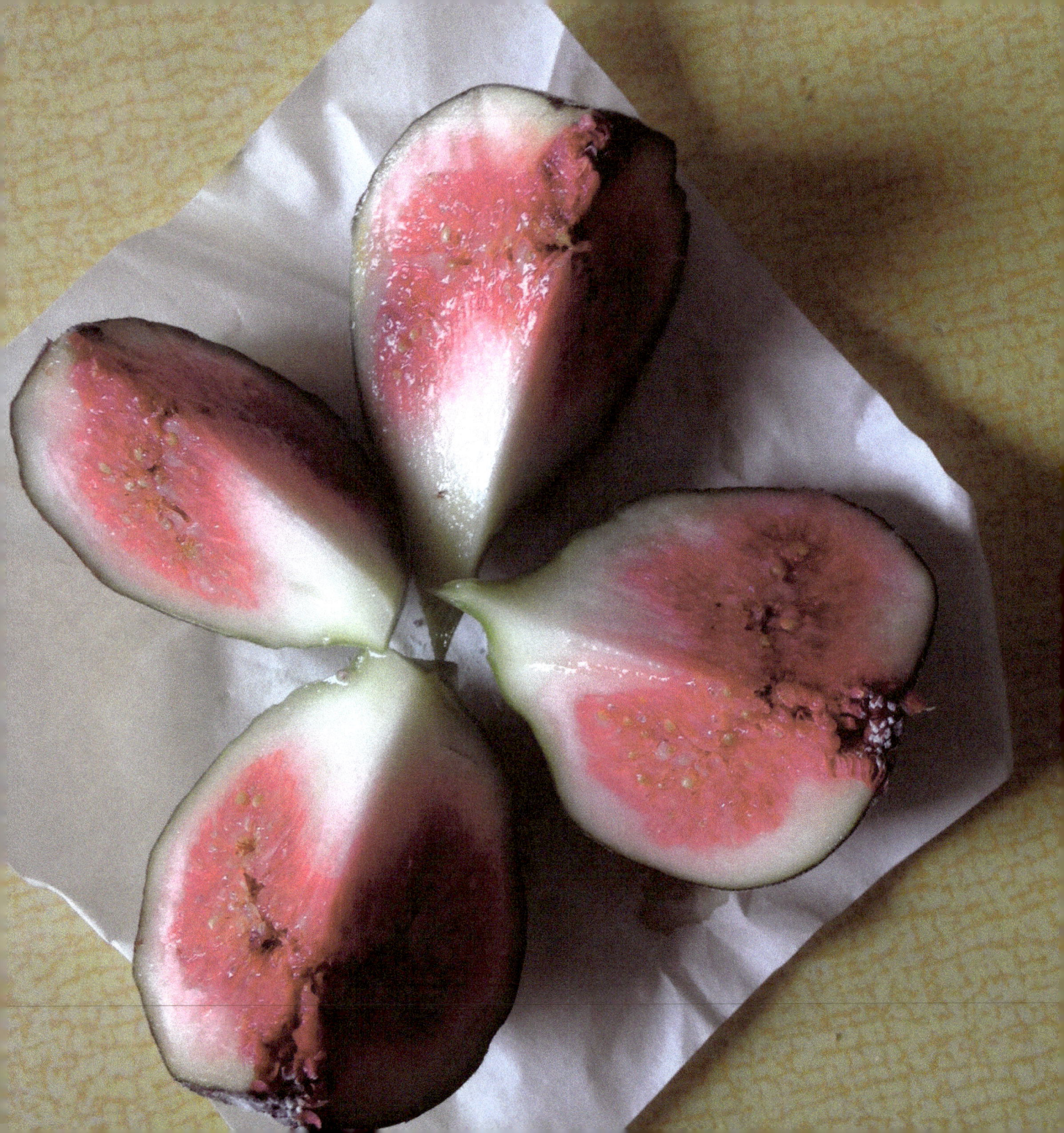

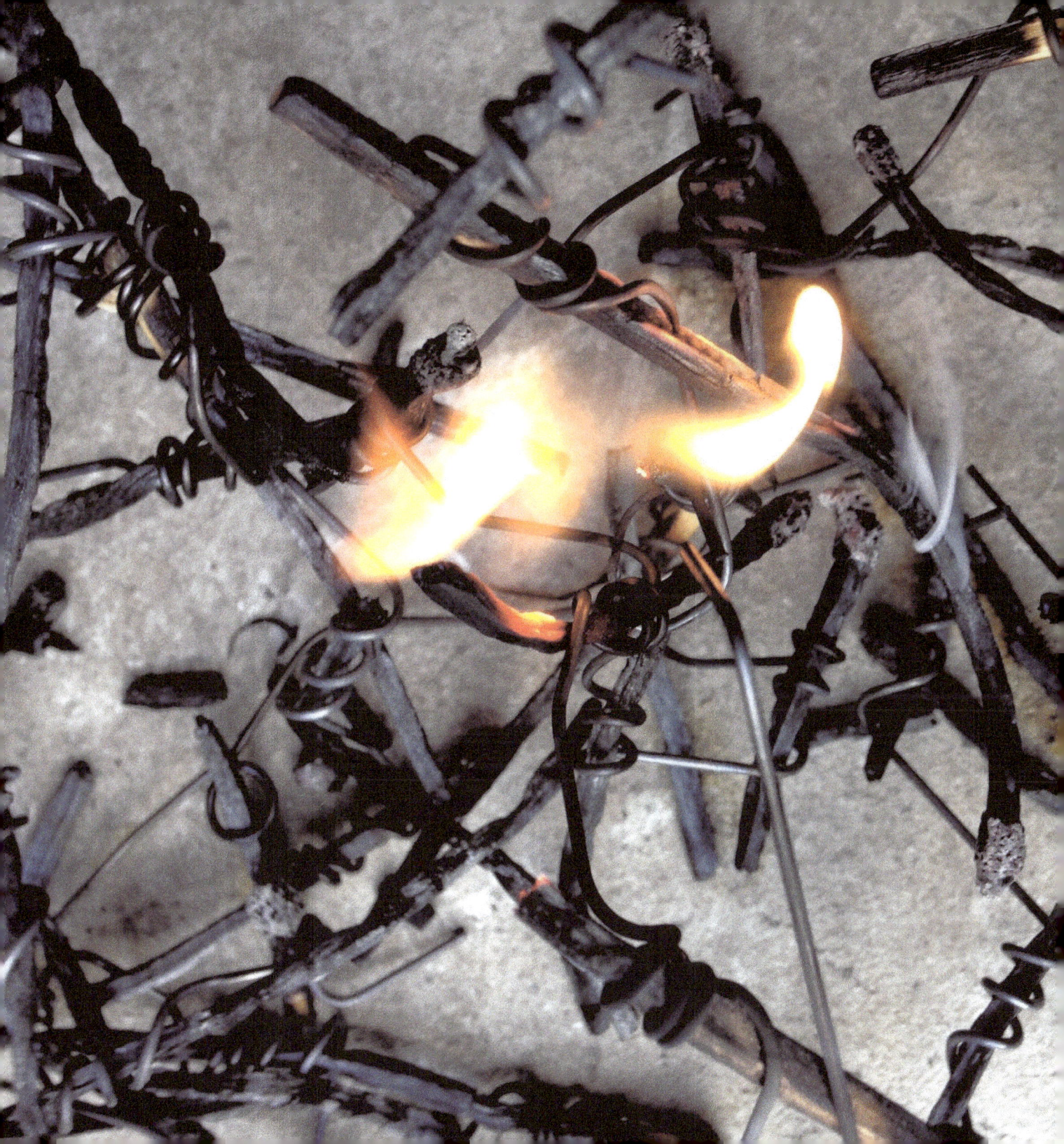

PRIVACY

FEAR

MODEL TIME APART

● BEING DROPPED & REJECTED &
         HATED

The iron slides back and forth,
nose nudging into the cuffs,
and behind the collar.

I press wrinkles out with grim determination.
Smooth cotton.
Smooth and perfect.
More perfect than I'll ever be.

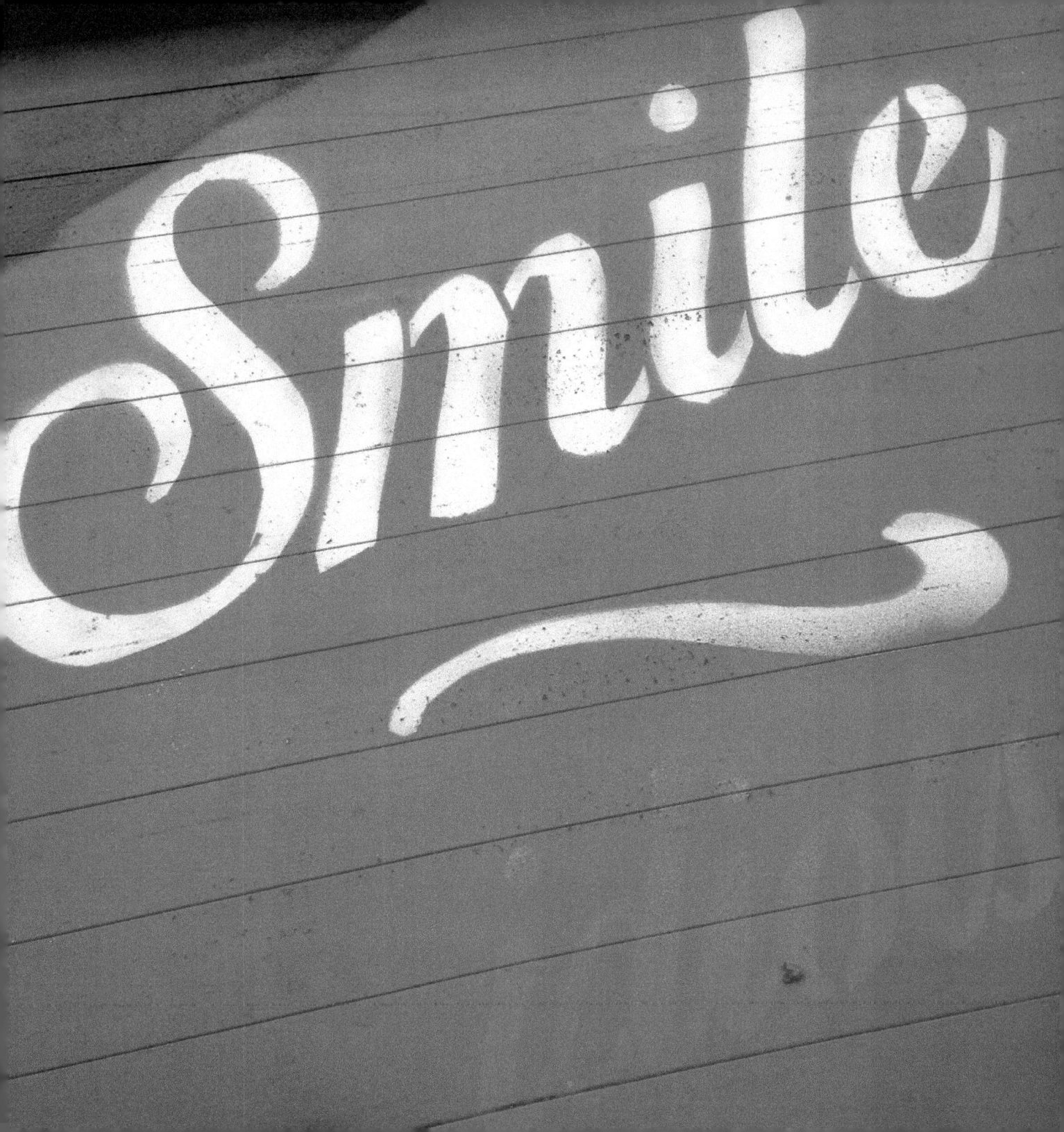

We'll merge together—be as
one. You'll do all the laundry.
I'll have all the fun.

misertus

nostri

No comfort colder than the ring
on my hand—first link in a chain.
Pulls me down for a man.

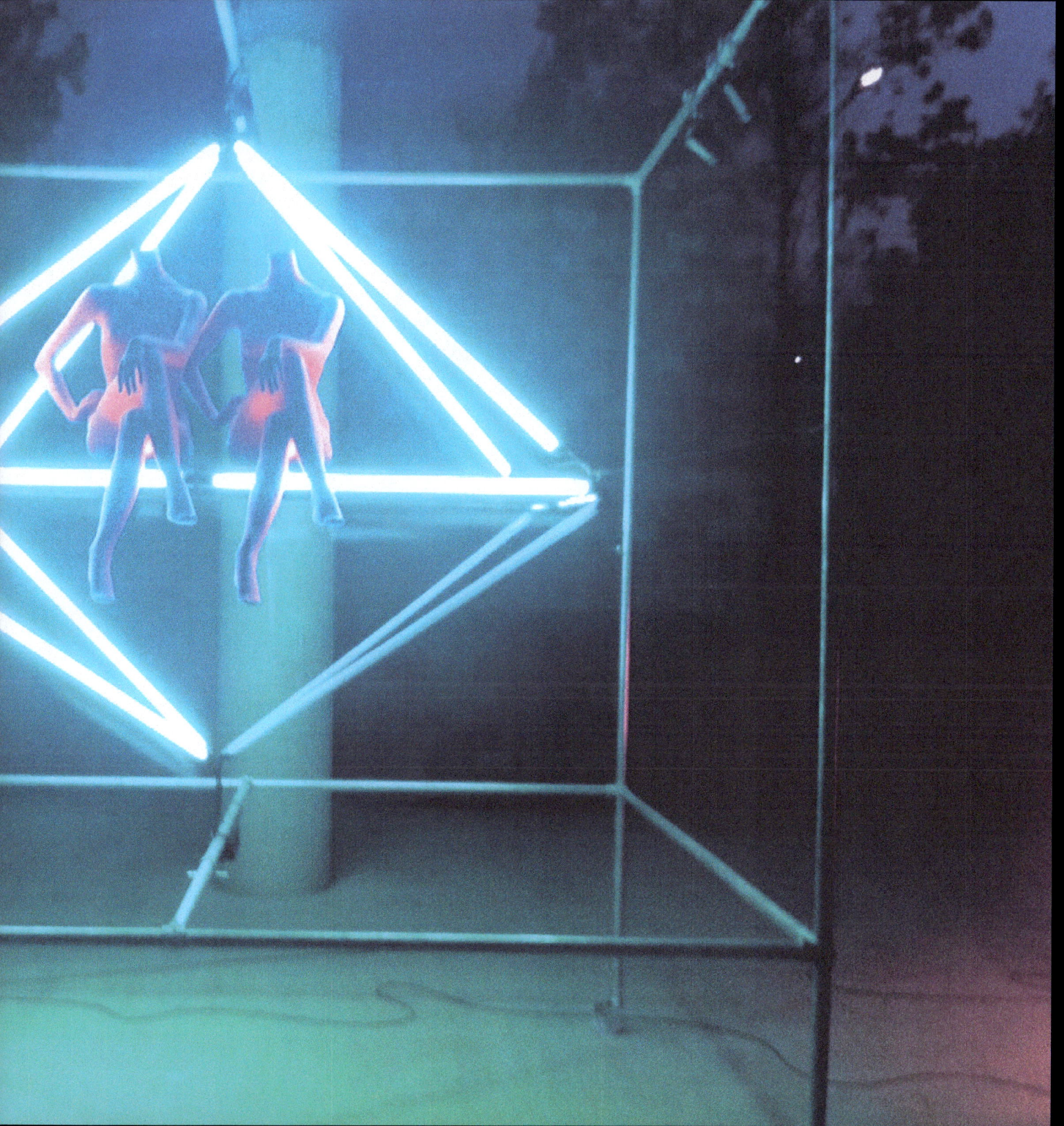

In some ways you and I chose to be dead. We chose to be together because we felt so alive, but then we tried to capture, and bottle it, and it just went off. Aliveness isn't something that can be contained. It needs to be lived.

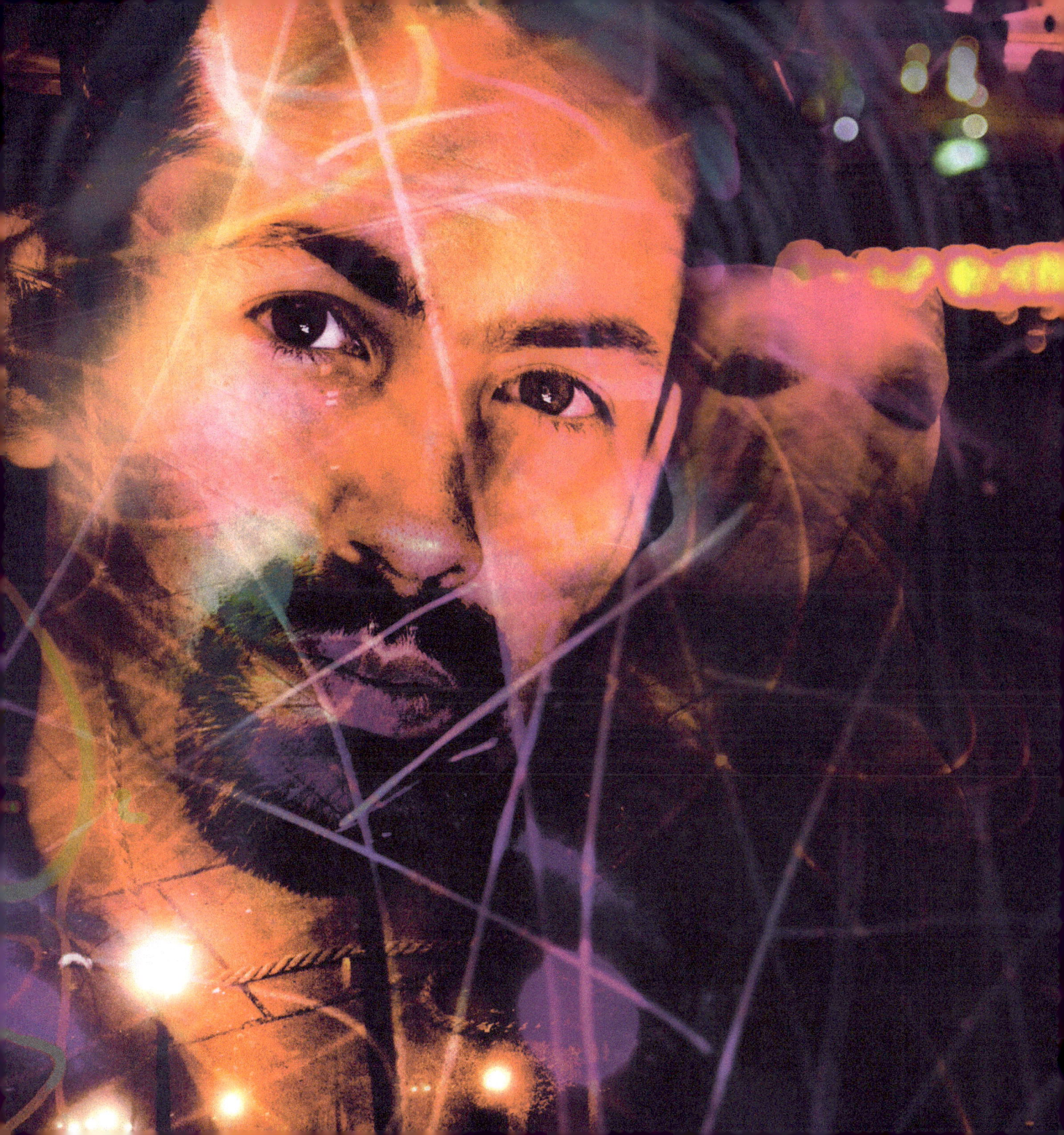

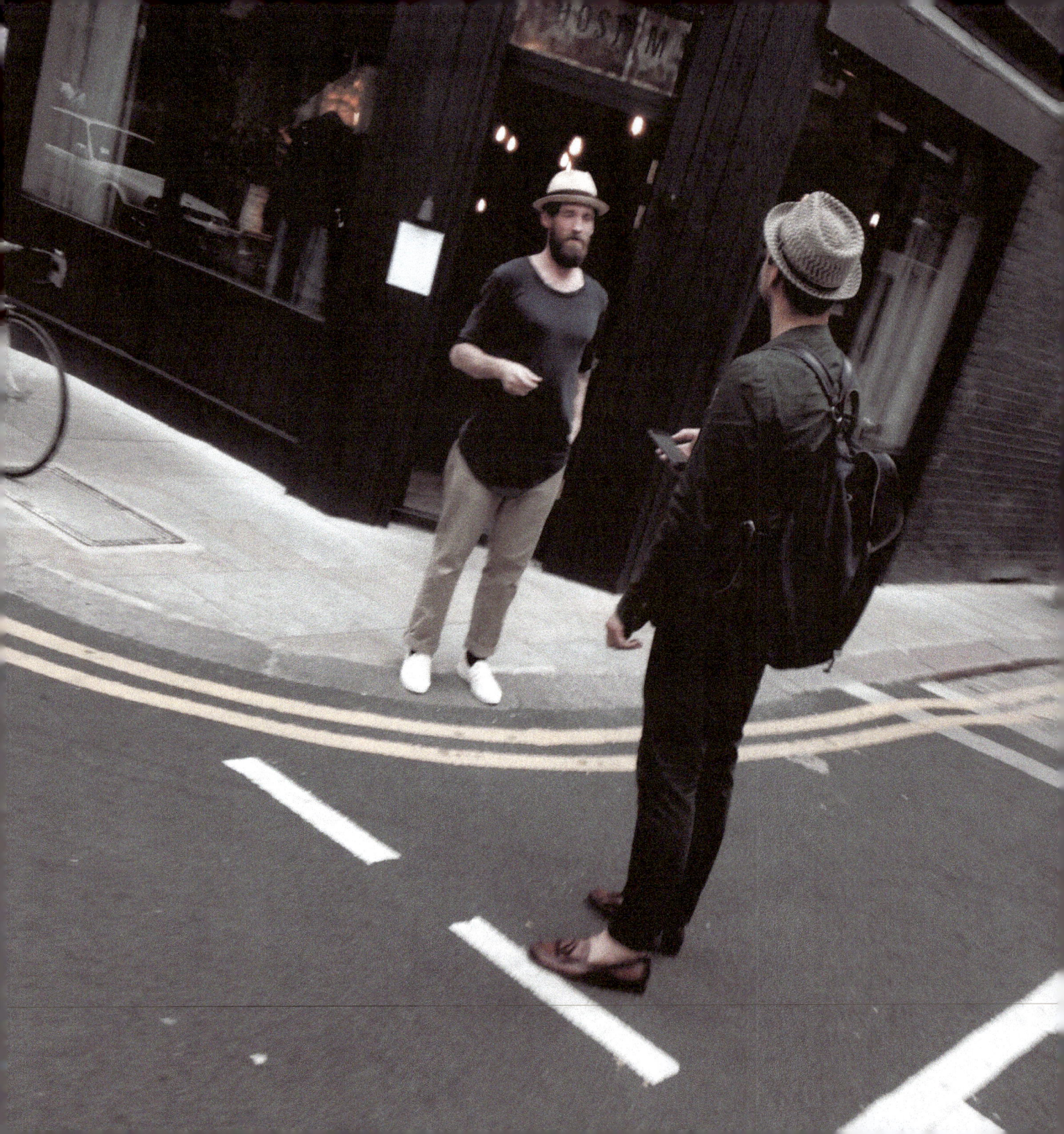

I sometimes wonder if he's gay. Nah. Not like that. He seems interested enough. Nope. That wouldn't bother me. I'm not like 'Stone him! Burn the sinner at the stake!' I've got nothing against gays. I'm really liberal and everything. It's more like the *mind-wandering-as-I-fall asleep-really-late-after-really-hot-sex-that-he just-didn't-seem-to-notice* way. Know what I mean? Maybe? Ummm.... ok.

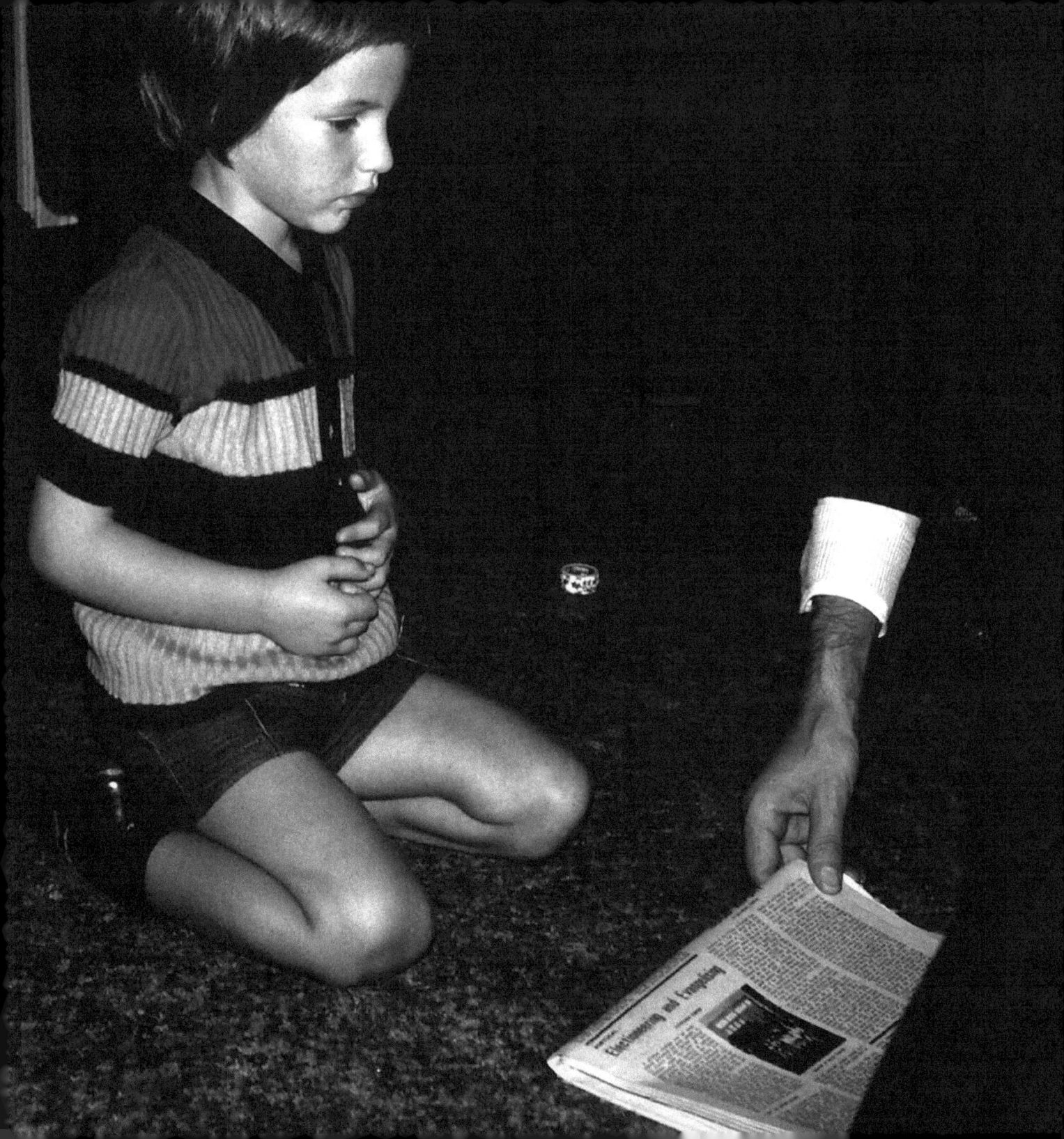

My pain is fear. Terror, encoded in my body. Fear of being negated, of not being seen, not being valued. The terror of never being whole. Alone. Scared of being me. Scared of not. Frozen.

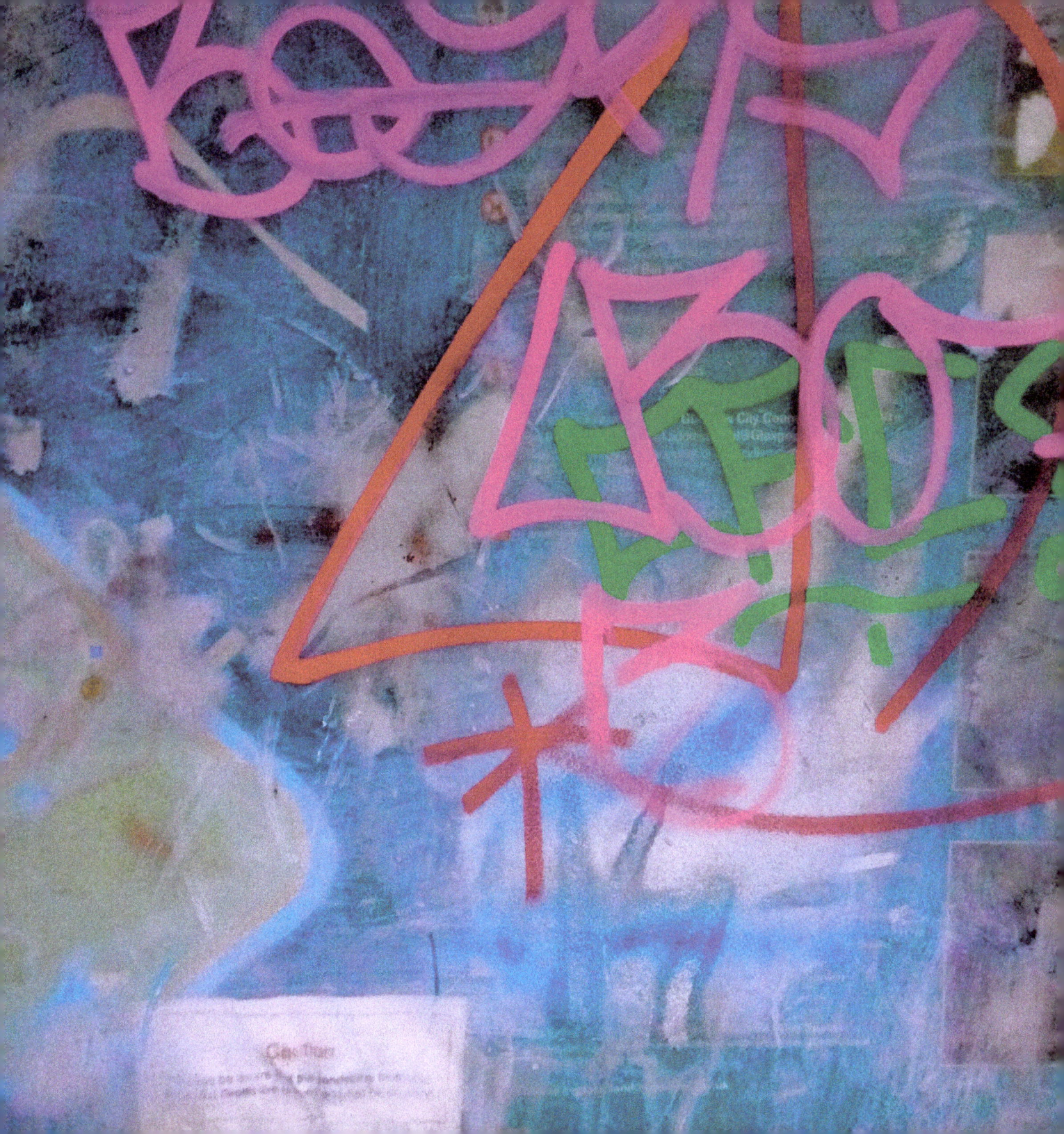

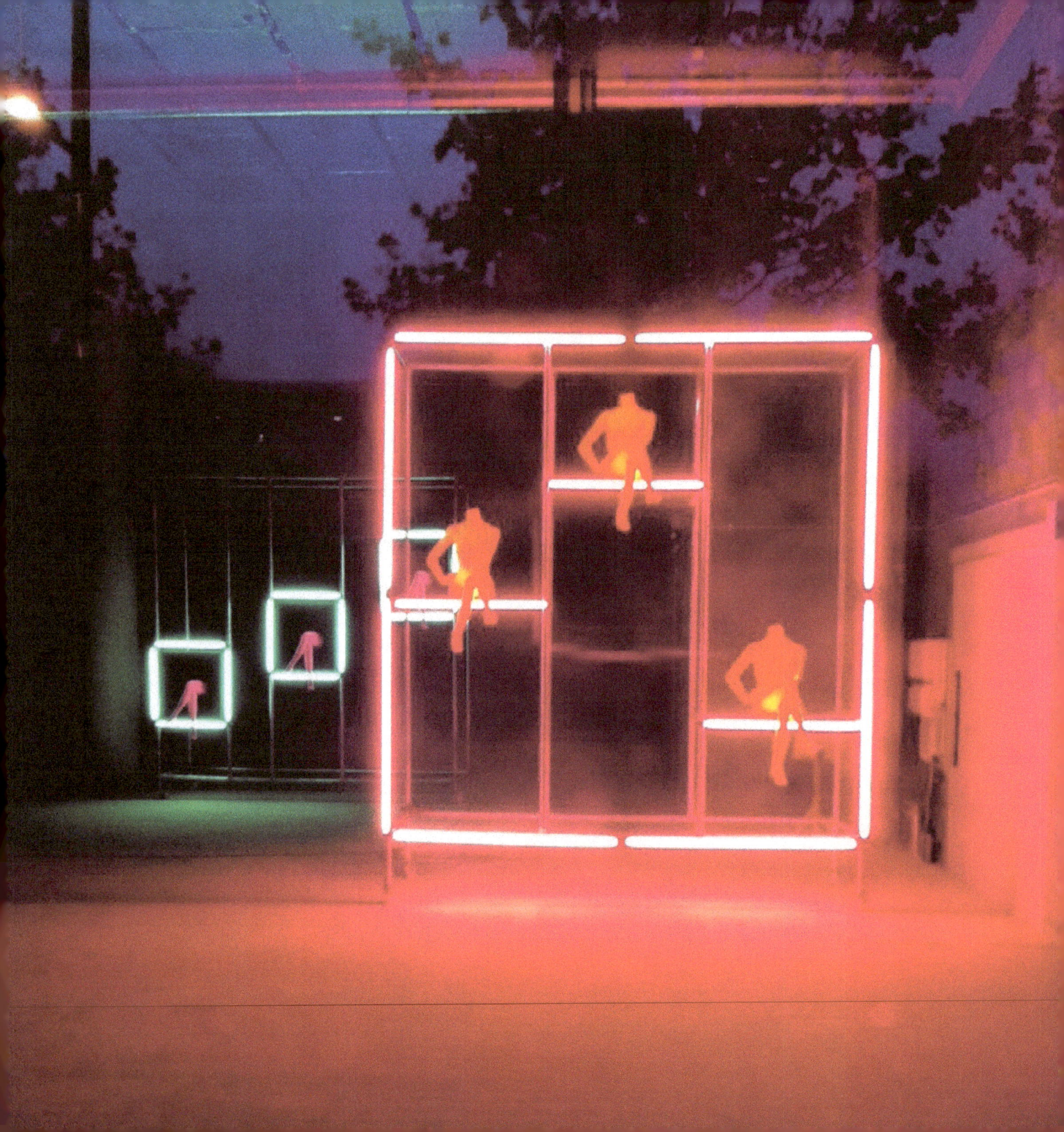

Your body
calls to my body—
even in sleep,
sleep begun in anger and fear.

Your hand curls around my hip,
pulling me closer
before pushing me away.

Hair on the back of my neck. I
wonder what he's done. Who has
he raped, or murdered? What will
he do next? To whom? I shiver—
get on the train.

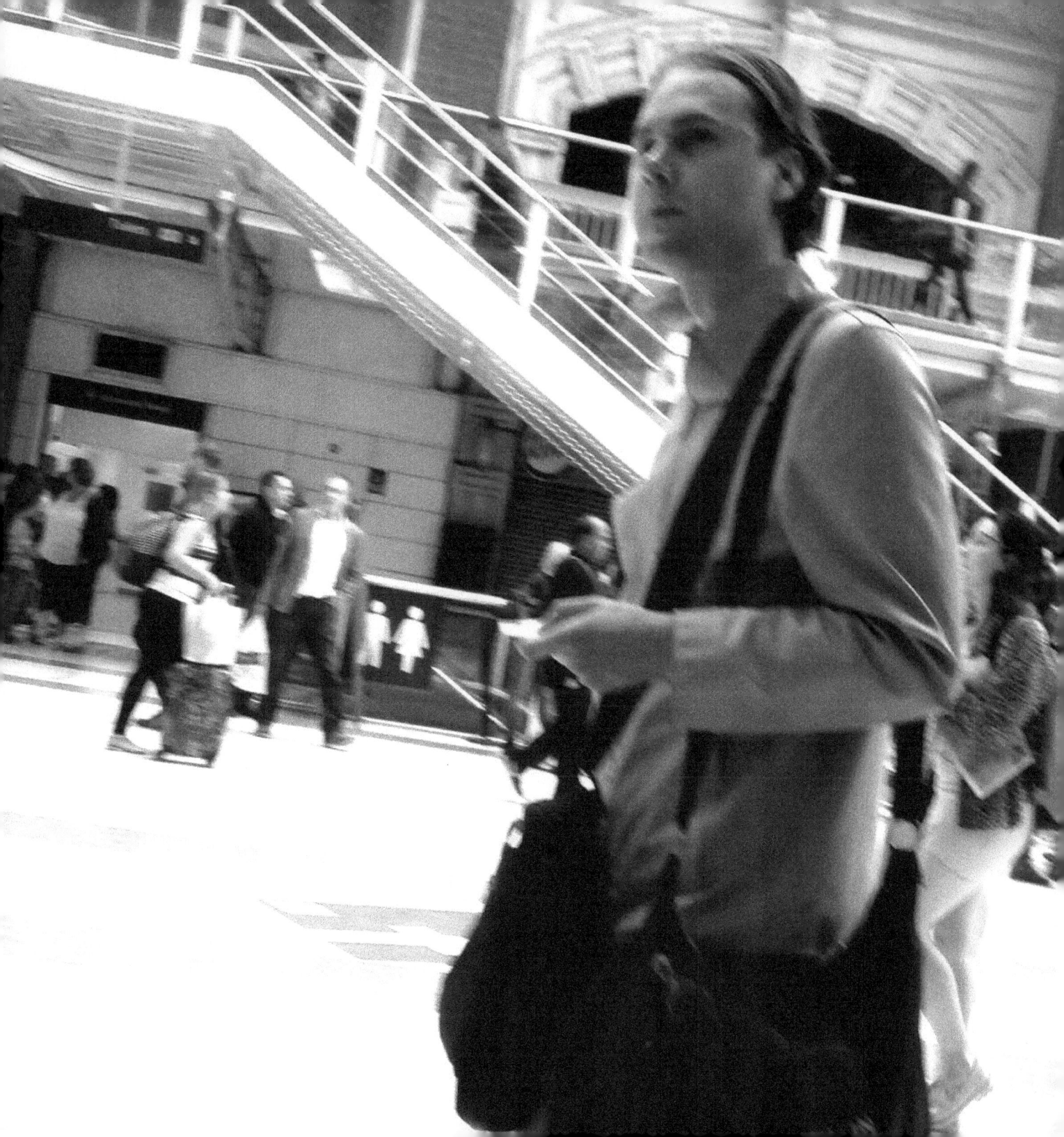

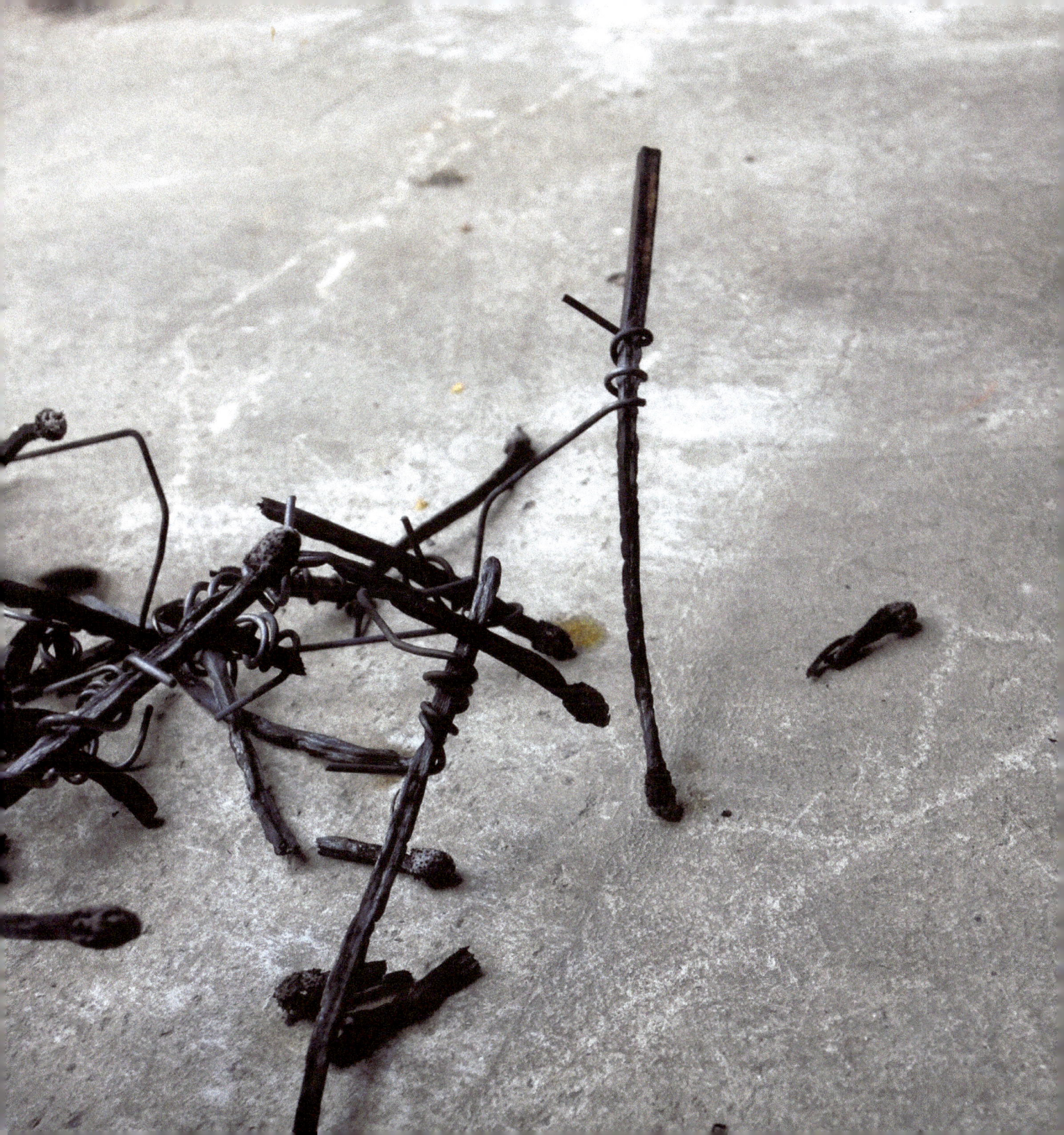

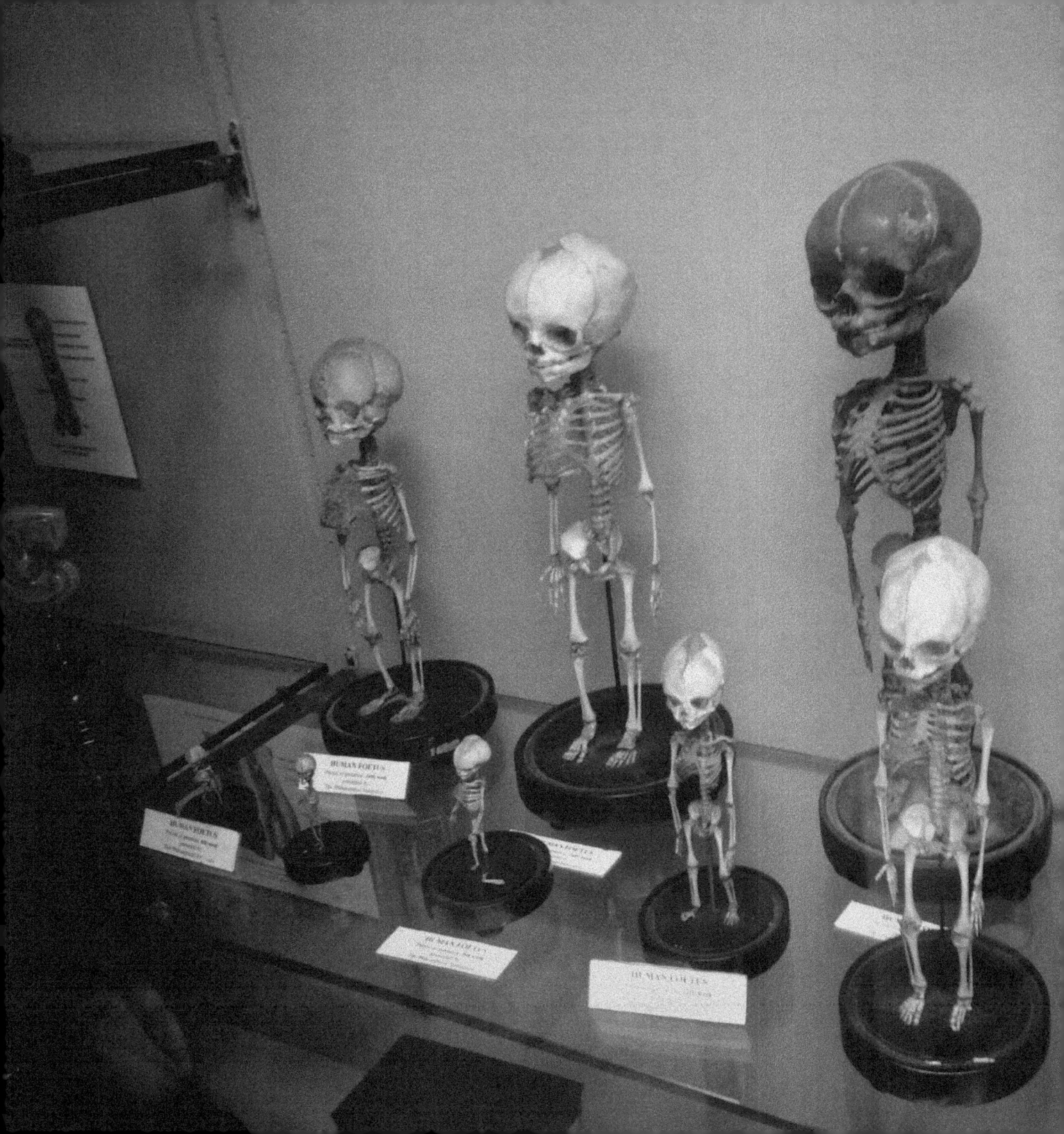

I worry about her—
she looks cold.
He's turned her into a dolly,
with a seam-mouth,
and too-blue eyes.

Naked bones,
naked bones,
such
tiny, tiny toes.
Dangling.
A puppet from a pole.

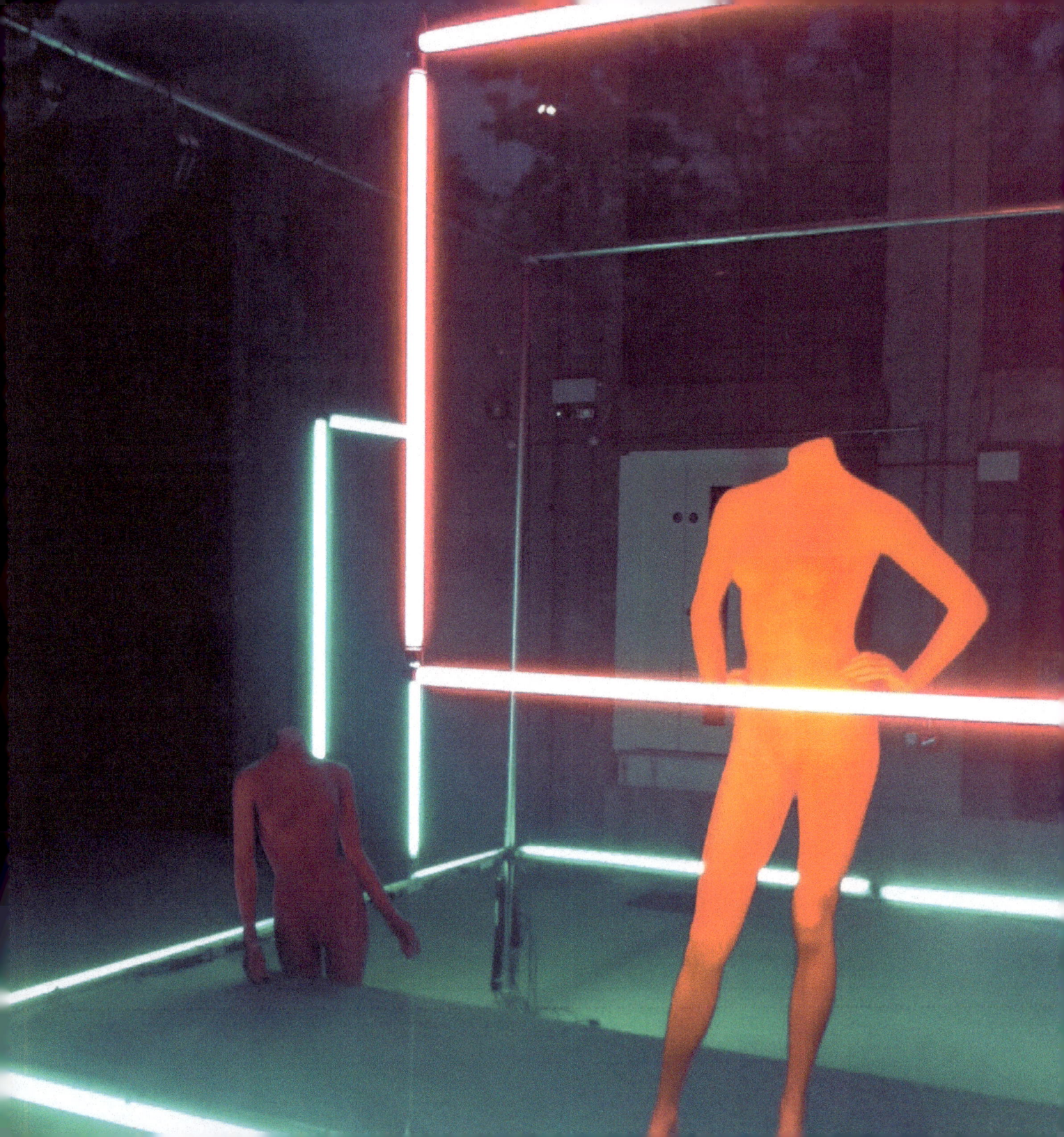

I am reliably informed that
15 years cannot offset
the 10 minutes
of joyless rutting
with random 20-somethings
you imagine will change your life forever.

It will—
cover my face with your thumb
on all the photos, squint, and you'll get the general idea.

Or perhaps you'll find someone better,
more compliant,
who will pretend along with you,
that intimacy in the absence of love is possible,
or love is something irresponsible and easy,
that anyone can have with anyone.

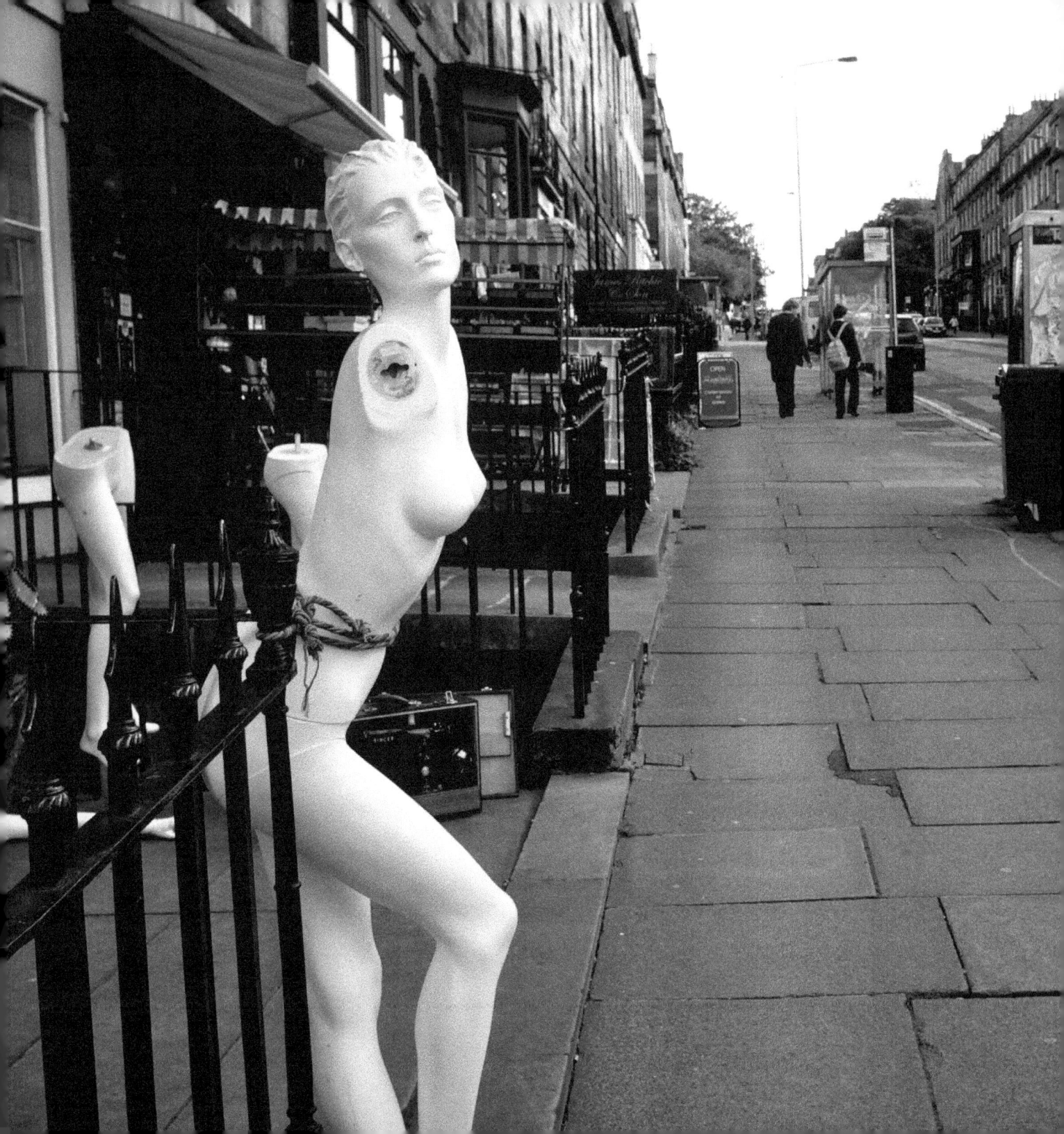

You didn't want sophistication.
You didn't want skill.
It's always been the shrill ones,
the *ooohs!* and *aaaahs!*
willing to jack you off, metaphorically speaking,
stroking your ego in public,
who command your attention.

Who am I, after all, burning inside as I do?
I lick you with my eyes,
but you don't notice,
fuck you with my mind—
but you don't feel it.

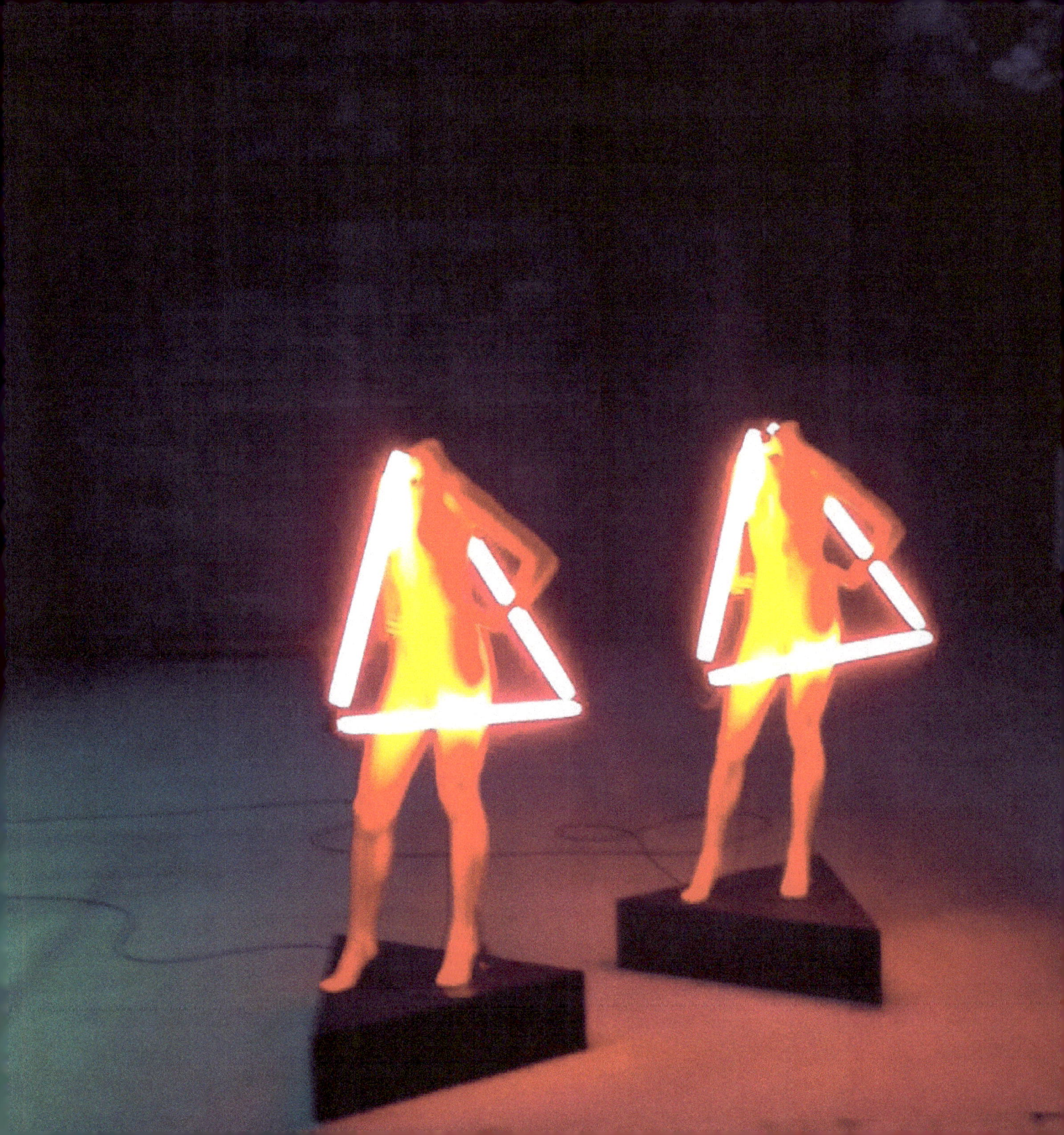

Do you prefer
the love and lust you steal
when I'm asleep?

Sex, picking my pocket
when no one else can see,
and dark hides you from yourself?

We commit this body to the
ground; earth to earth, ashes to
ashes, dust to dust.

– Book of Common Prayer

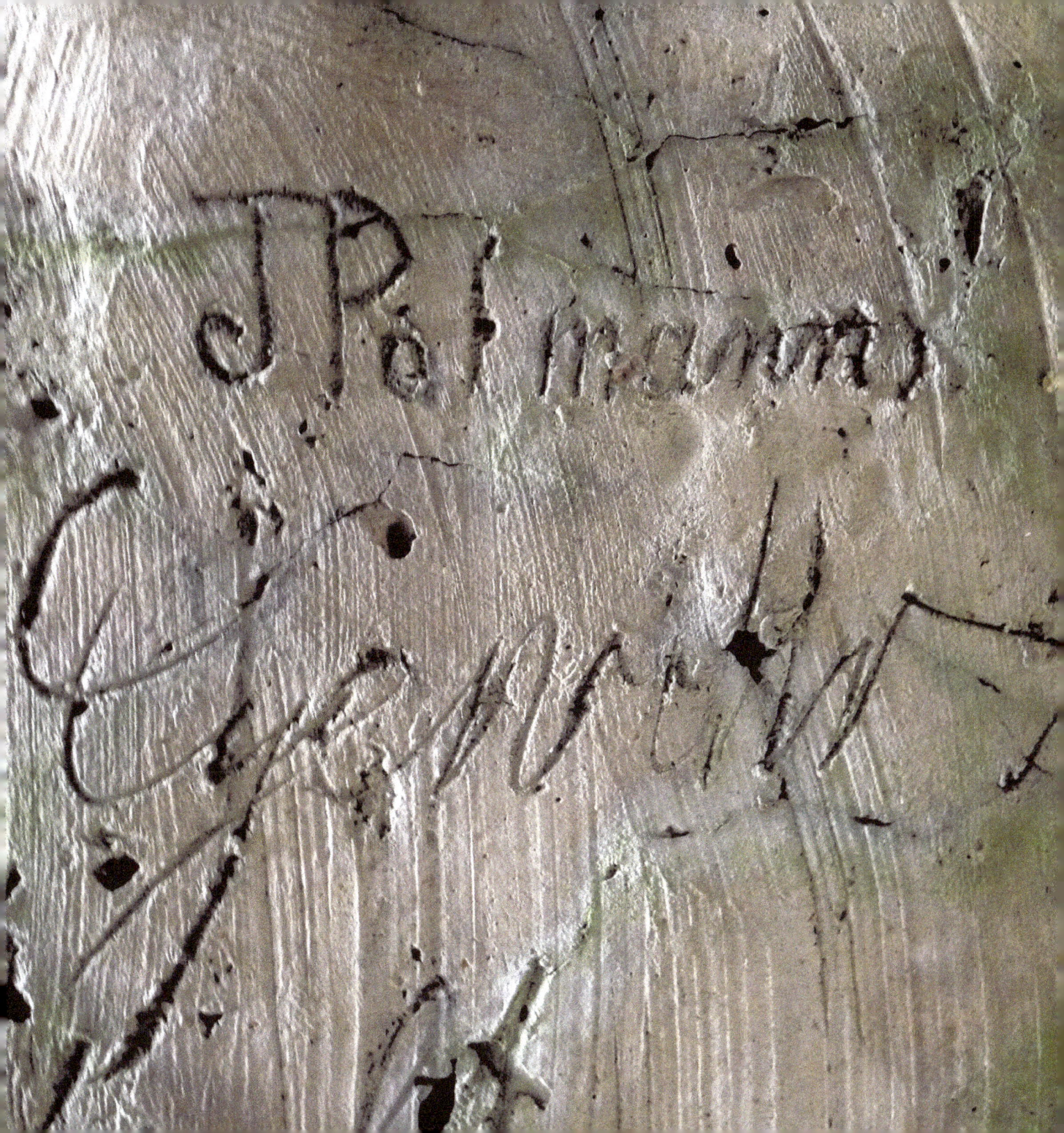

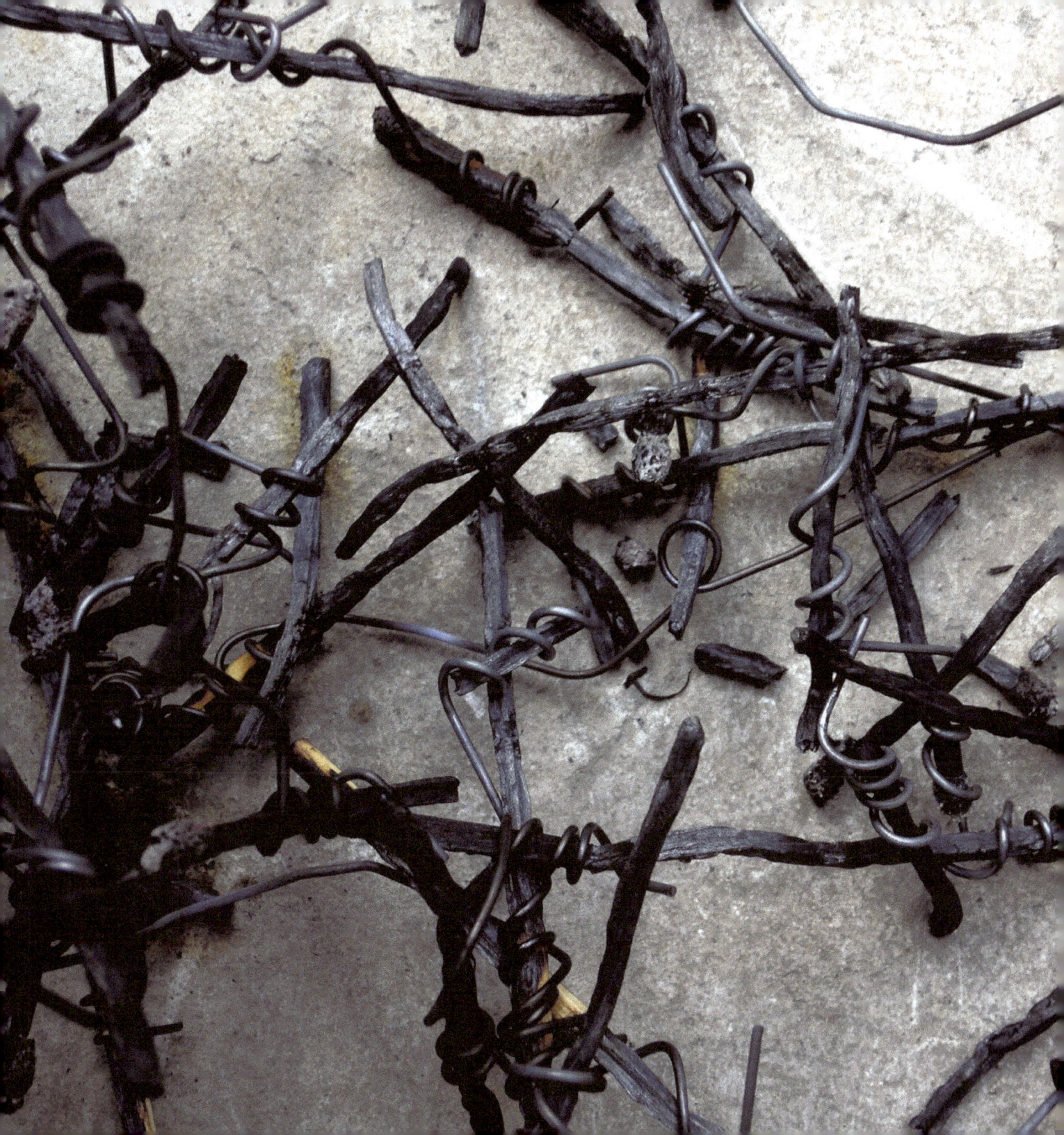

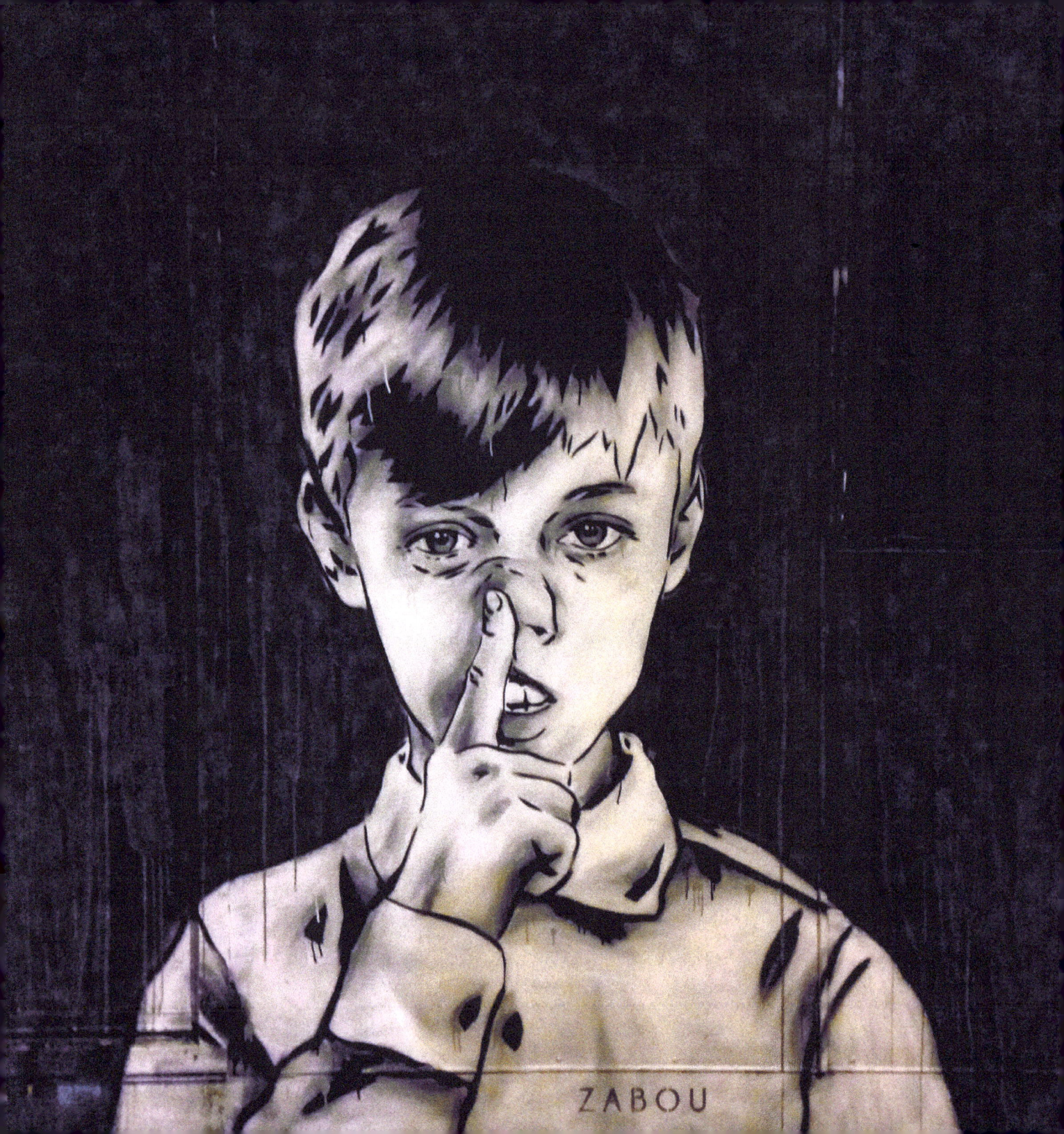

You threw us away
trying to find your self.

vivo sunt liberandi

animas suas

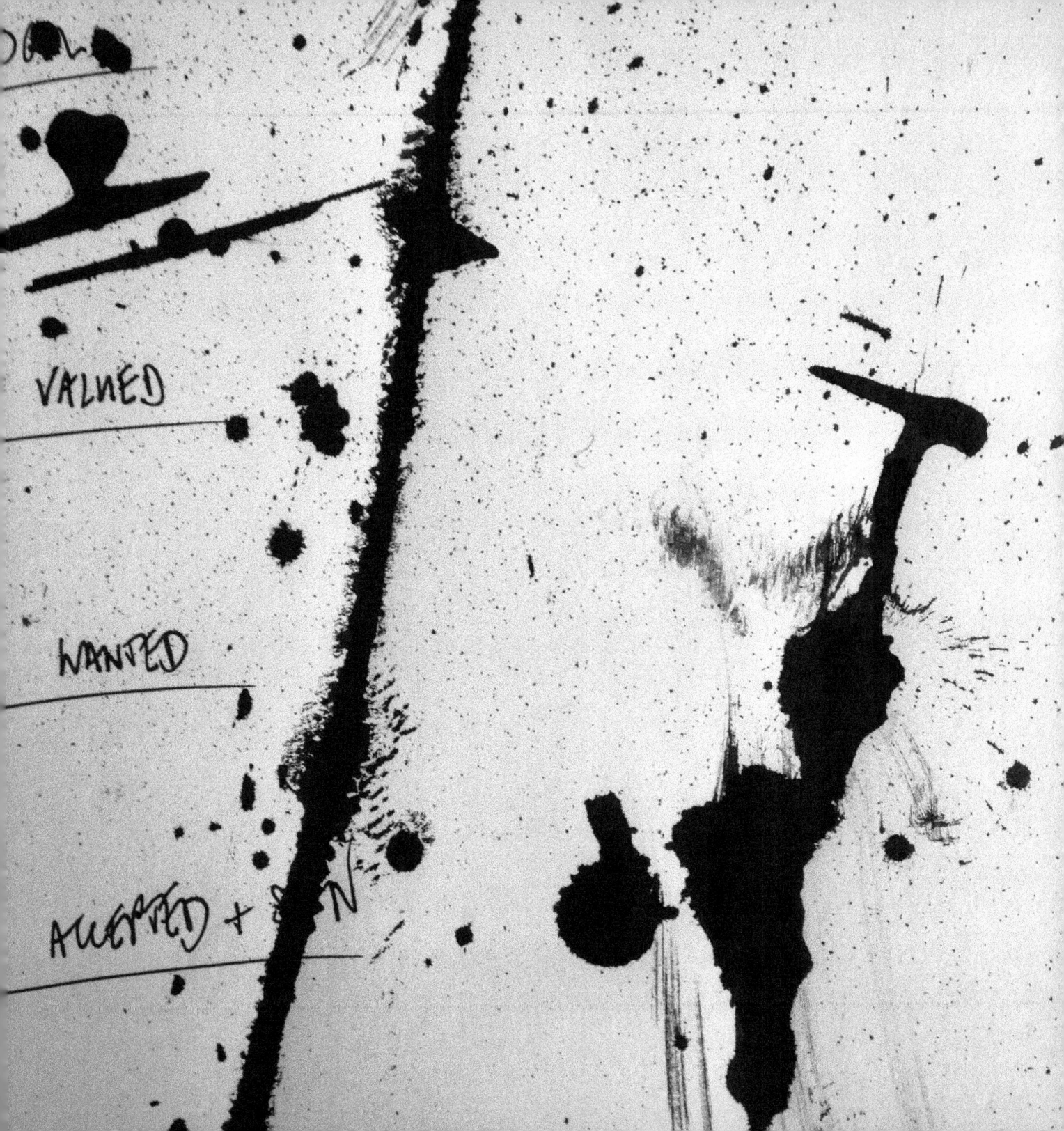

I love you—with your
vulnerabilities, the things that
make you human and capable
of being hurt. Fragile.

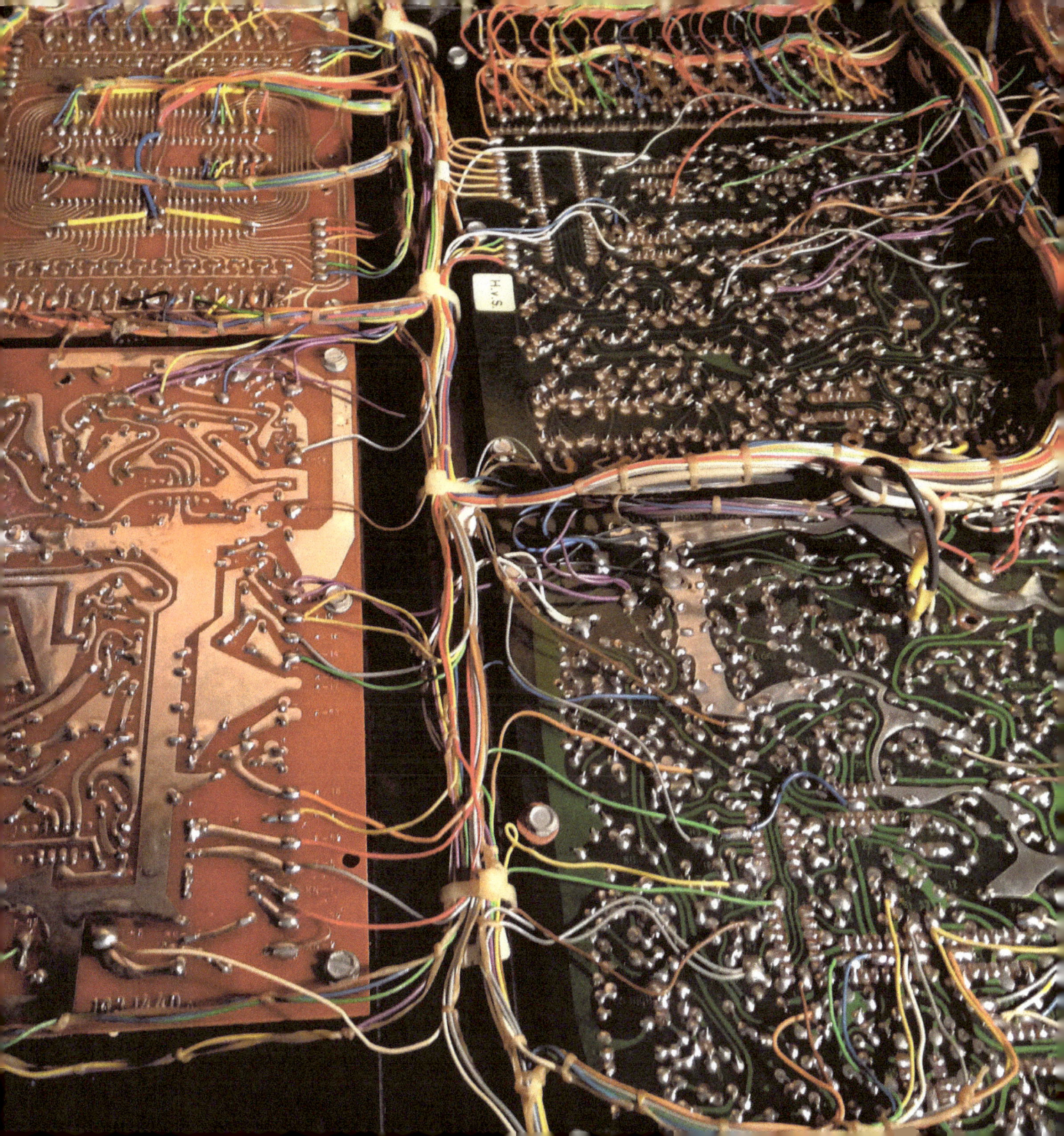

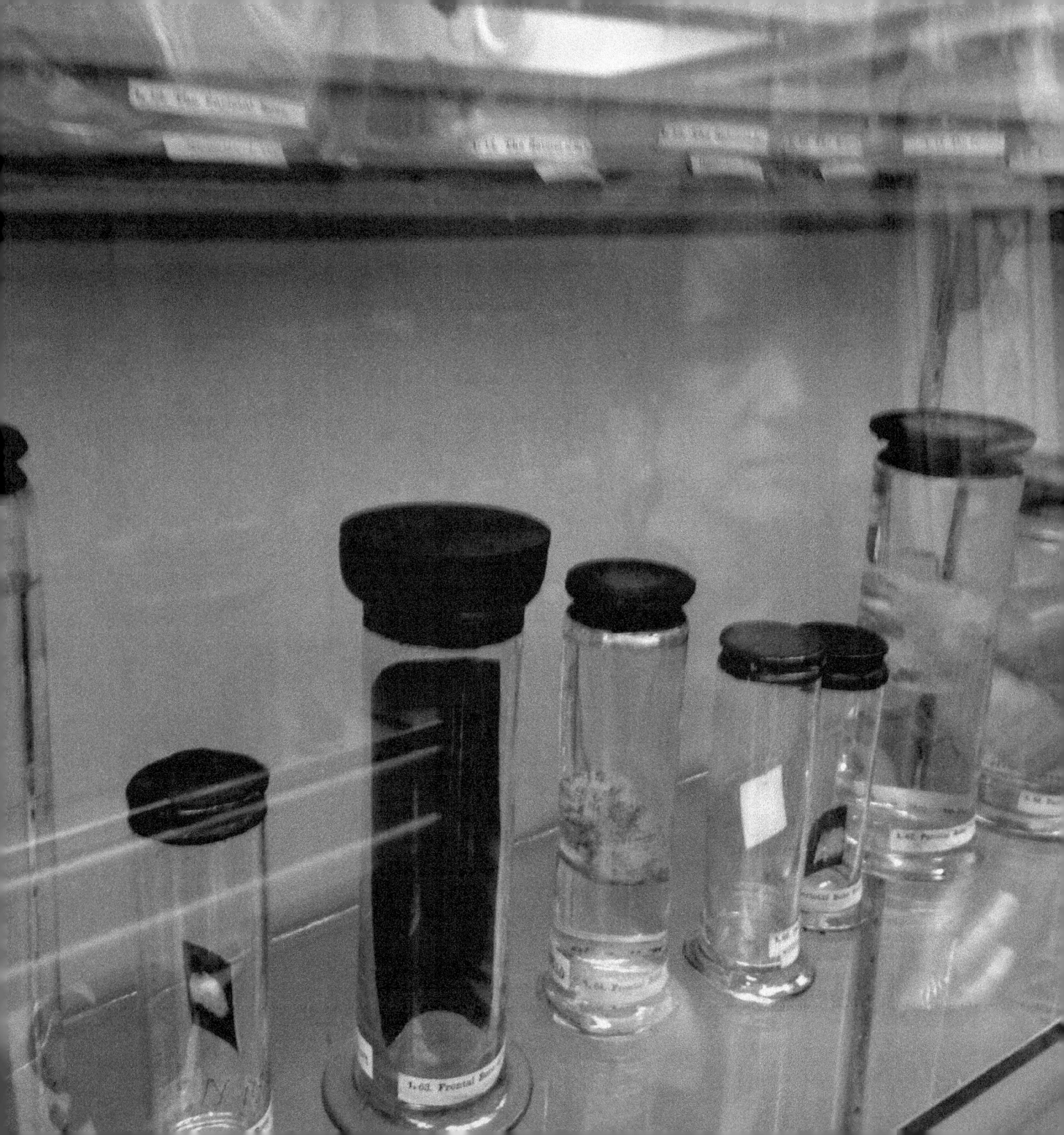

Just like Grandma's storm cellar—
miles of wobbly metal shelving
filled with jars,
in William's basement.

Specimens, floating.
Home-canned.
Each an anatomical curiosity.

This shelf holds
Queen Charlotte's pets, recycled—
the dissected eyeball of a nilgai.

I imagine myself stretched out on one of the shelves,
reclined on my left hip, leg covered in inky squiggles,
filing my nails, waiting patiently to be examined.

Grisly remains.
Not too particular about where his corpses came from, they say,
especially the pregnant ones.
He didn't mind,
overly much,
if they were still whimpering when the cutting started.

Gravid uterus, a label says,
but all I see is Death, perfectly formed, sleeping-with-eyes-closed,
thumb-in-mouth, permanent five months gestation.

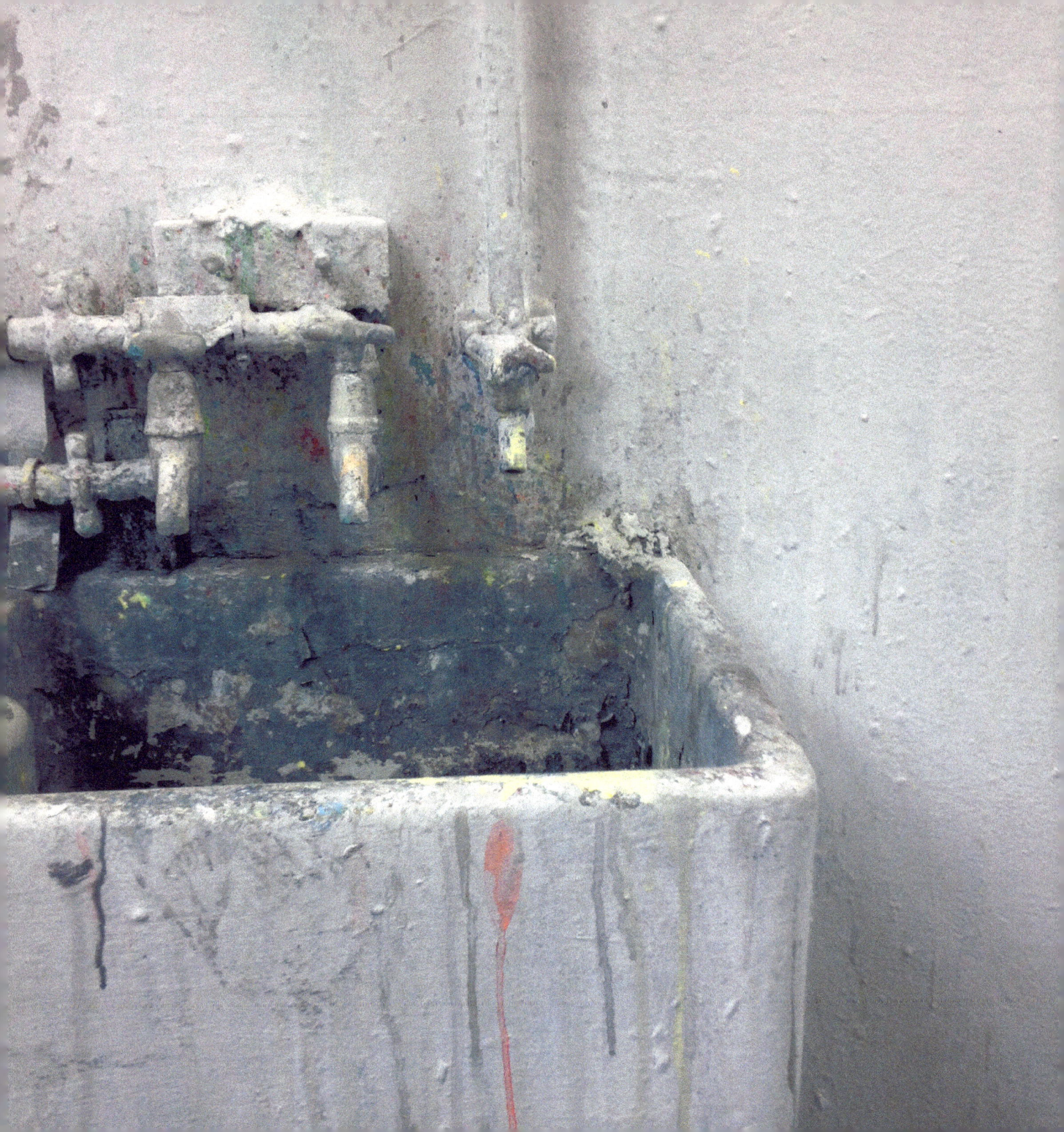

I am, now—
filth-bucket,
landfill,
lightning-eater,
burnt to a cinder.

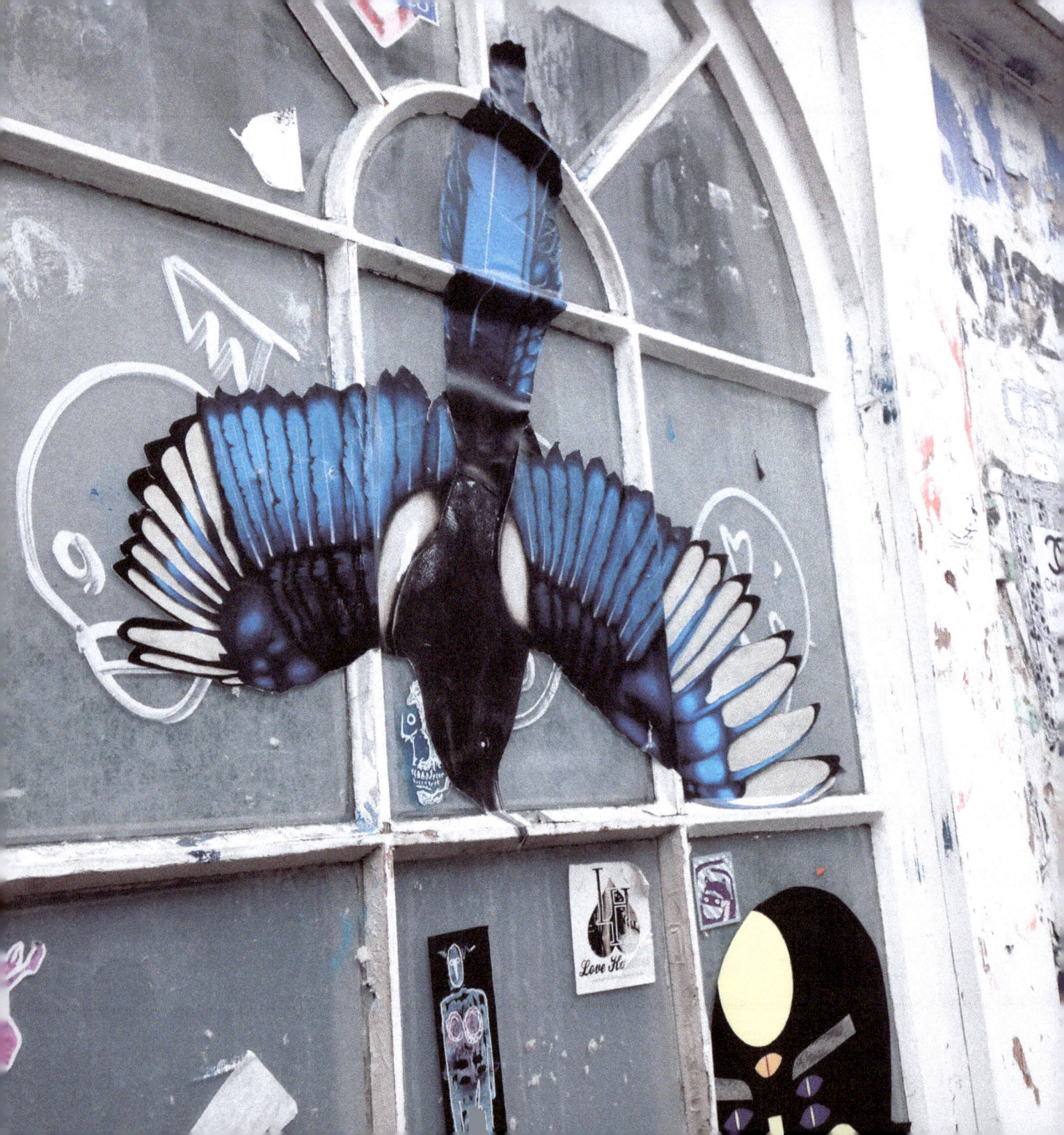

We are—

6 fingered glove
5 wheeled bus
4 cornered triangle
3 legged horse
one-armed bank robber
2 headed coin

A broken sparrow that flies no more

EREA

VION

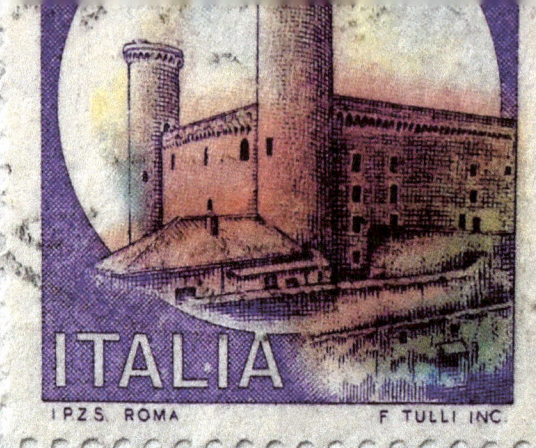

ITALIA

I.PZS. ROMA   F TULLI INC.

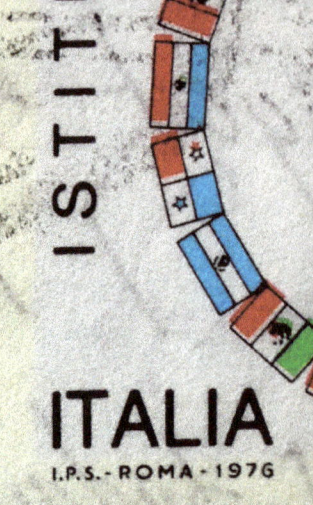

ISTITU

ITALIA
I.P.S.-ROMA-1976

Mary McDonough
℅ 1015 West Benton
Iowa City   IA 52
U.

If the falling out of love
were as gentle
as the falling in love had been—
I'd leave tomorrow.
I'd leave now.

But there's no gentleness to be had.

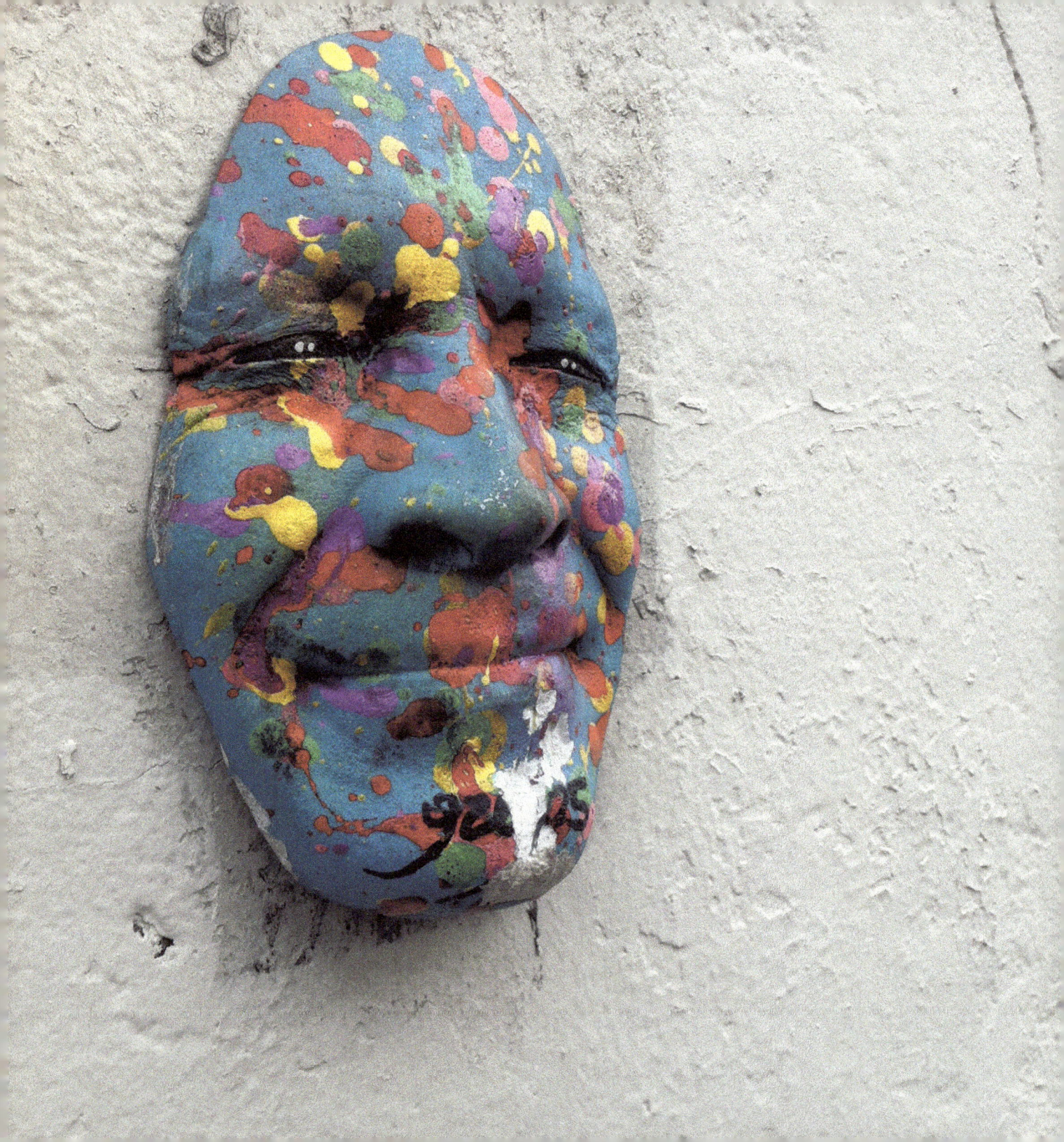

When I had given up hope of ever
being me again, alive again, something
snapped. I tore myself open. Light
came out.

I'm sewn back together. All threads,
and crazy coloured knots, and zigzags,
and gaps.

*Nobody ever told me before
that my CHOICES are what's
creating my problems—I need
to remember that.*

Her well-rehearsed victim spiel had fallen on deaf ears.
In the past, I'd have felt too much guilt and shame to
help her. Now I see *hers*, and I tell her the truth: it's
her problem, and I can't, and won't, fix it for her.

*I need to make REALLY different
choices, don't I, if I want my
life to change?*

I tell her I don't give money to people who beg, but
she can have £5 if I can take a photo of her for my
book. She promises to use the cash to pay for a hostel.

We hug.

I hope she's not lying about that too.

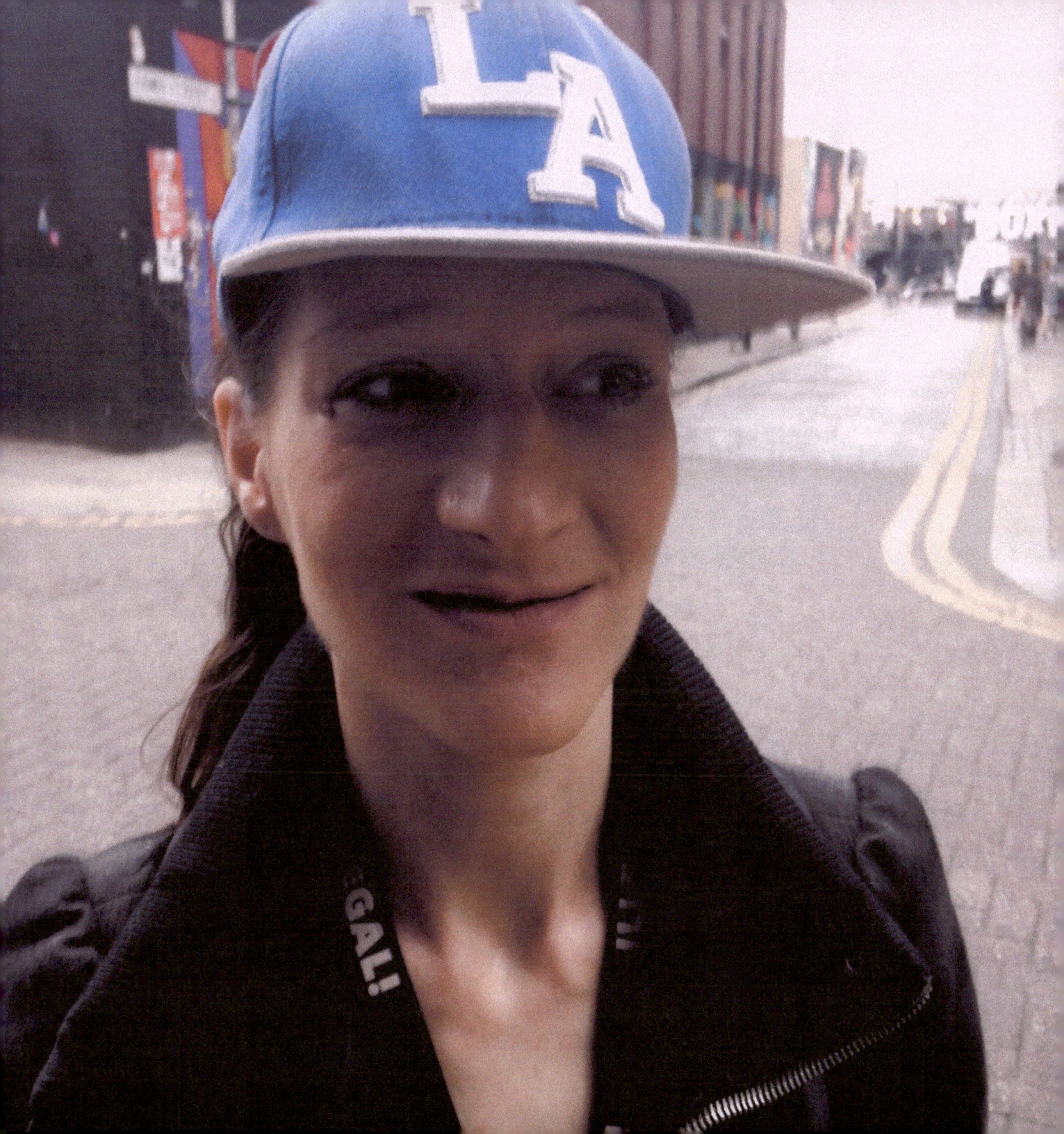

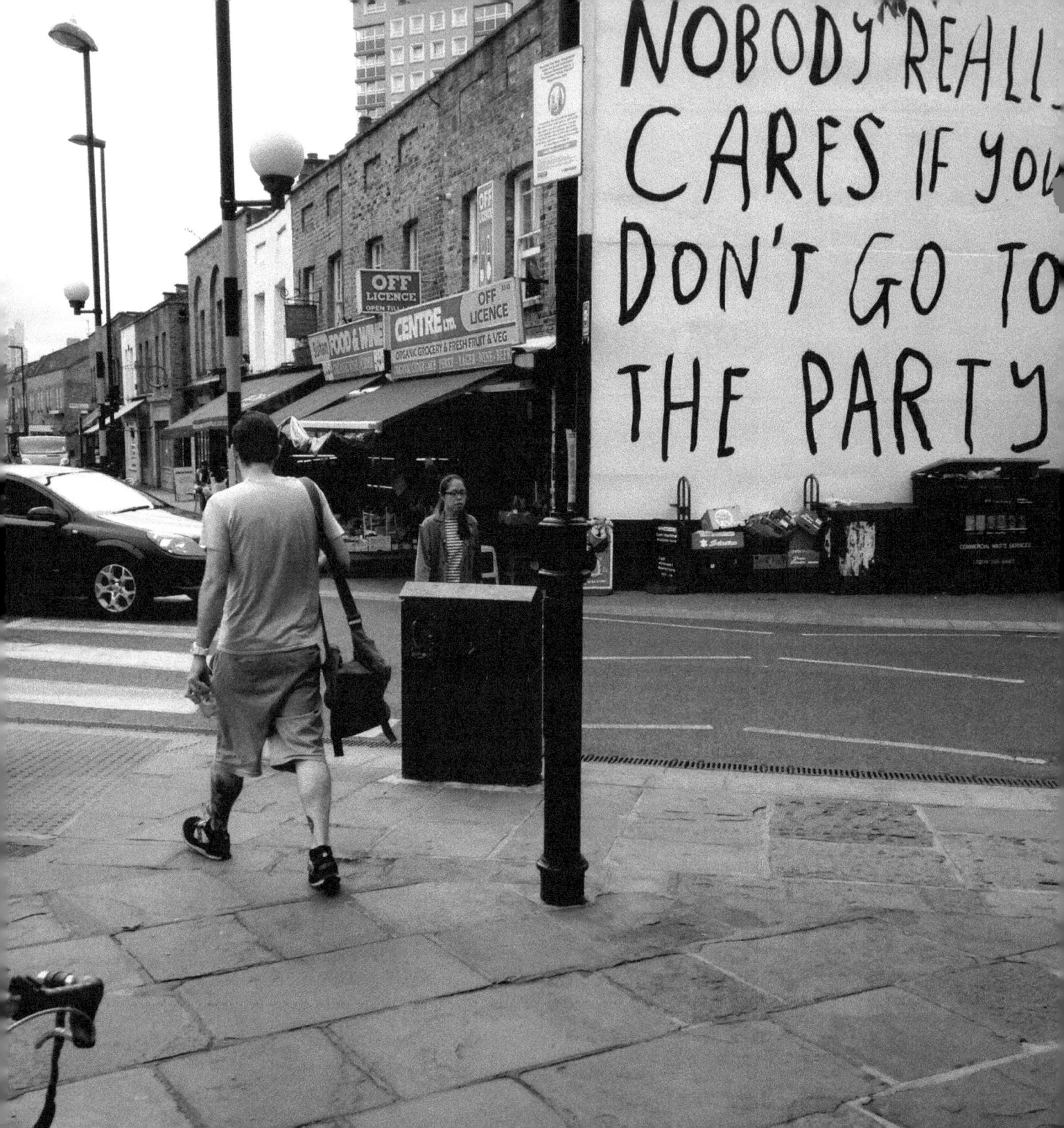

There's never a right time. Only now. No right. No wrong. Just choices that work for us—or don't.

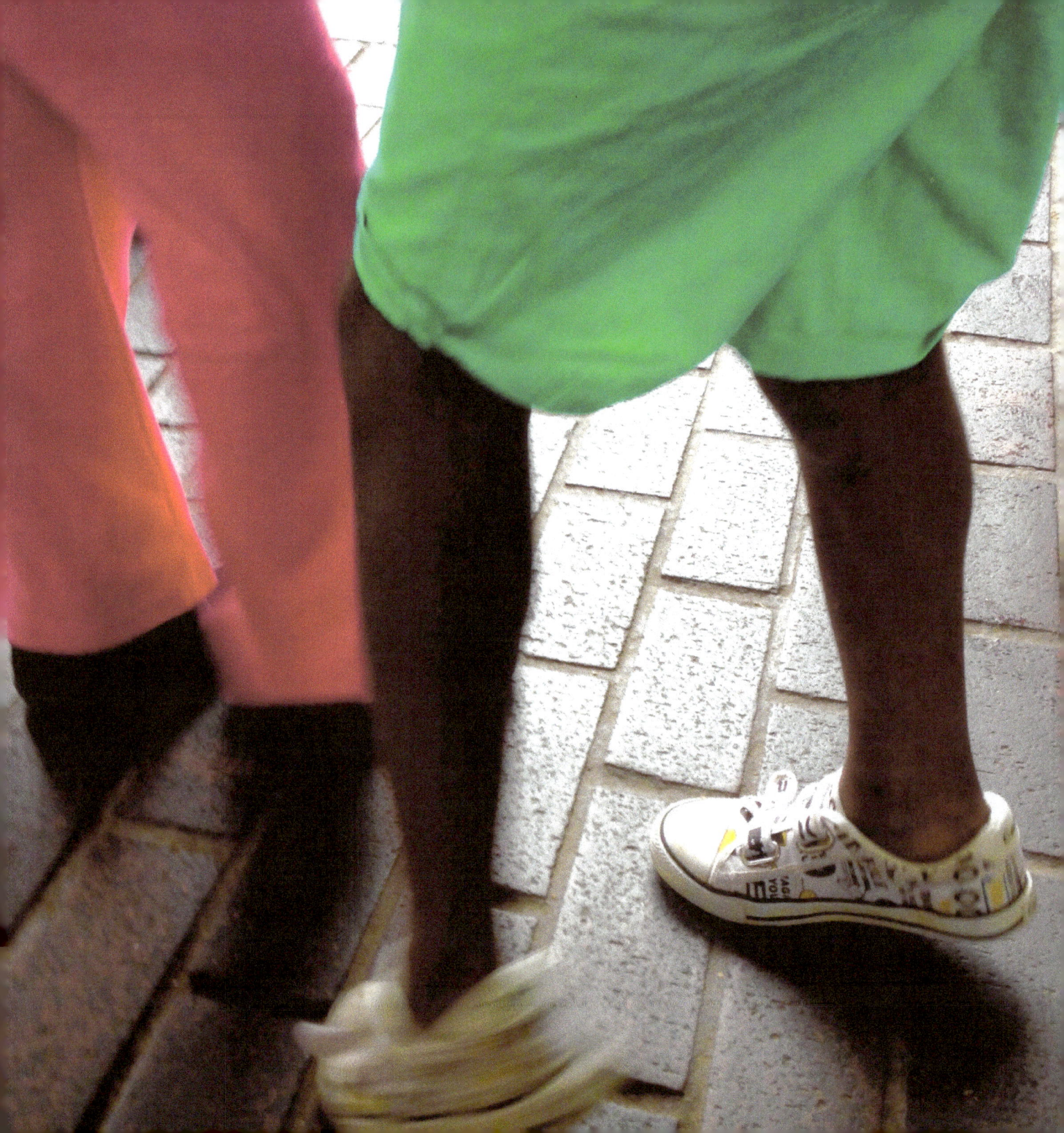

If Kurt Cobain was in my first grade class, he could have come over to play. I could have said

> *It's ok if you want Jesus to have you for a sunbeam; I don't mind being the dark one.*

We could play cops & robbers. I'd be the baddie. I'd tell him

> *You can use my cousin's best gun— as long as you don't eat it.*

But that will never happen.

The Undertow. Always in capital letters, hushed tones, the same way people talk about cancer or alcoholism. *The Undertow will get you. Bite into you. Pull you down.* It can have me.

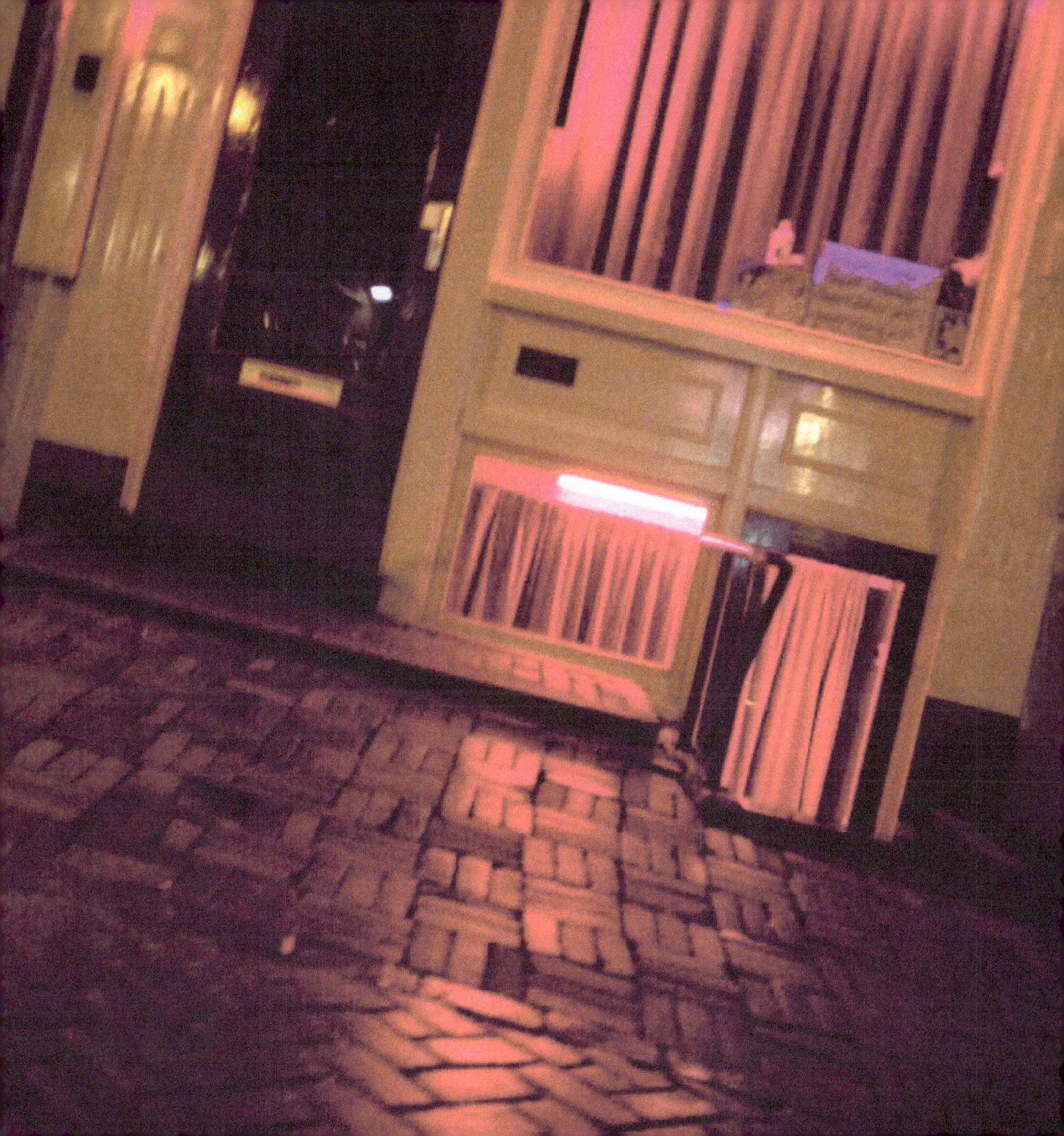

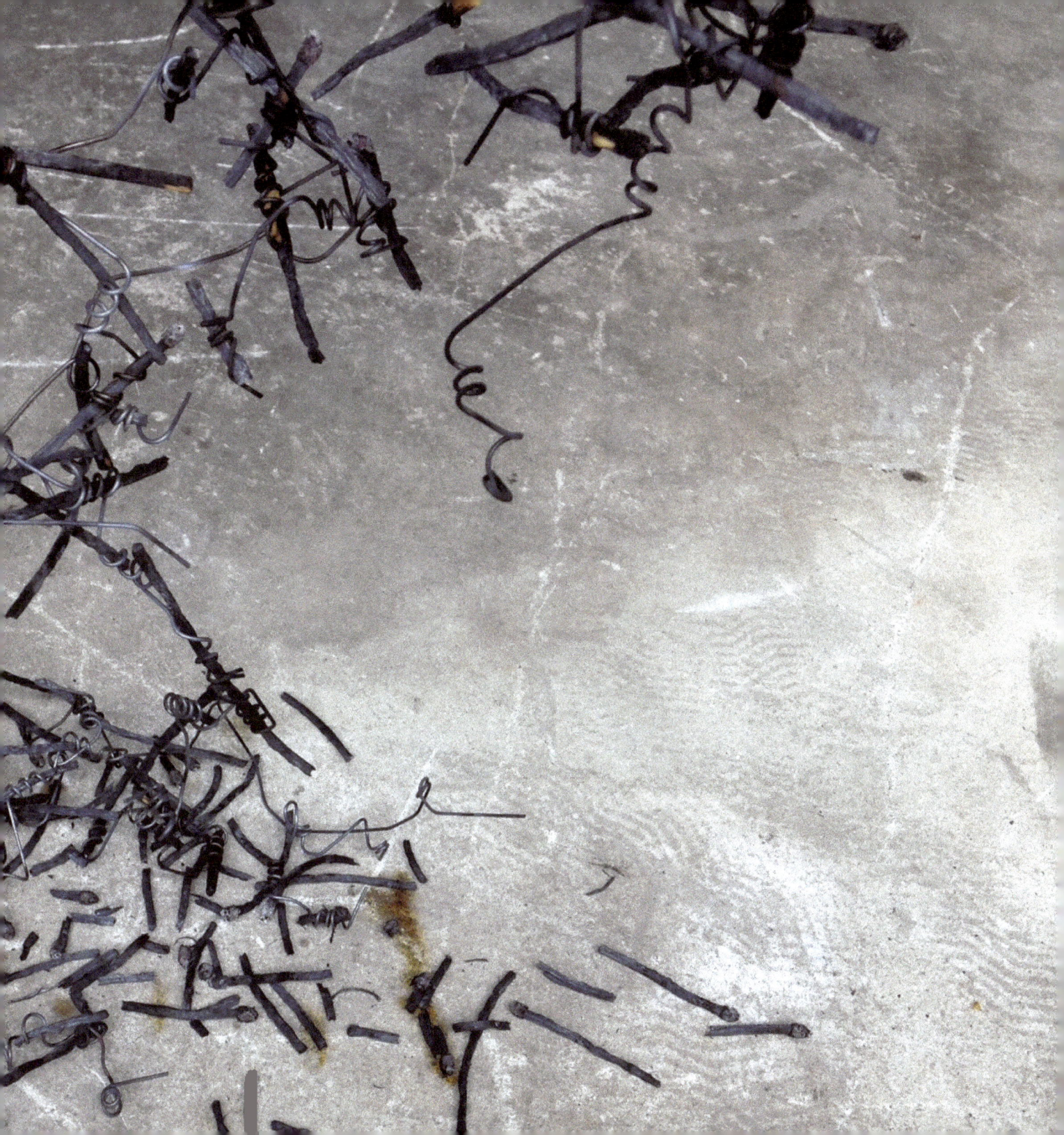

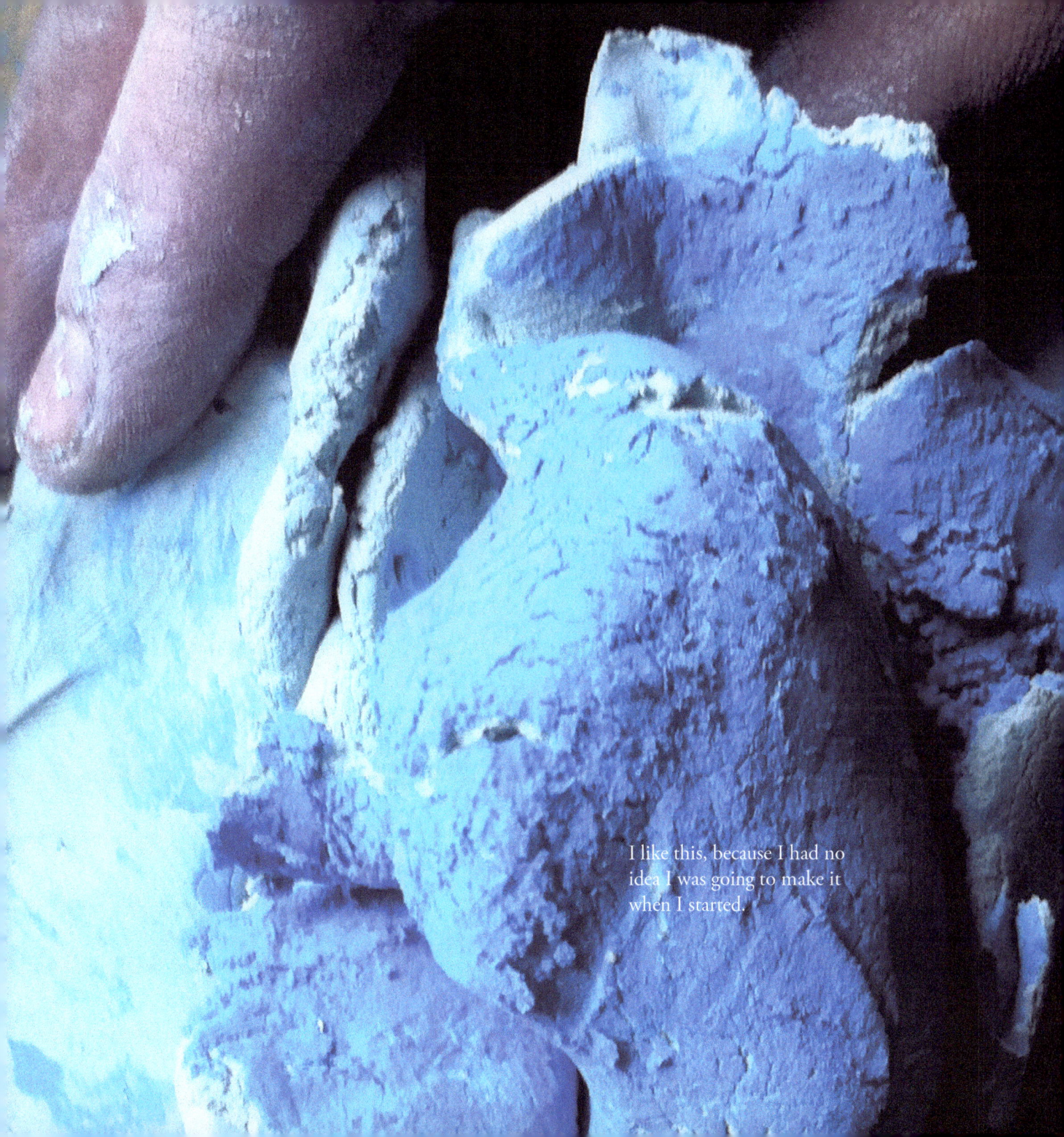

I like this, because I had no
idea I was going to make it
when I started.

48. 78. Uterus containing Twi

We're all sorts of ones and twos.
We live in a big bottle.
They let us be. I don't know why.
I didn't want to lose her. She's my friend.

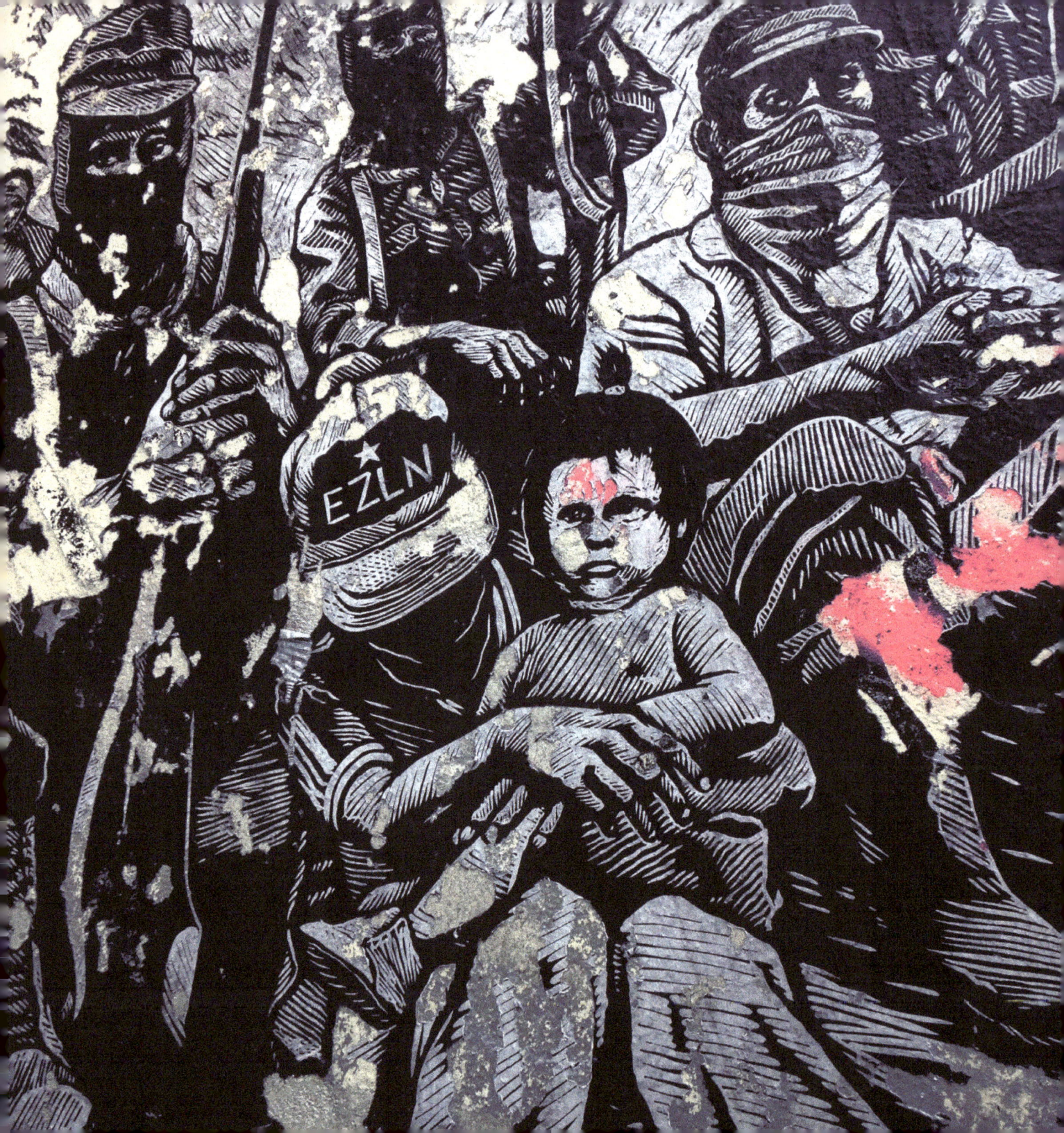

I want to touch all of
them, to take them
home, to wrap them
in blankets.

I've been as profligate as any drunk, staggering home, holes in his pockets, spilling love here and there; and now quarts, years later it is gone. I threw love after your retreating back, left crumbs of it, a trail to lure you home after the wicked witch had finished with you. I begged for it, grovelling like the patient dog I am, a kick as good as a kiss, because that's all I knew. I made it easy for you to use me. I am awake, and still alive enough to feel, to know what's missing— what I will never have.

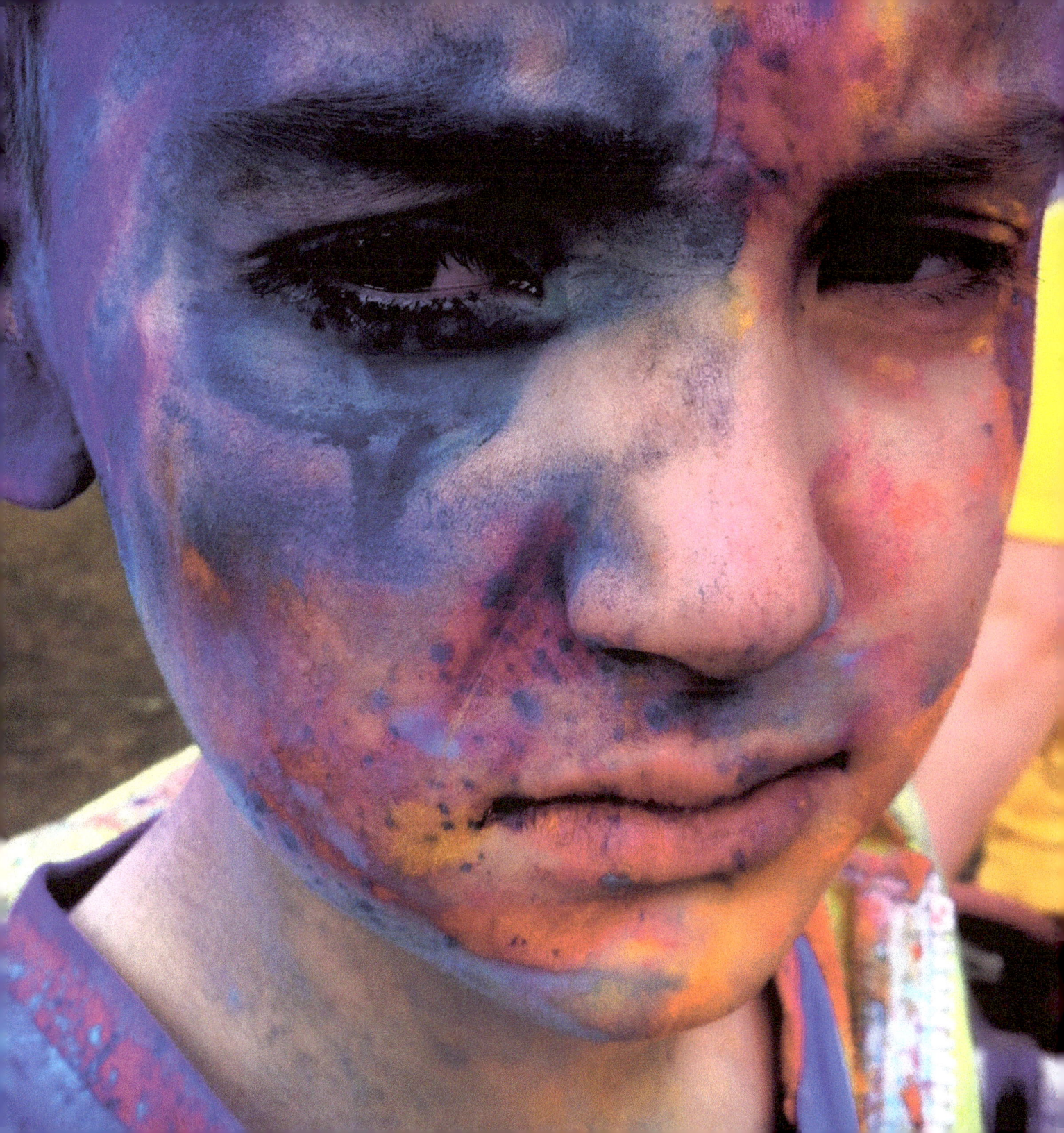

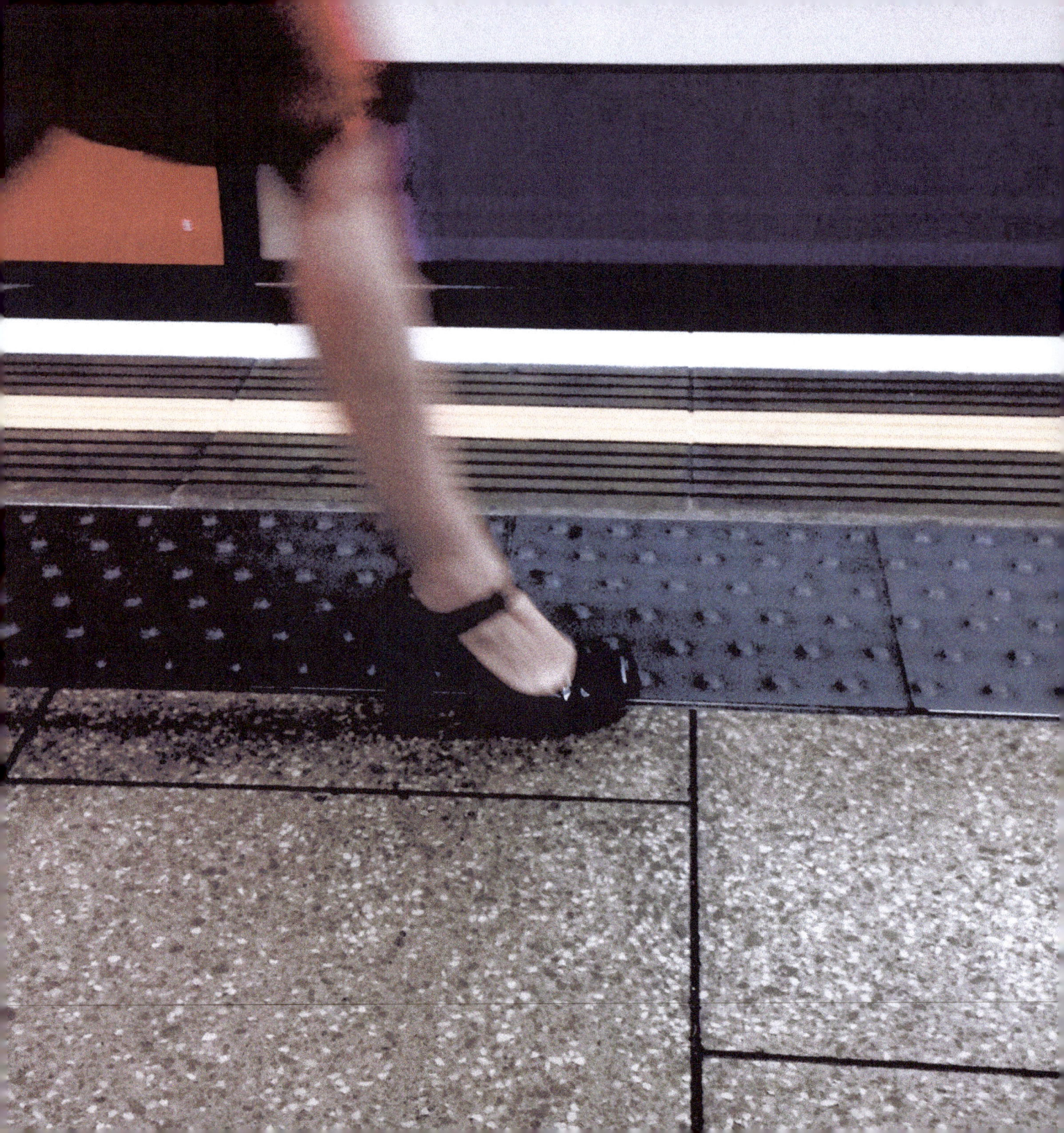

Débridement,
précisément,
pour éliminer ton taint,
the stain of your adulterous caresses.

Débridement,
because I'm no longer l'objet
de ton affection.

No granulation of the tissues
is apparent, post infection.
An open wound takes time to heal.
Death by a thousand shallow weals.

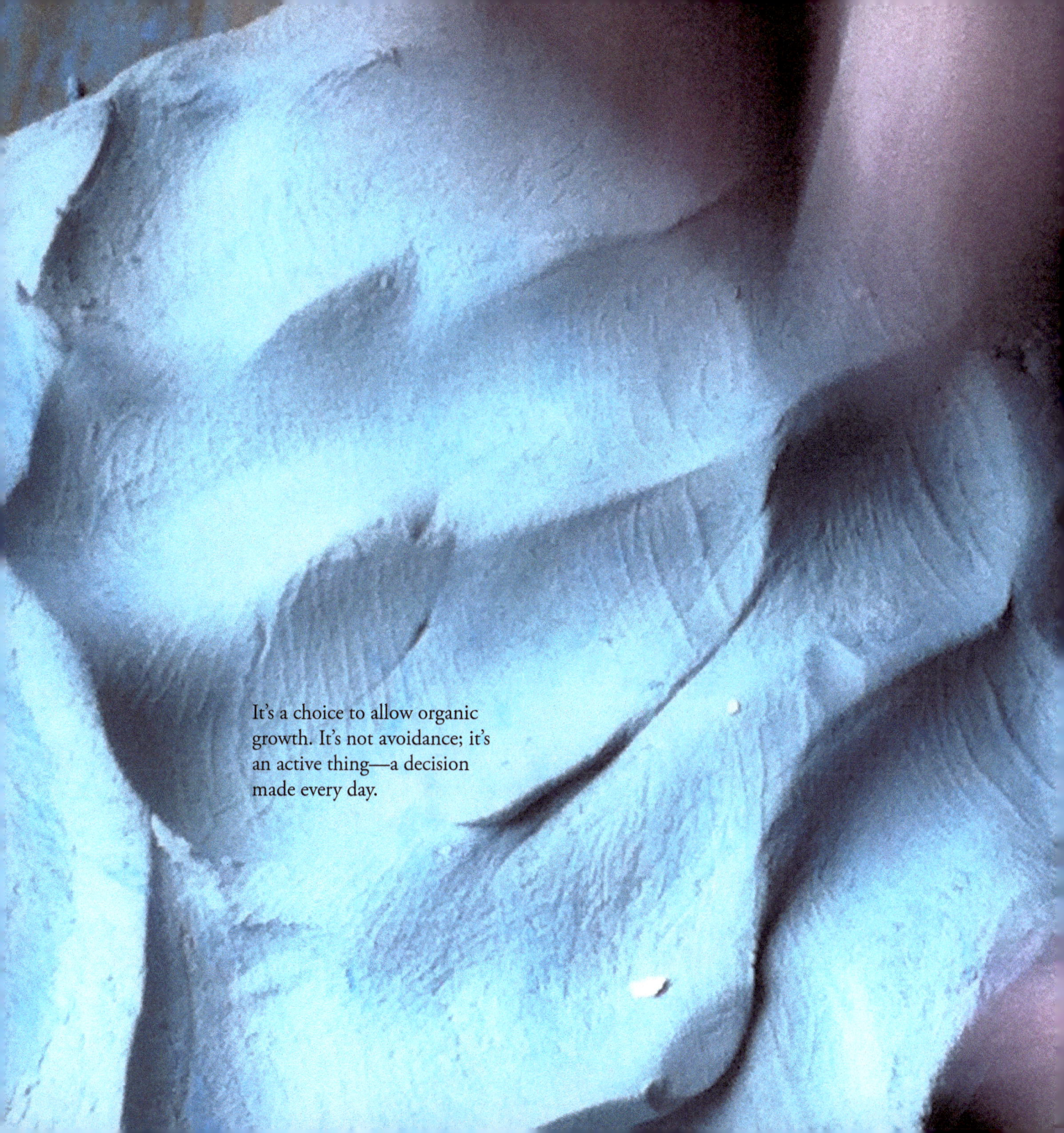

It's a choice to allow organic growth. It's not avoidance; it's an active thing—a decision made every day.

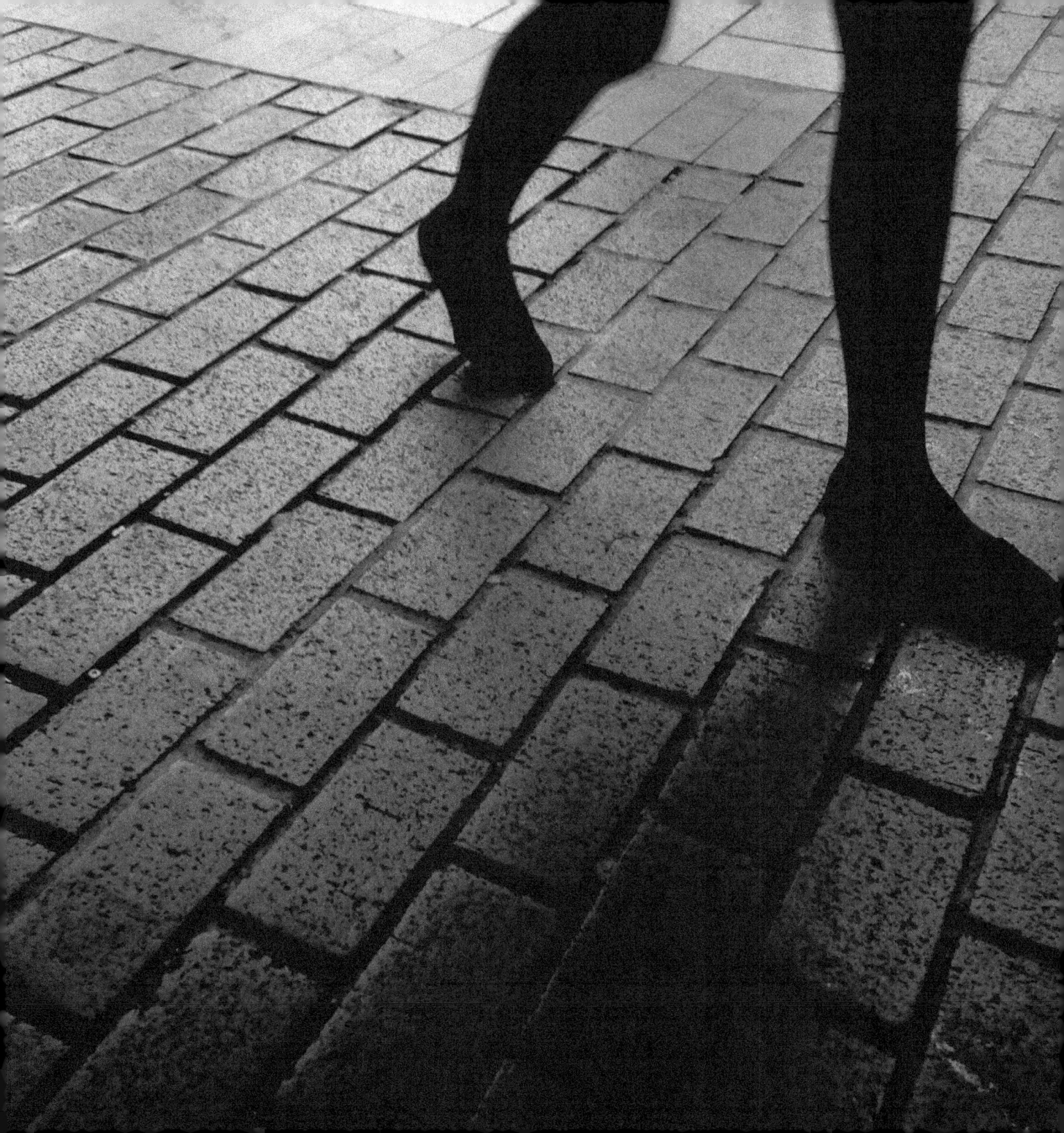

Bones spread out thin, a film over the bottom of a trough, not enough of me to deepen or extend. Molecules barely touching, bonds stretched to the point of evaporation.

Condensation. Stasis.

sanus, sanus,

sanus

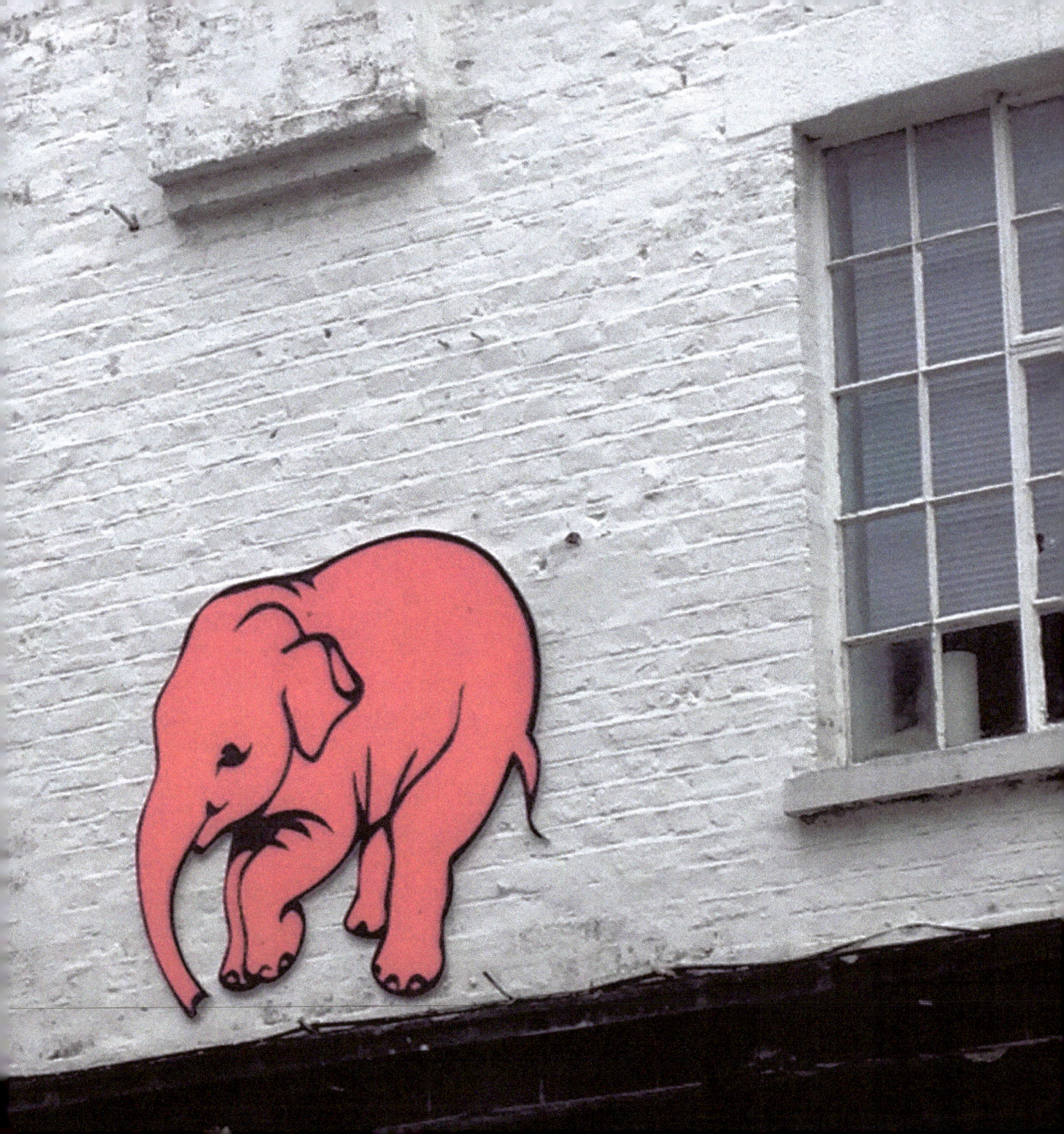

Makes sense that you in
some way were heavy because
I made you heavy, and you
allowed me to.

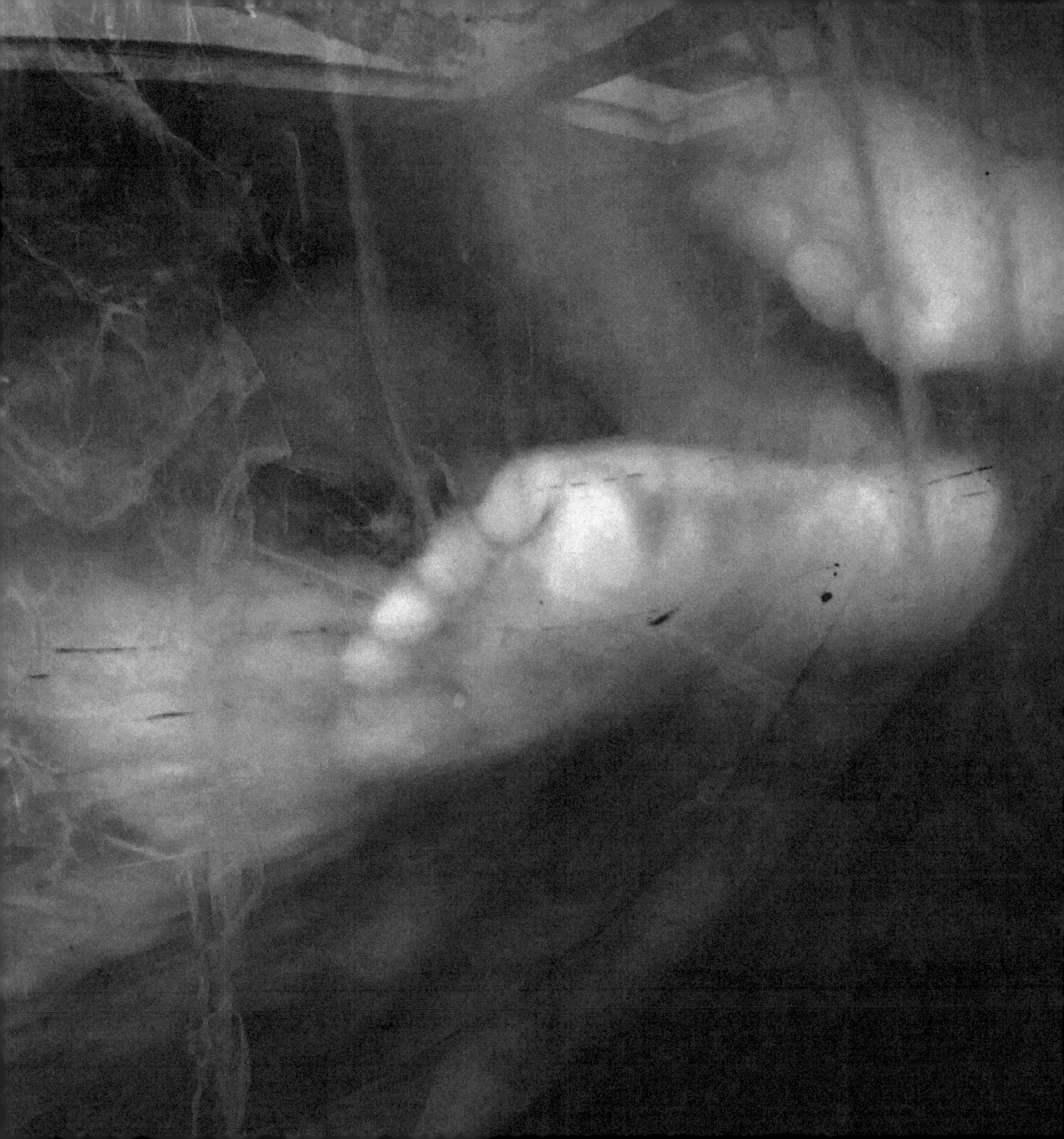

Bottom of the pool.
Perfect breast stroke under water.
Teacher spoke in bubbles.

I didn't train as an artist. I don't have a certificate,
or an MFA. Maybe I'm a fraud. I'm scared of pretending:
I did it most of my life. Pretending to be a Christian
'cause my dad was a minister. Pretending to be rich,
'cause I went to school with children of millionaires.
Pretending to be a scientist, 'cause I wasn't allowed to
study art.

Pretending to be an artist? I can't. It matters too
much. And I AM an artist. I just don't have a fixed
medium. I make it up as I go along. And I'm ok with
that; that's all anyone does.

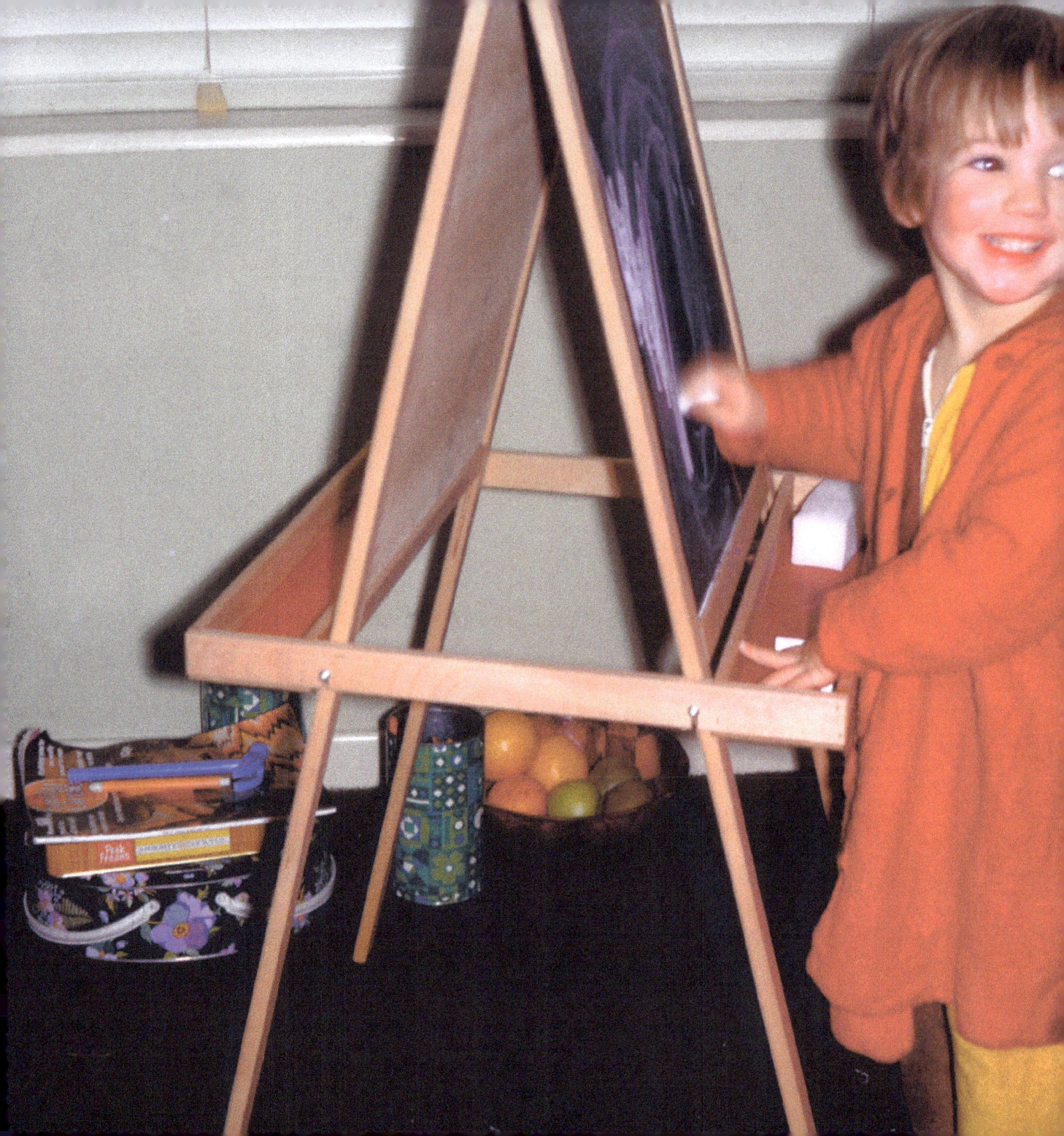

If you count a mississippi, you're counting a second.

That's what Jerry says.

I'm trying to stay down for more *mississippis* every day, so my lungs get bigger. I let my air bubbles out—one at a time—so I can stay down longer.

If you let them all out in rush, you have to hurry up out of the water.

Thirty-three-mississippi—

Thirty-four-mississippi—

Thirty-five-mississippi—

If I stay down long enough, my counting gets in a bit of a hurry. My words smush together—

For-y-four-missippi-for-y-five-misippi-for-y-six-mssippi—

then I have to push off the bottom hard with my feet to get up to the top fast enough.

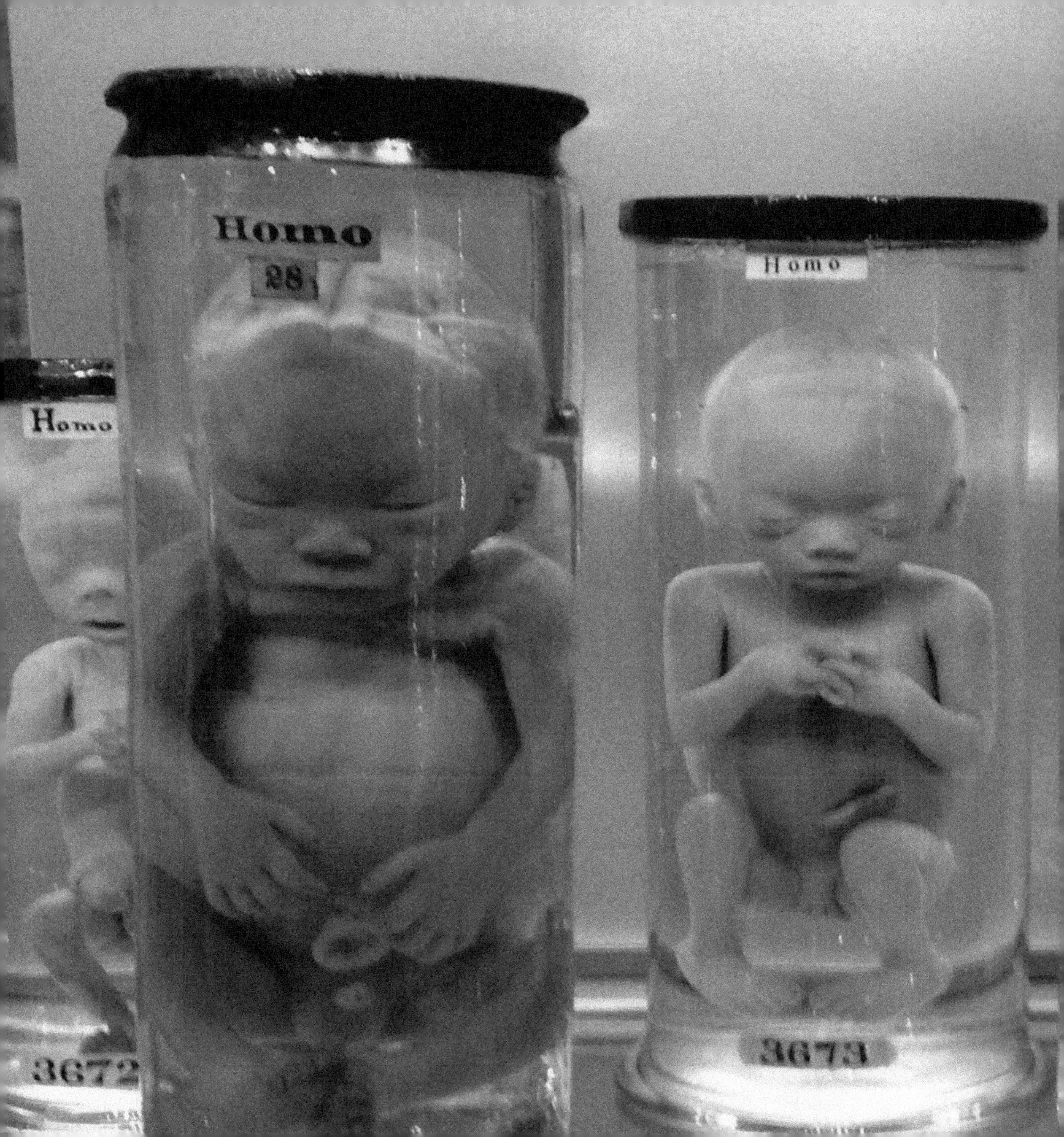

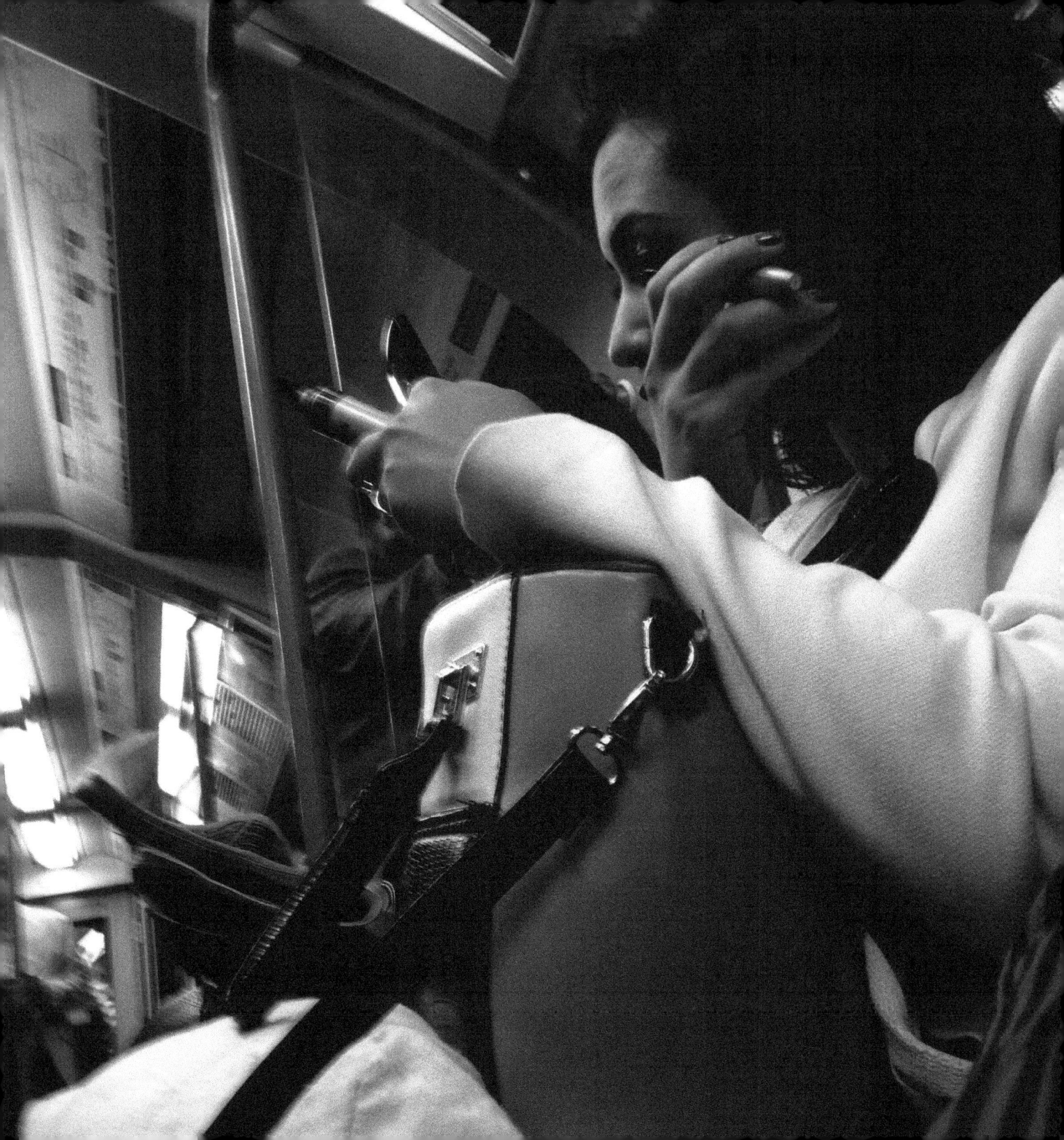

I wonder, is being human not "in" any more?
Is it somehow outmoded to have something to
say, something valuable, beautiful, even ugly.
Just something? Maybe narcissism is the new
black.

I've been there, too scared to share myself.
Putting on a suit to feel better about the
nothingness inside. Maybe that's actually
congruent? Insides matching outsides. Empty.

I wonder, is freedom
the acceptance of
being trapped?

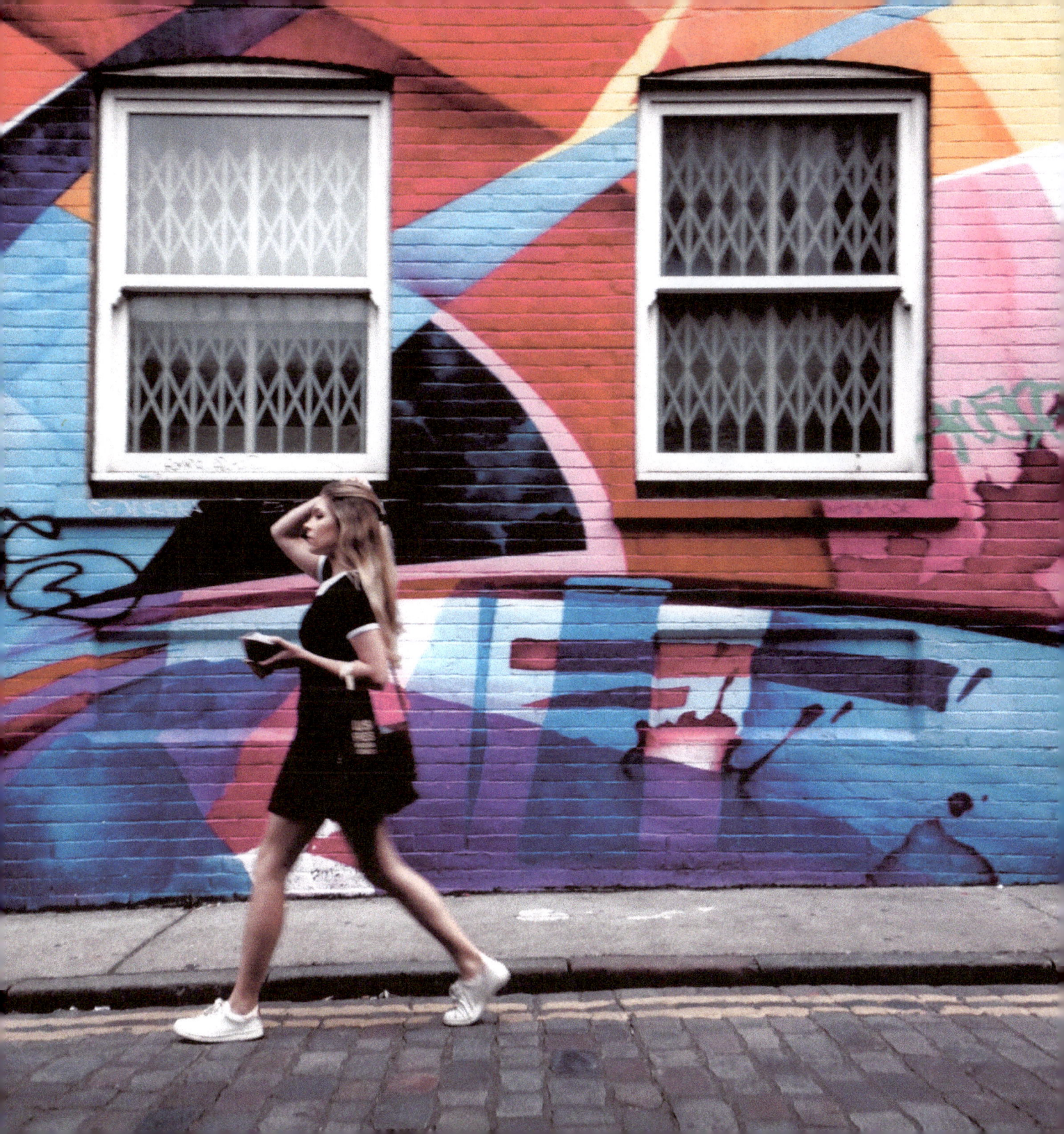

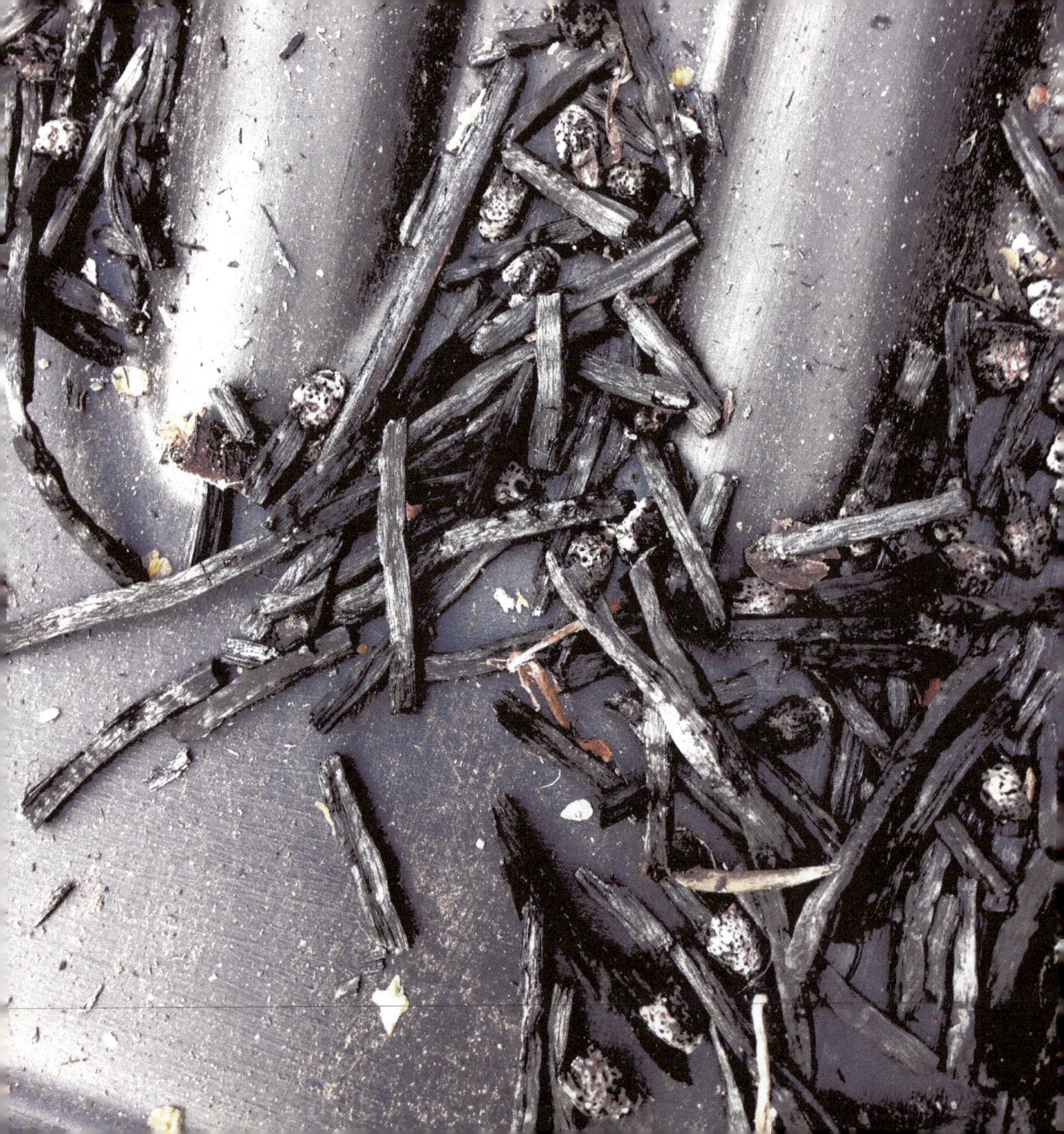

Ashes of us
Bones of us
Cremation
Purification
Beltane
Soot
Sharing dirt
Our dirt
Our secrets
All secrets leave marks

Nothing hidden
Nothing gold can stay

1 day we will burn
Away

Phoenix

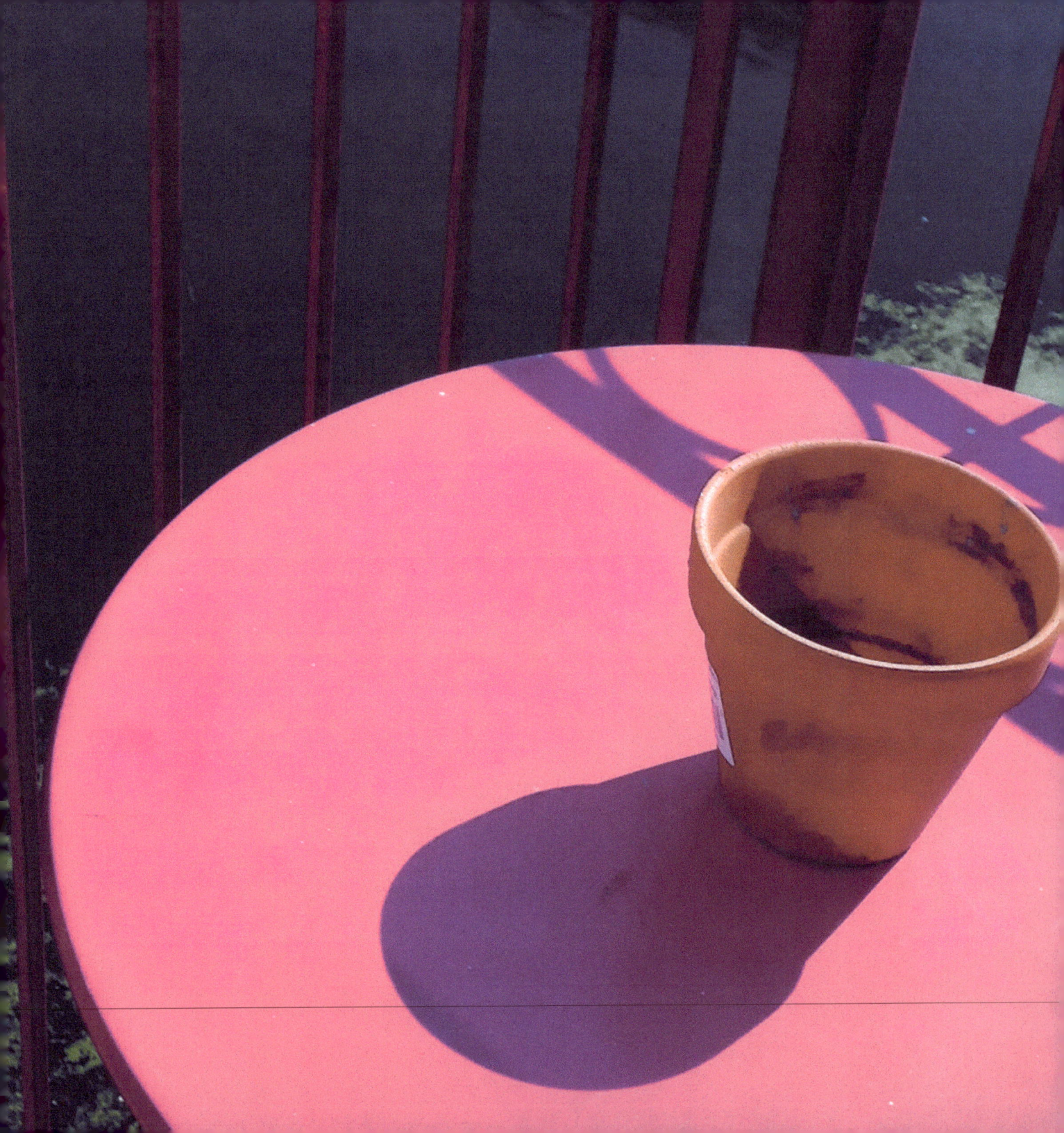

I want that scary future where I'm
always a bit insecure, always a bit
surprised when you come back to
our bed, but I love you and you
love me and no one can steal love
like that.

I never imagine people with their clothes
on. I don't mean that I visualise them
in their 3D technicolor glory... just that
I don't edit clothes in to the picture.
Seems like a sort of self-censoring to me.
We are just primates, really, who don't
have quite enough fur.

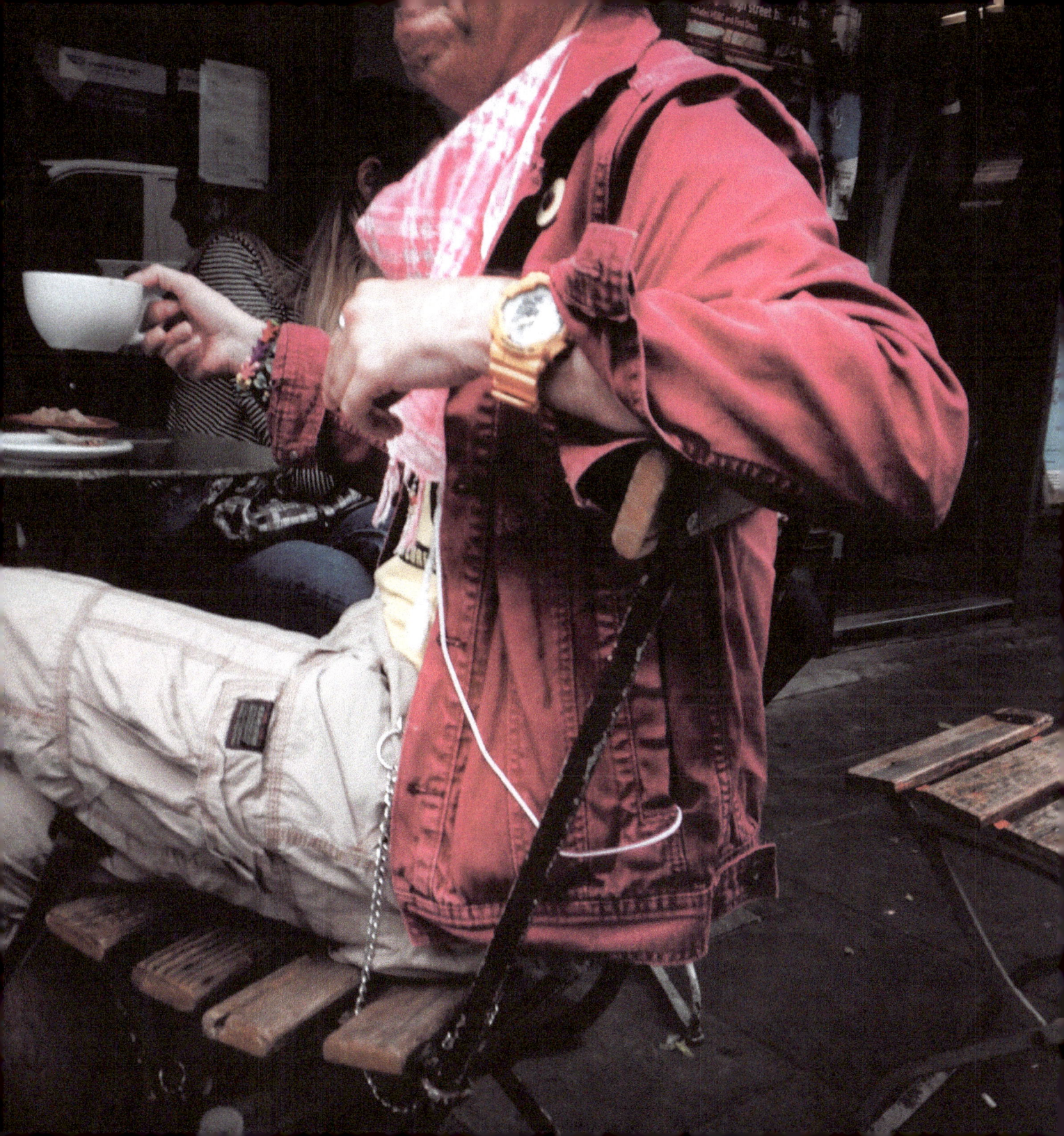

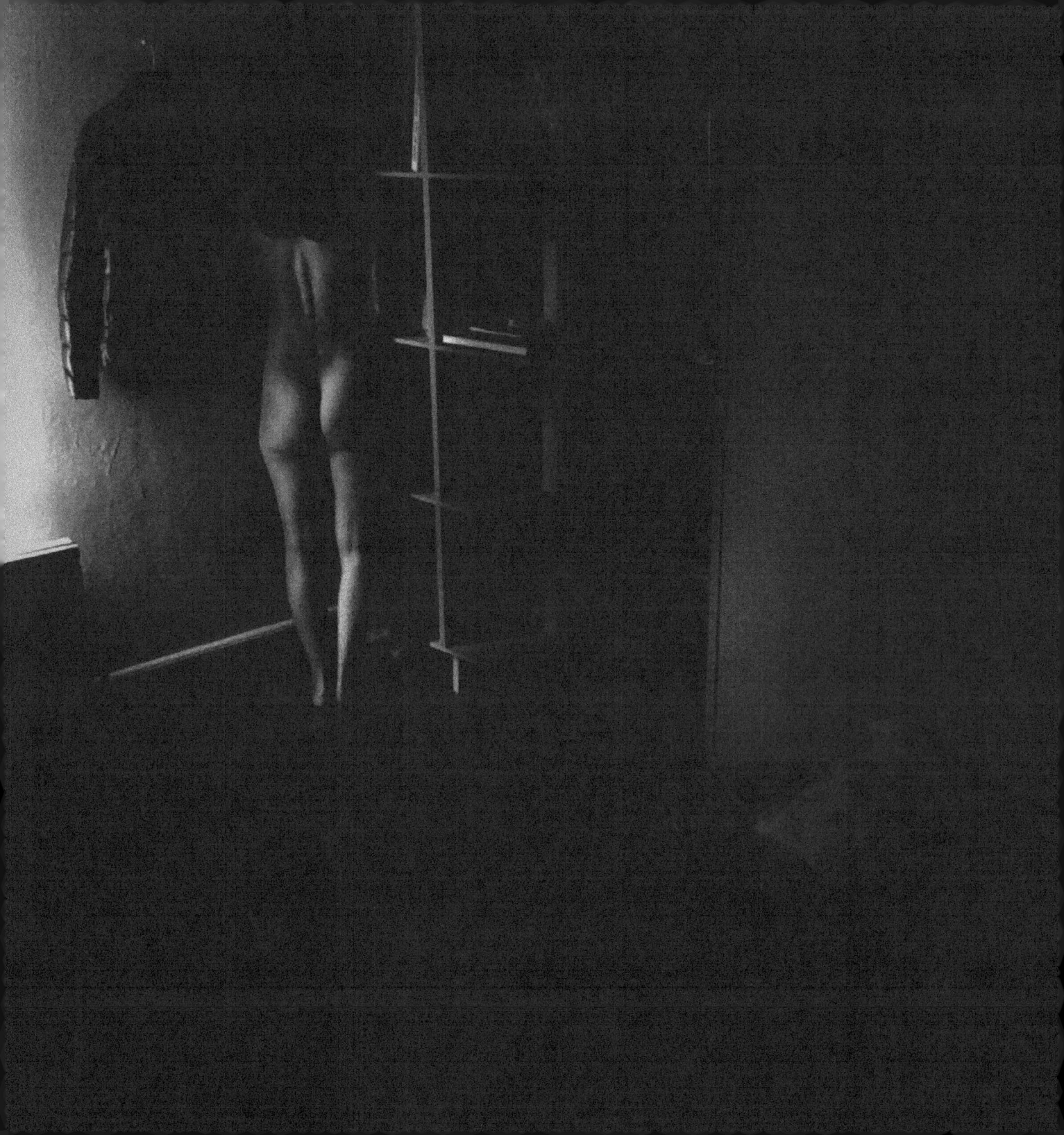

I didn't see beauty until I looked through other eyes.

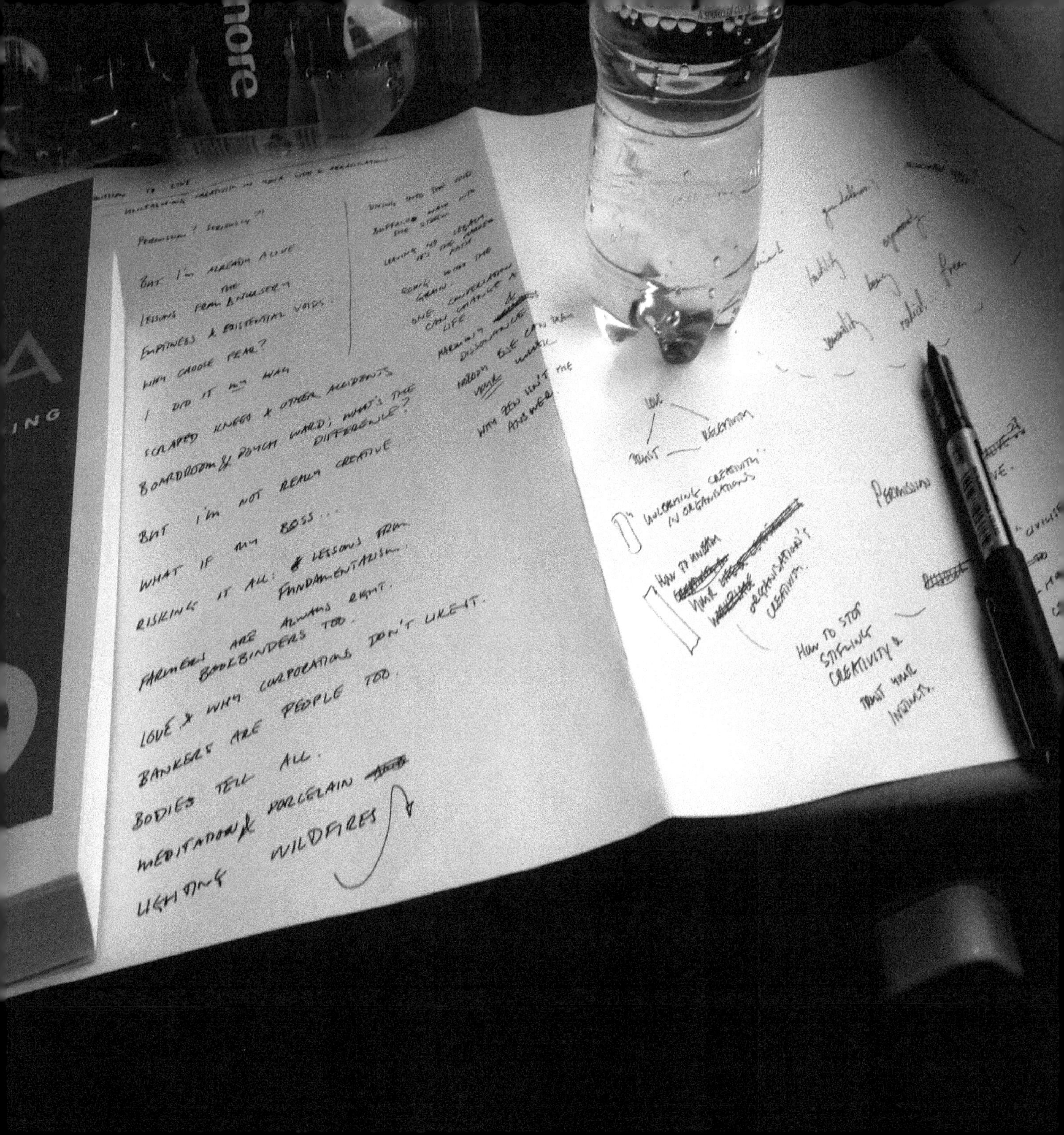

Handwritten notes (left page):

...... TO LIVE

MANIFESTING CREATIVITY IN YOUR LIFE & WORKPLACE

PERMISSION / SERENITY ??

BUT I'M ALREADY ALIVE

LESSONS FROM A NURSERY   THE

EMPTINESS & EXISTENTIAL VOIDS.

WHY CODDLE FEAR?

I DID IT MY WAY

SCRAPED KNEES & OTHER ACCIDENTS

BOARDROOM & PSYCH WARD; WHAT'S THE DIFFERENCE?

BUT I'M NOT REALLY CREATIVE

WHAT IF MY BOSS...

RISKING IT ALL: 8 LESSONS FROM FUNDAMENTALISM.

FARMERS ARE ALWAYS RIGHT.

BOOKBINDERS TOO.

LOVE & WHY CORPORATIONS DON'T LIKE IT.

BANKERS ARE PEOPLE TOO.

BODIES TELL ALL.

MEDITATION & PORCELAIN

LIGHTING   WILDFIRES

(right column, left page):

DIVING INTO THE VOID

BUFFALO'S MORE FUN

FROM THE STORM

LEAVING NO LEGACY

IT'S THE CAMERA MAN

PEOPLE WANT THE GRAIN

ONE CONVERSATION CAN CHANGE A LIFE

MARKING TIME

DISSONANCE

HEROIN ... ELSE CAN RAD

WINE   WHERE

WHY ZEN ISN'T THE ANSWER

(right page notes):

LOVE

TRUST → REVELATION

1 UNLOCKING CREATIVITY IN ORGANISATIONS

HOW TO UNLEASH YOUR ORGANISATION'S CREATIVITY.

PERMISSION

HOW TO STOP STIFLING CREATIVITY & TRUST YOUR INSTINCTS.

(scattered words top right): HUMILITY   GENEROSITY   BEING   FREE   SENSITIVITY   RADICAL

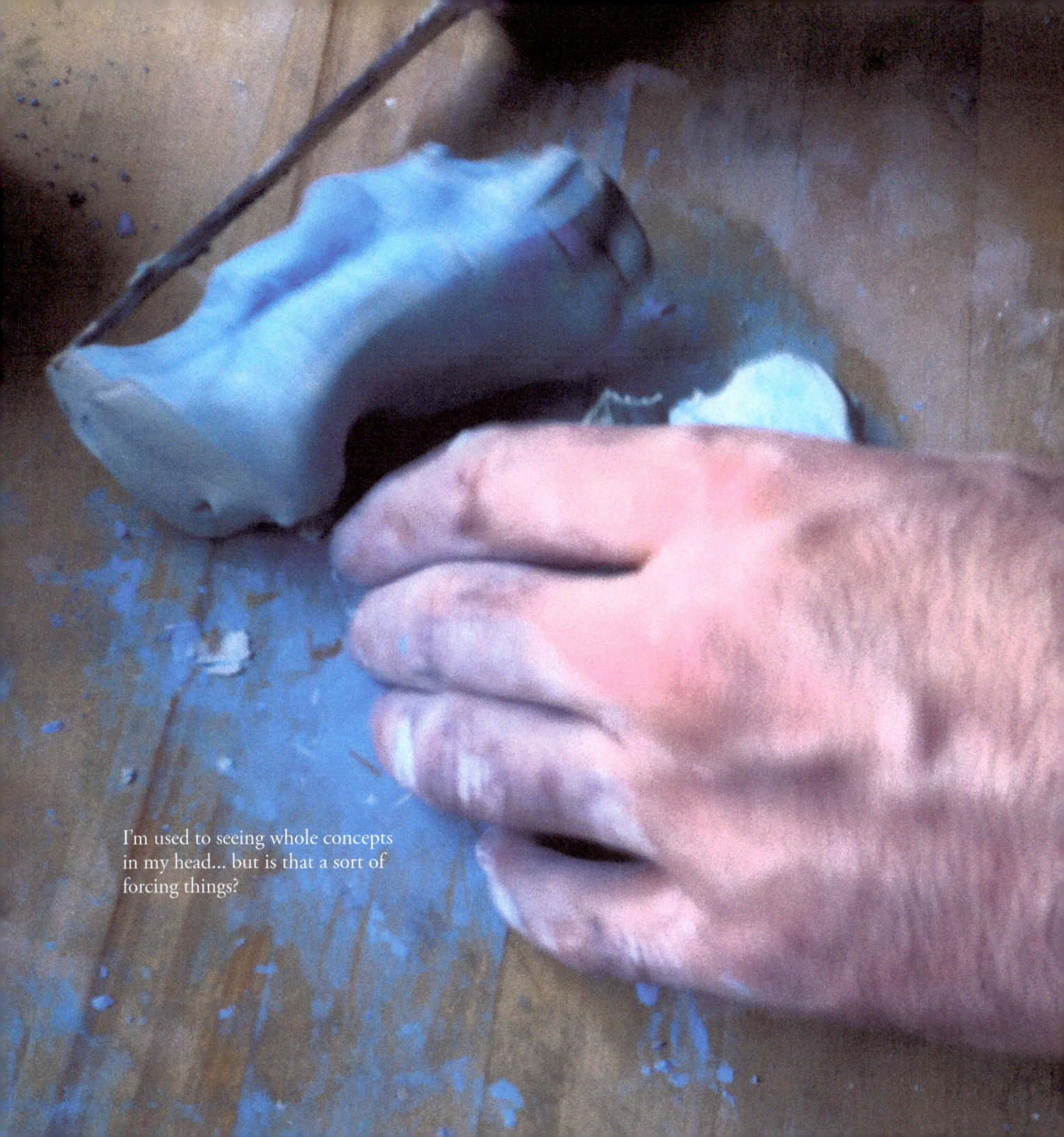

I'm used to seeing whole concepts
in my head... but is that a sort of
forcing things?

The wind is wild. The hurricane that has been predicted for weeks may be arriving on the Outer Banks. I don't care. I dive in, porpoising out, back in again, riding the waves back to the beach. The sand the surf carries scrapes along my skin like a giant tongue; maybe The Undertow is a cat. I think about swimming out, straight out, towards the flickering lights of the shrimping boats. I decide to swim parallel to them, along the coast. I have no one to swim with; no one to play with. I'm fizzing with energy, and my skin is melting with the force of it. I'm just water, myself. Nothing solid, nothing human is left of me, other than frustrated lust. The water strokes me everywhere, and I wish The Undertow were human, or whatever it is I am.

Bare bones,
lovely bones:
grounding us
in us, grounding us
in home.

Velvet flesh,
leather-bound.
Tie me down,
right to the lovely bones.

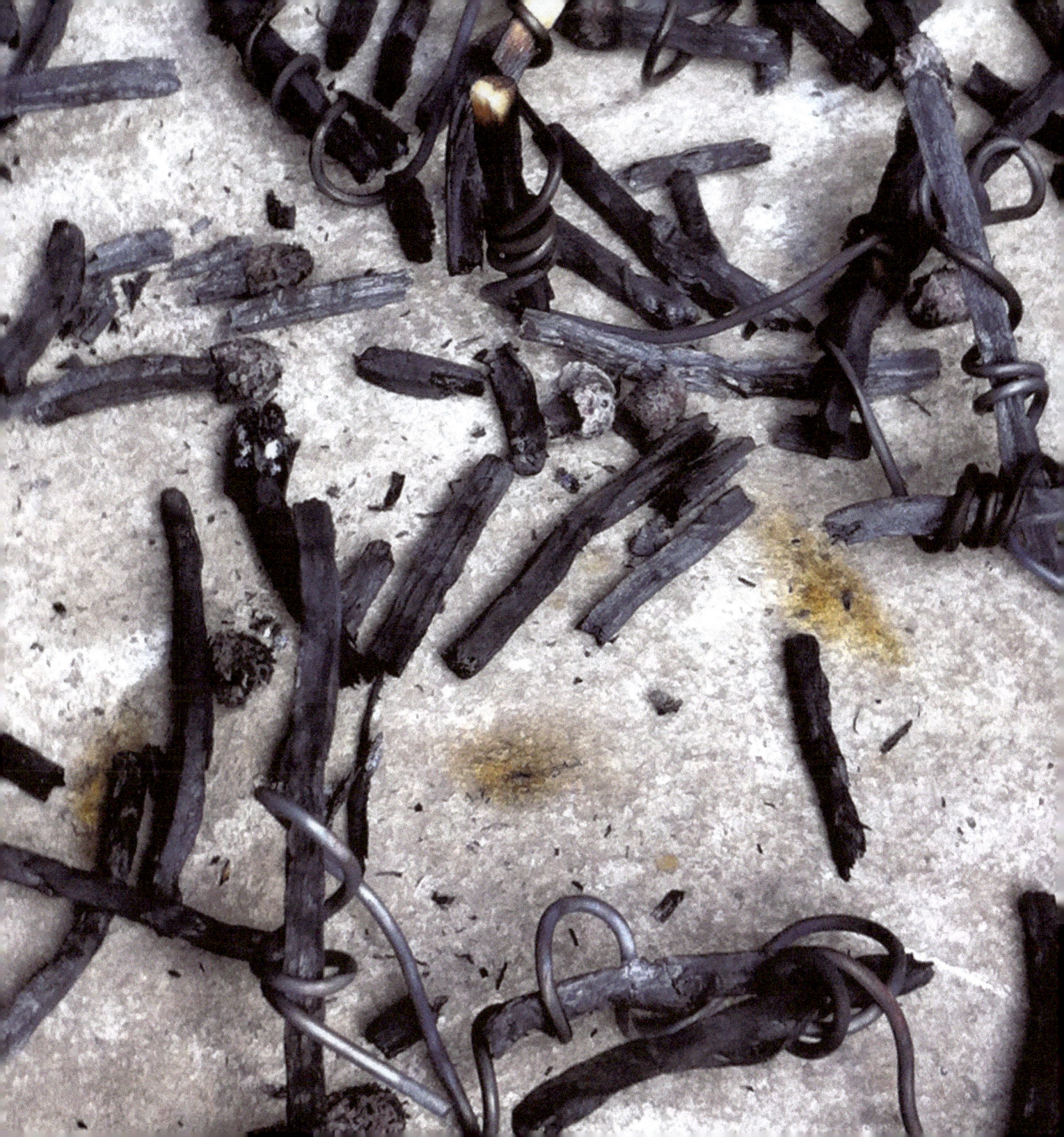

nunc

requiem

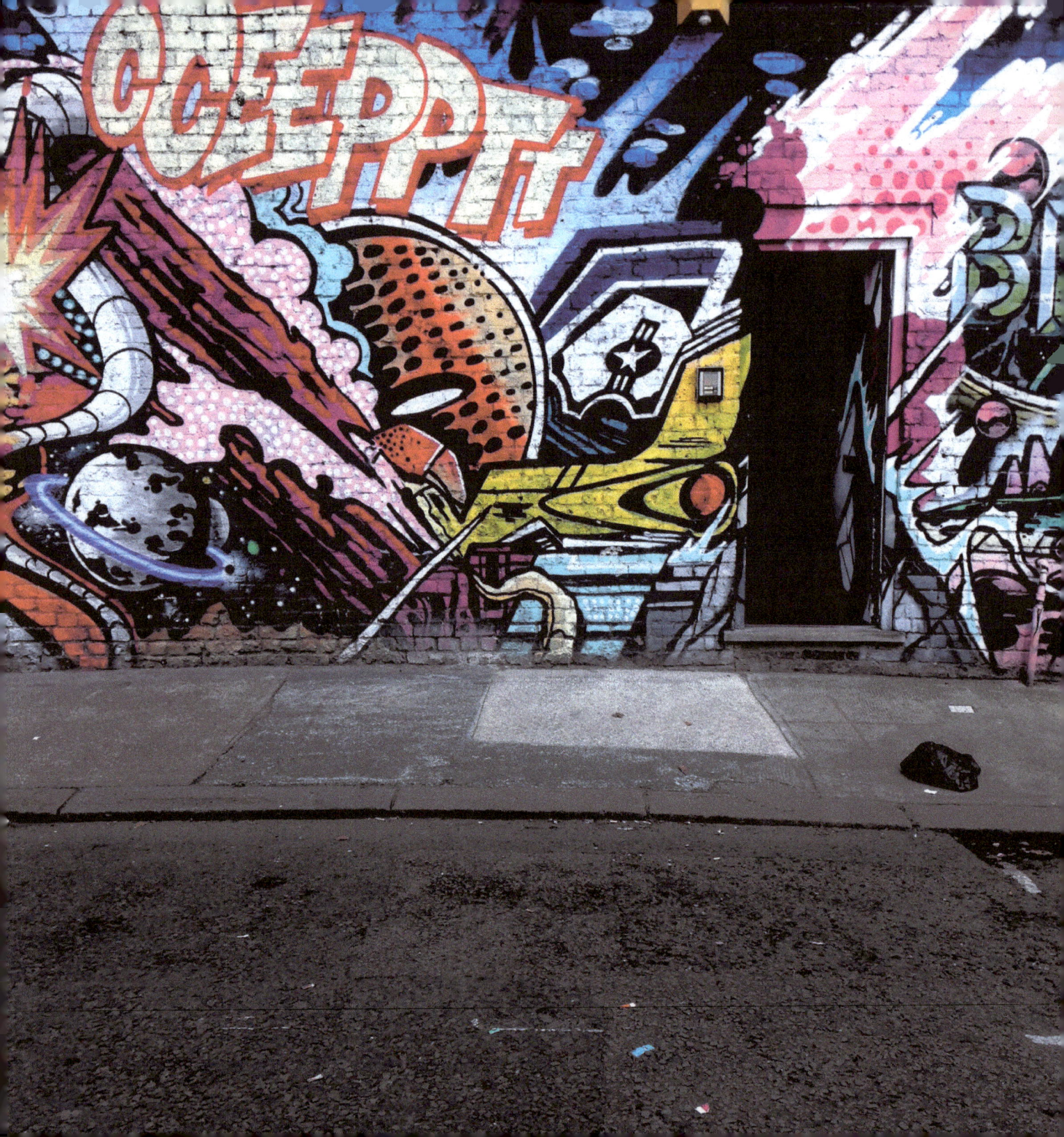

I can write my own story.
I won't wait for the giant to grind my bones
to make his bread:
I'll grind my own.
I won't wait for the prince to drop my slippers:
I'll drop my own.
I won't wait for the evil queen to tear out my
heart: I'll tear it out myself.

My skin
wants your skin
all over it.

My skin
wants to lick
your skin
all over.

God wants you to ... dowdy

Enjoying yourself is unwise ...ful.

...ther evil. ...peopl... want sex ...d that's a sin.

sex is amazing

...rting is evil

I LOVE moving.

I want to play with lots of different peop people's bodies

Shameful.

Bodies are...

I want talk about sex lots.

Sex is an act of aliveness.

I LOVE wanking

I want to sleep with lots of people

I want to be sexually free

...to be ... but ... fun.

I love inhabiting my body Powerful. Sexual.

Naked = fun feel + sexy ...

I want to be strong & sexy

I love my body!

...shame + hell.

I can't look at you:
you might see,
down inside,
the wanton rest I've hidden
from myself.

Split me open
with the tender brutality
of your lust;
leave me no hiding place.

If I bite your jaw
as you come inside of me,
will you
forget me
after the marks fade?

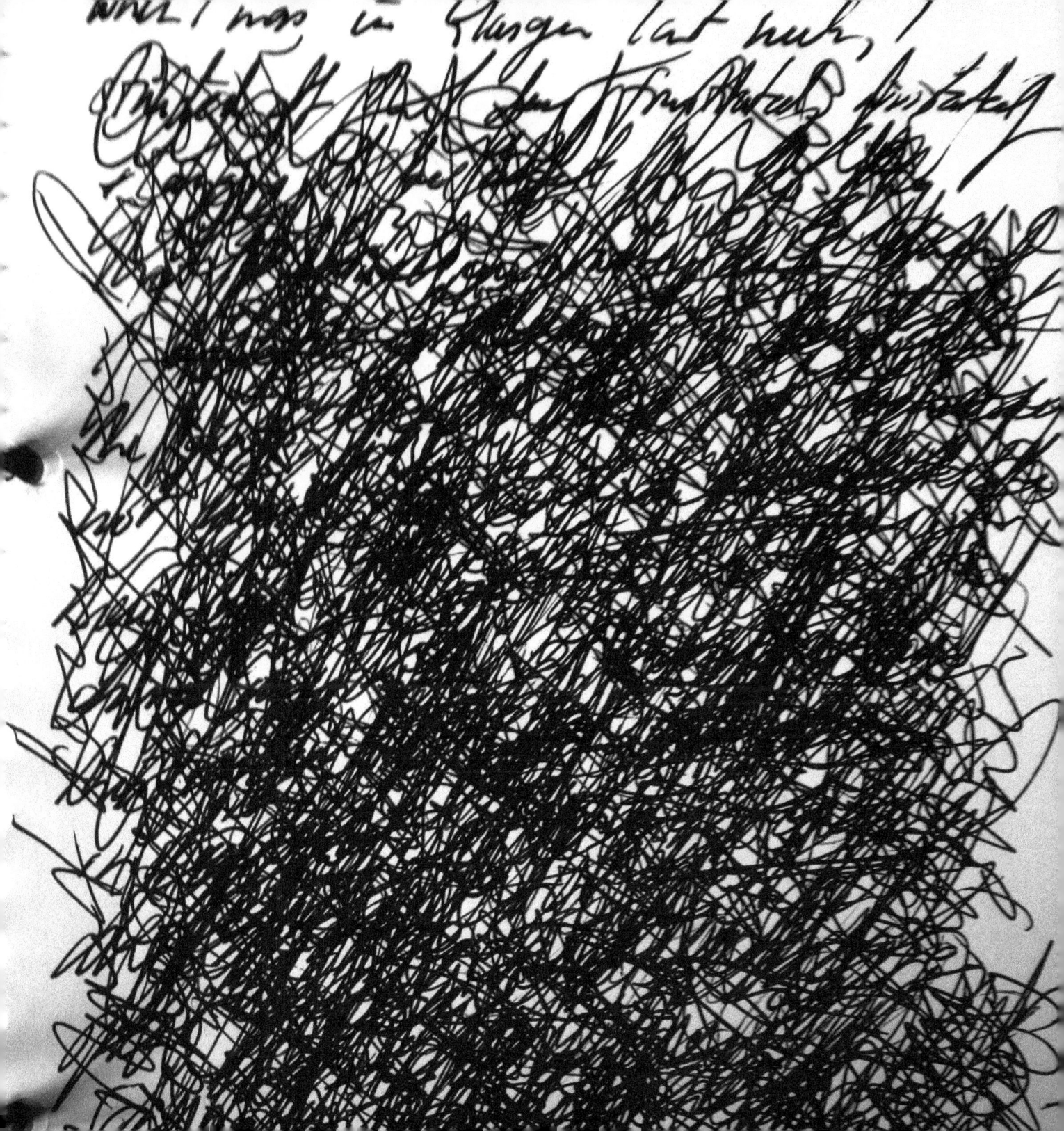

Bestial whimpering,
all fours.
Bone-juddering rhythm stutters
into tired simplicity of form.

Limp as cling film,
pulsating with lust,
cunt to brain
one wiry
nerve
of pleasure.

Profane cock,
reverent tongue,
your body the sum of
all that matters to mine.

R.I.P.

MAD

MADDIE
was
here
2k9

Bite me,
scratch, tear,
like the animals we are.
Hurt me,
push, pull,
like the man you are.
Pin me,
crush, slide
like the beast we are.

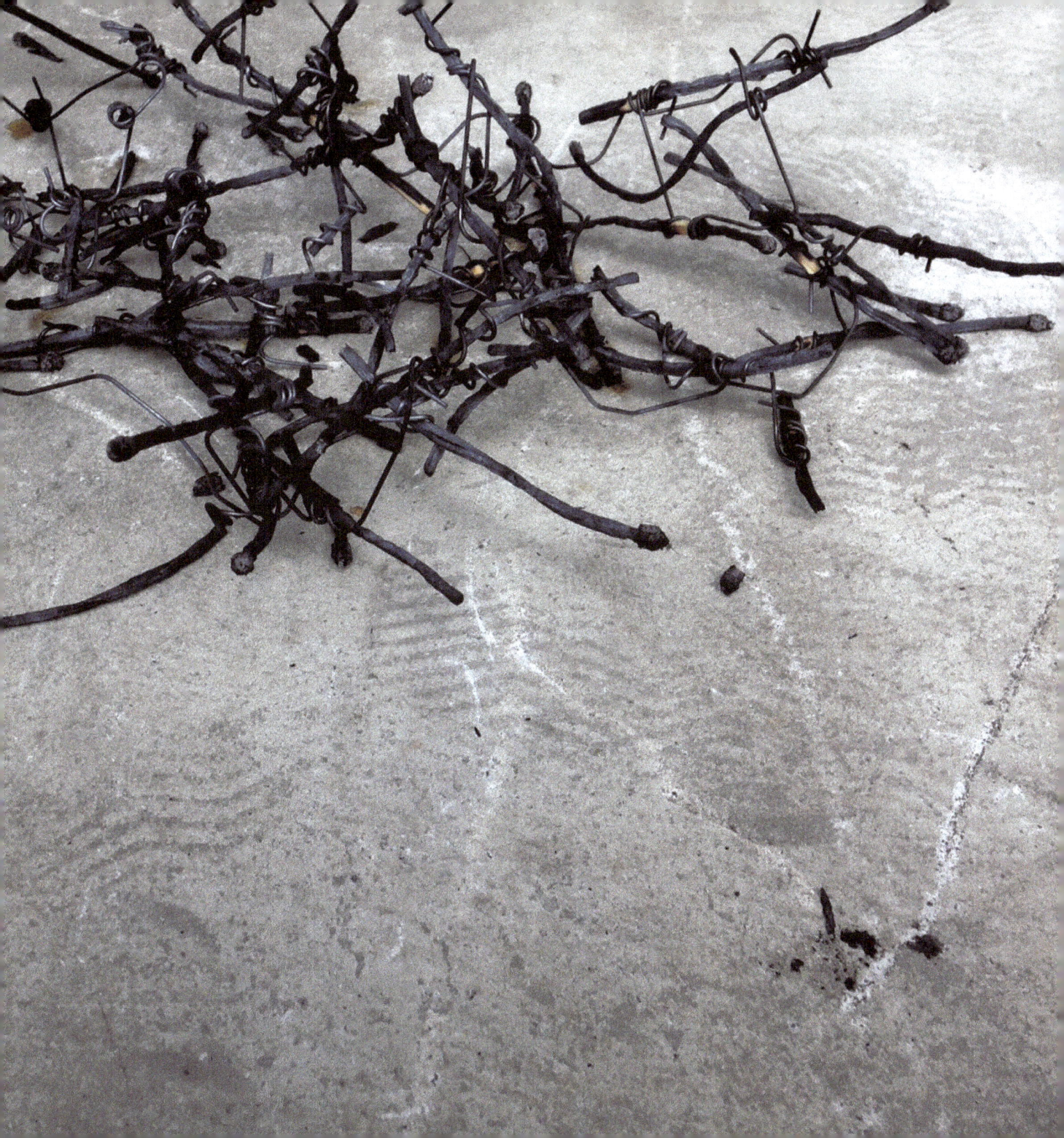

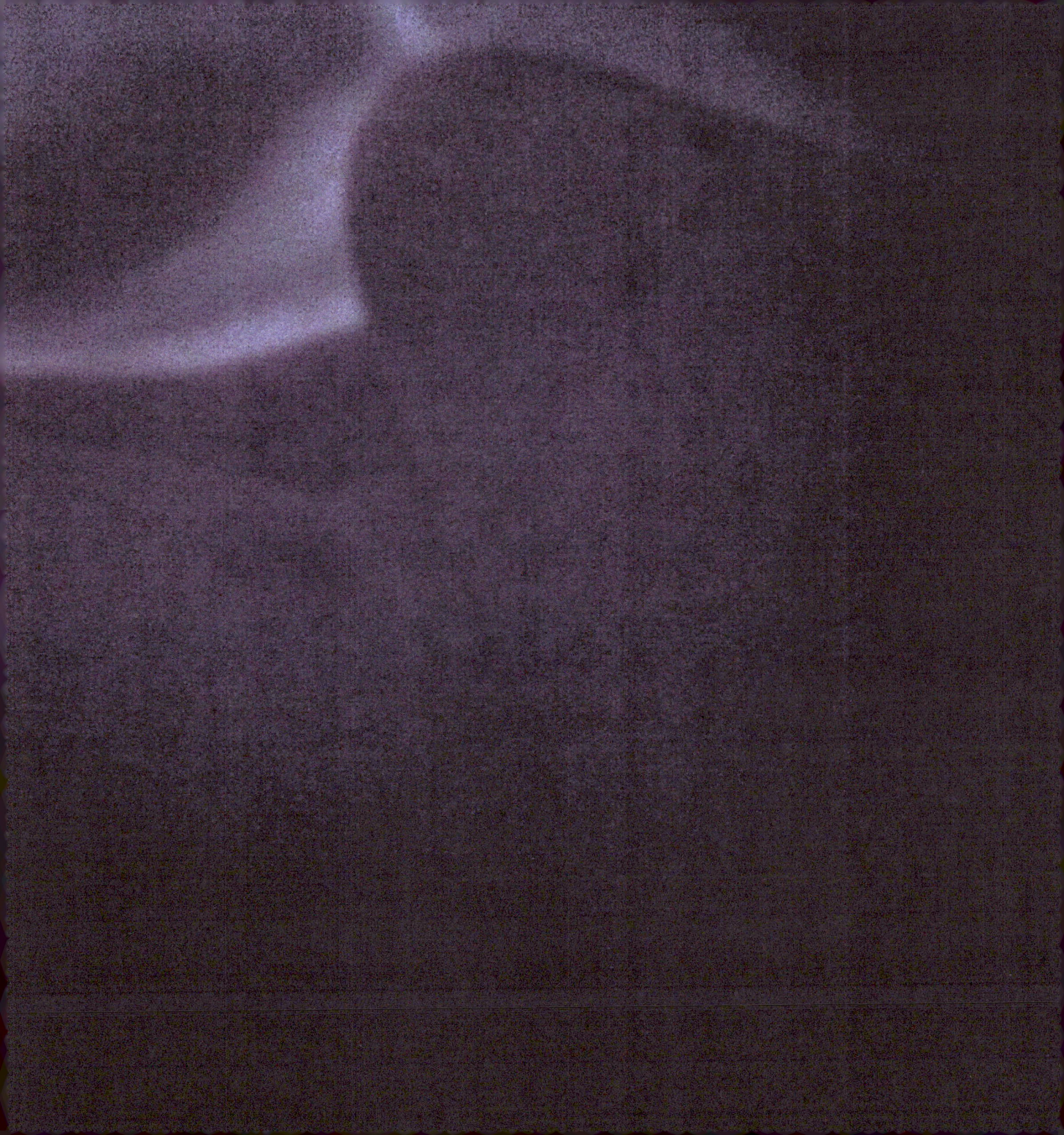

Two backs.
One cunt.
One cock.
Two breasts.
Two nipples to flick with my tongue.
Balls to roll in my hands.
One ass to lick or finger.
Don't hold back.

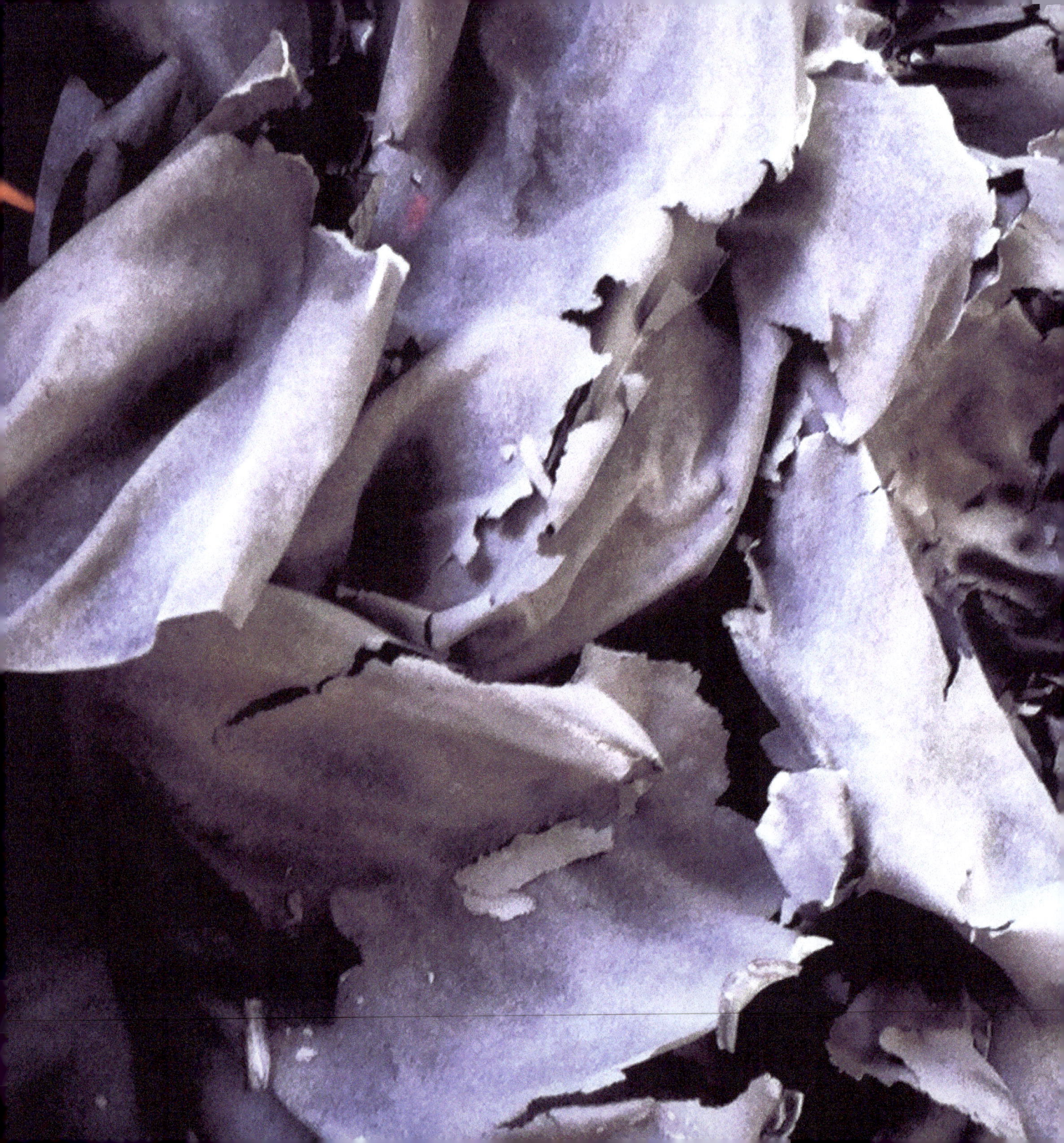

There is nothing else
but this moment,
a thing we make and unmake
again and again
that might be love.

***

Lust for breakfast
sex for dinner
love for supper
throw away the bones of me after.

***

I can't see what follows:
there is only the bald
certainty, the urgency
of now, of you here with me.

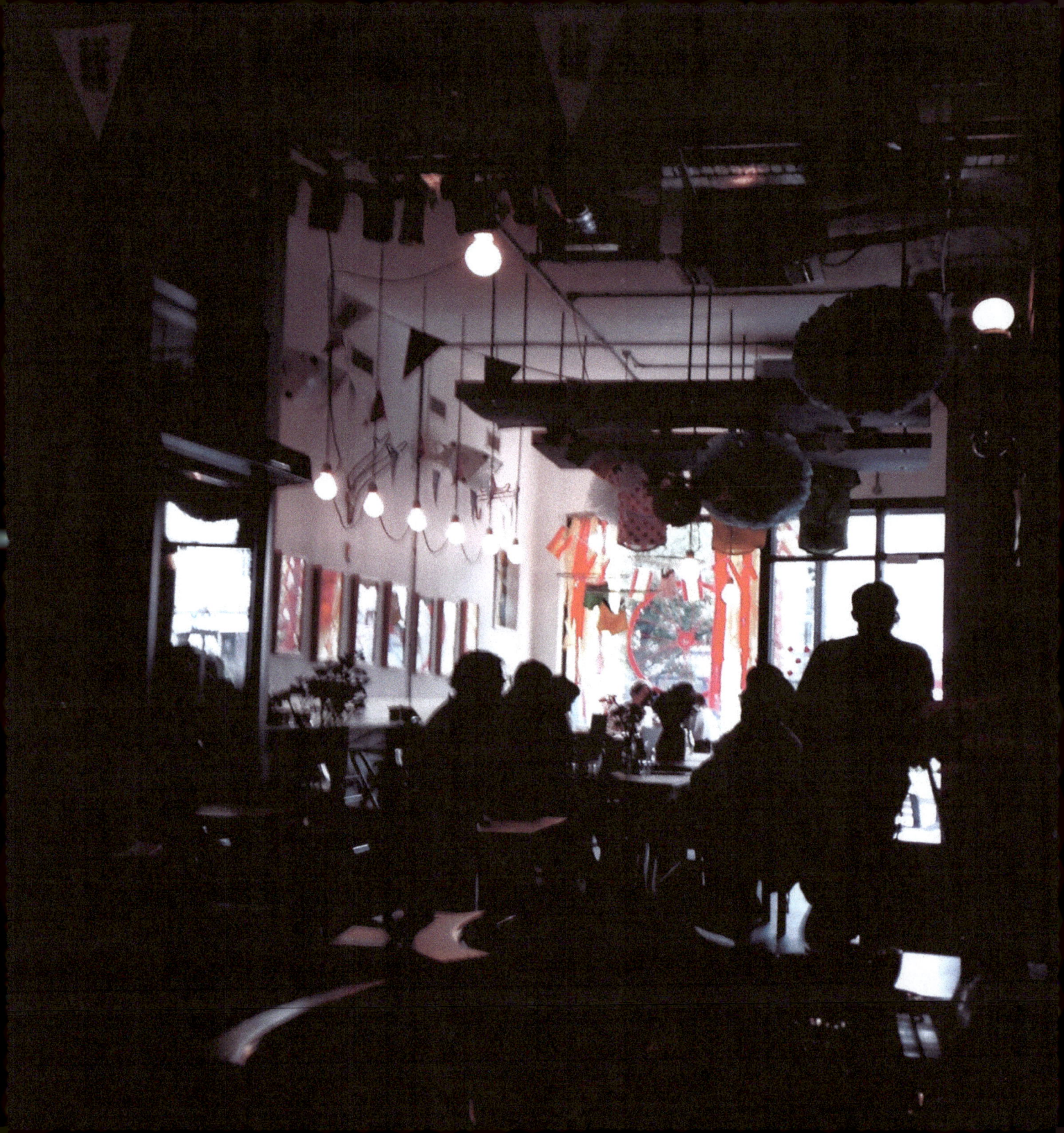

I was your door,
your out and in
your through here
there is freedom
and chaos
and being.

You can come in—
I'll be here.
Take the trash out,
away out,
I'll be here.

Your door.

Your in.

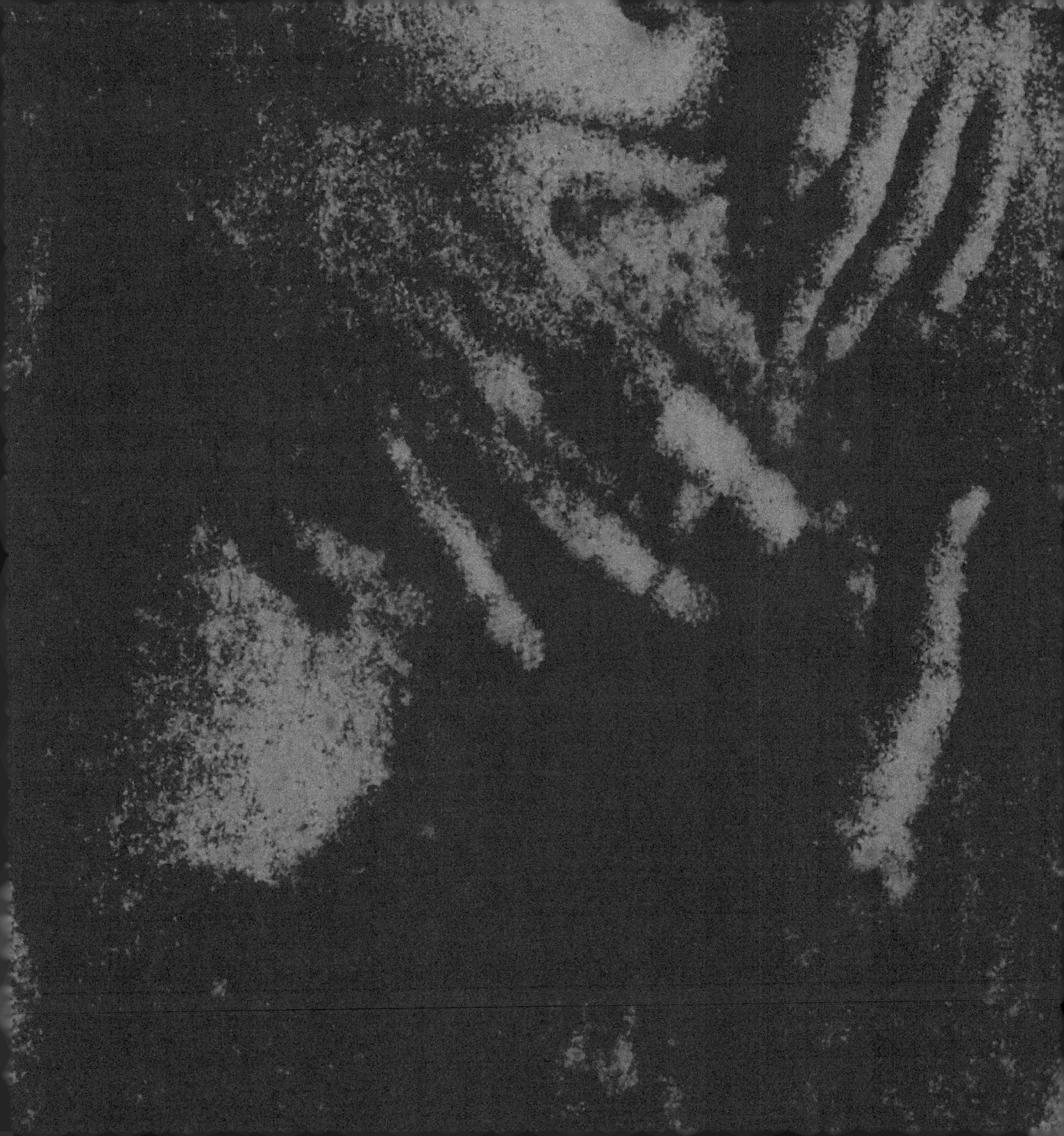

Push inside of me—
my body remembers how it feels
when you want me.

Dig your fingers into my hip,
clutch my bones
like they're your own.

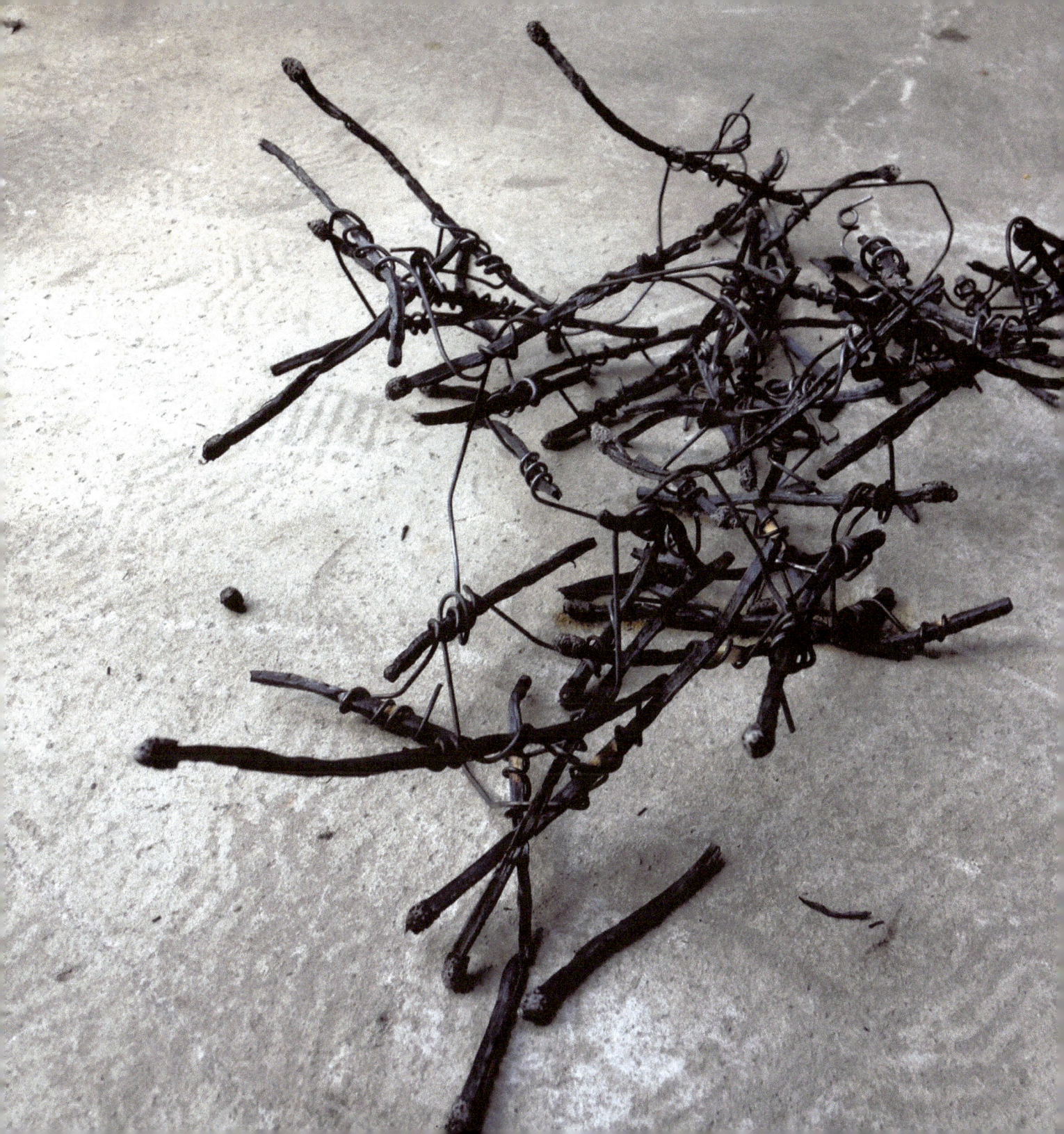

amor exponit

dolor

Eating by fridge light,
two bathrobes
huddle in the night.

Yogurt.

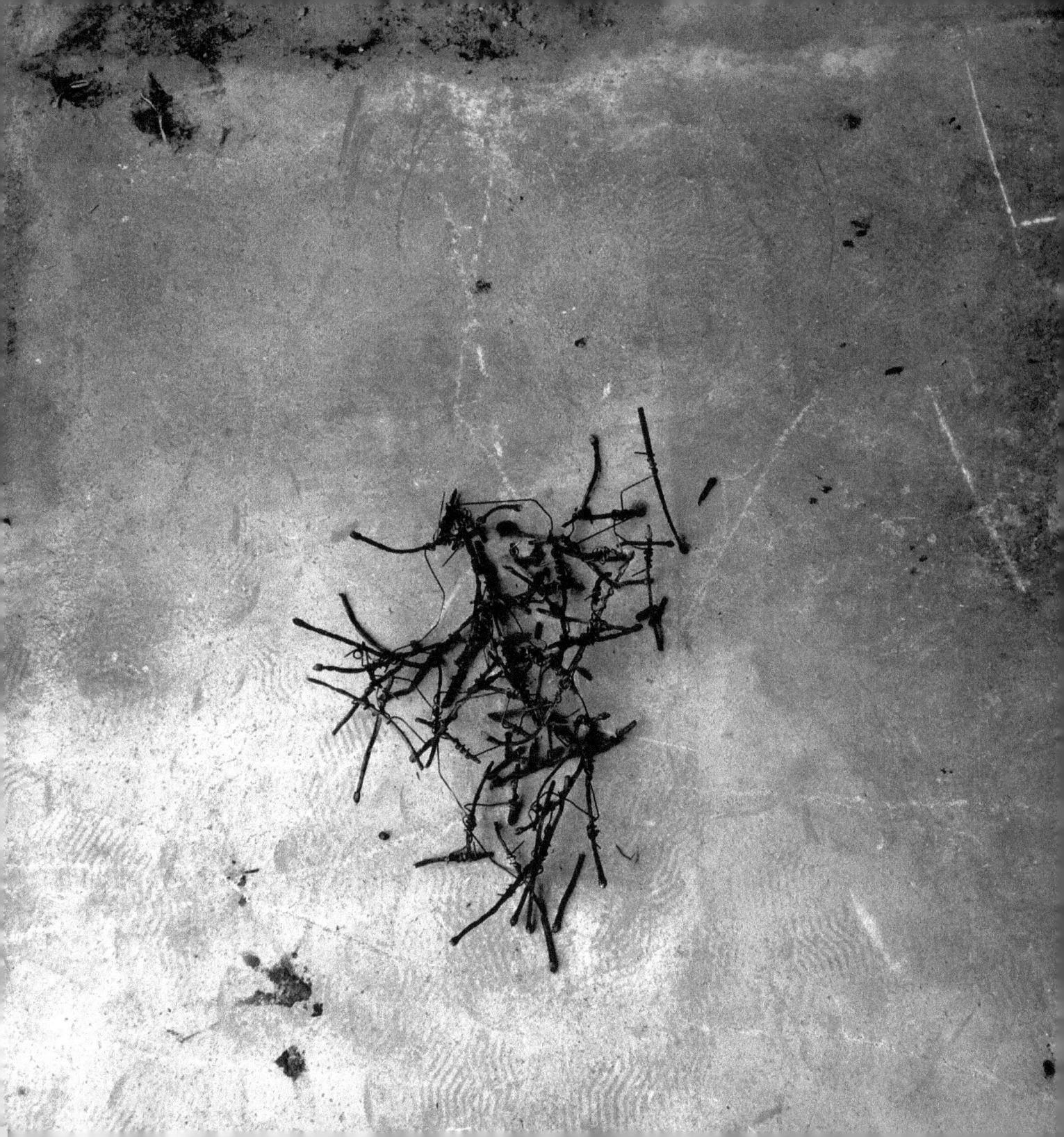

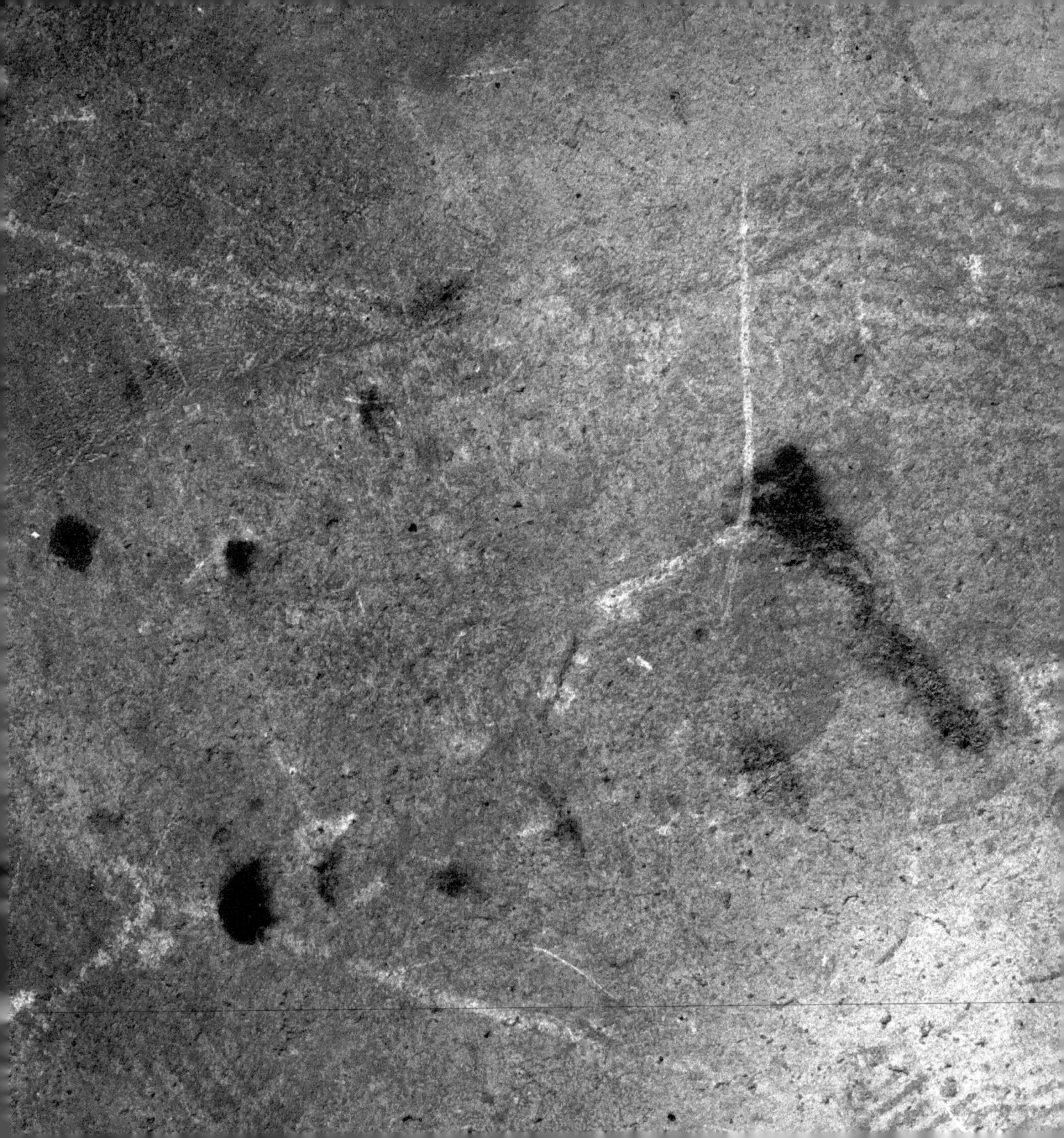

Love burns away shame, guilt and fear. If we let it. Sparking, hissing, spitting, flaring, spreading light, and warmth, leaving only a memory of what was there.

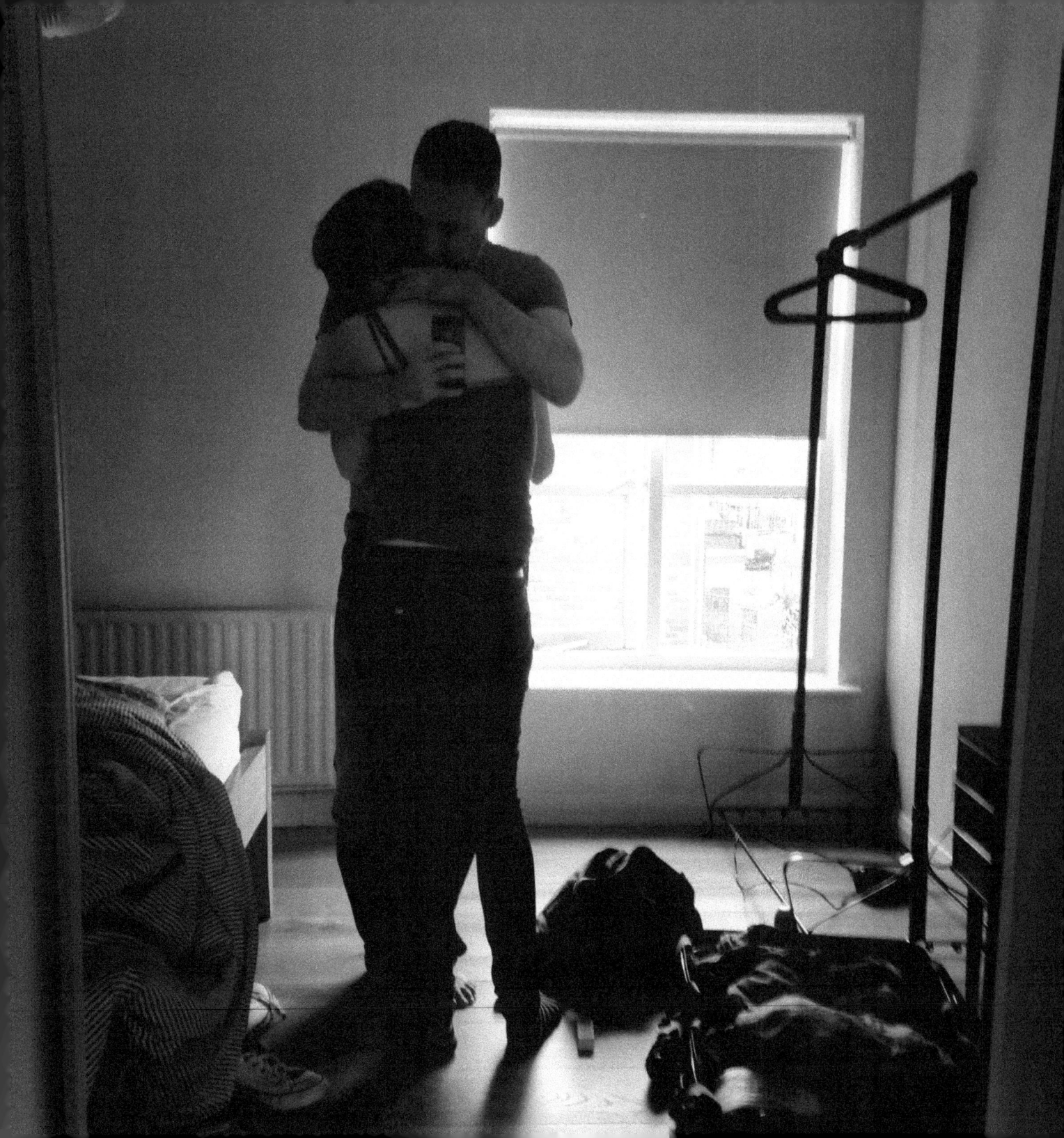

I want the bond we have.
I want to nourish it.
And nurture it.
And take care of it.
And grow it.
And feel it fully.
And prune whatever we need to prune in our lives
to make way for new growth.

PRIVACY = HEALTHY

It's similar to communication

I NEED

(If you don't want to answer)

what you want —

or

PRIVACY = CHEATING
INDEPENDENCE = DANGEROUS WILL LEAD TO SOME KIND OF RELATIONSHIP

you just
hide yourself
so nobody else
can have you (see what
you saw)
I'm not worth
staying with, so
I have wanted to
have your undivided attention
you can't leave
you're here for
me to be in control of
I have all power for
or you'll leave

I'm afraid of ...
I'm not worth
anything or good enough.
I'm not valuable.
No one will want
me. I'll like myself.

Wait for...

If you want
to leave, please
leave. You are
free.

PLEASE DON'T
CLIP YOUR WINGS FOR
ANYONE. EVER.

PRIVACY IS A NECESSITY

I'M WORTHY, flaws ... it's healthy. I AM GOOD OR...

I NEED SPACE.
me too

LOVE IS FOR GIVING/SHARING.
with lots of people.

SEX IS MY FAVOURITE THING ... A SENSE ... PARTIES

it's one of my favourite things too

I'M NOT YOU. — I AM ☺
OR ONE OF THEM.
I'M A PERSON.

I'm worth
being with

You are
nobody's
property, and I
can't control you &
don't want to.

Thank you

I want you to be
the longest poem I ever
write,
with the fewest words,
or maybe just
one.

lumen ex

nobis

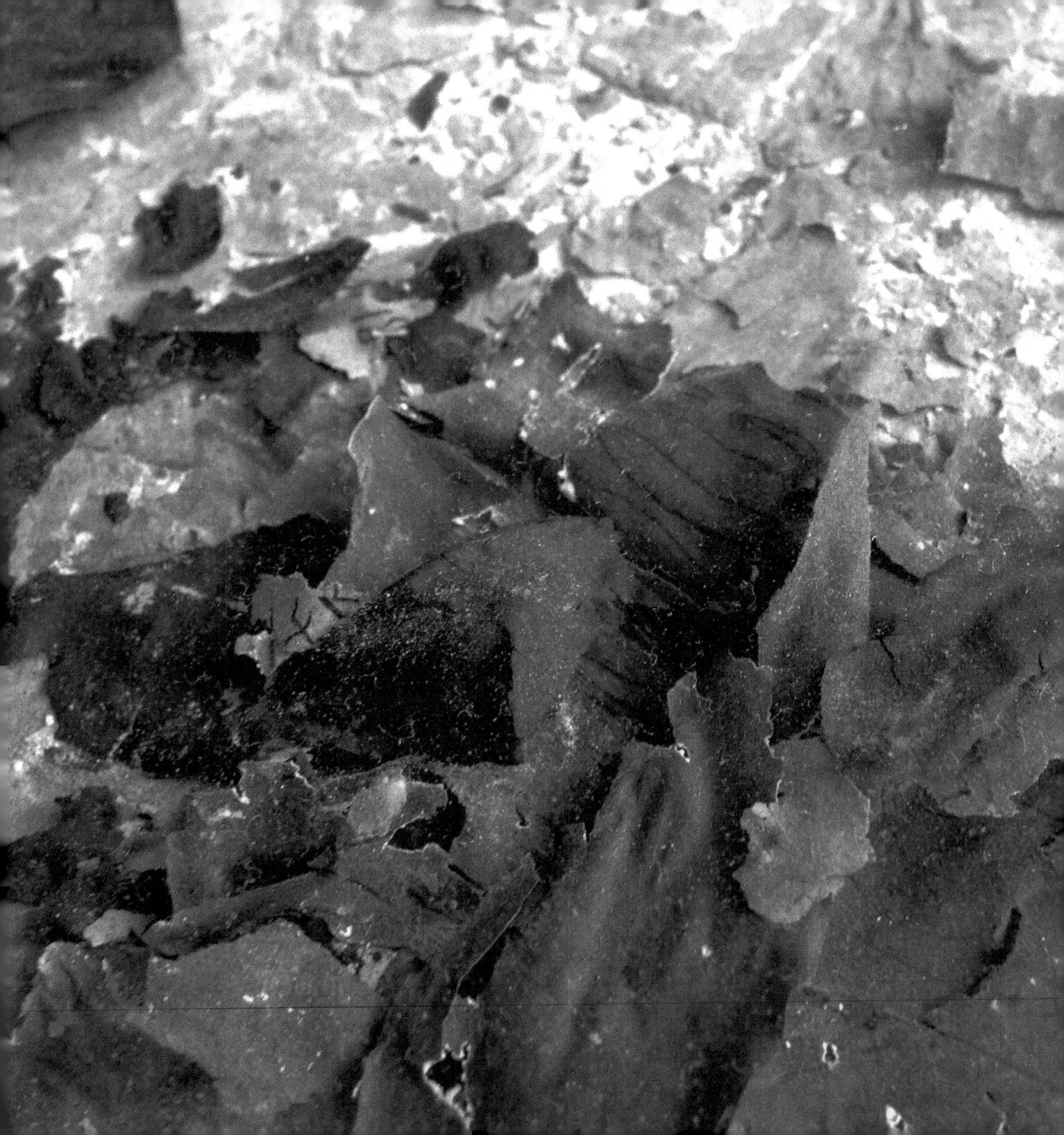

Dirty is bad. Dirty is good. A dirty girl
might be very good indeed, a dirty whore—
not so much. Slut. Slag. Slapper. Naughty.
Totty. Hooker. Woman of the Night.
Streetwalker. Ho. Older words. Slattern.
Trollop. Cunt. Doxy. Harlot. Scarlet. Jezebel.
You. Me. Us.

paradoxum

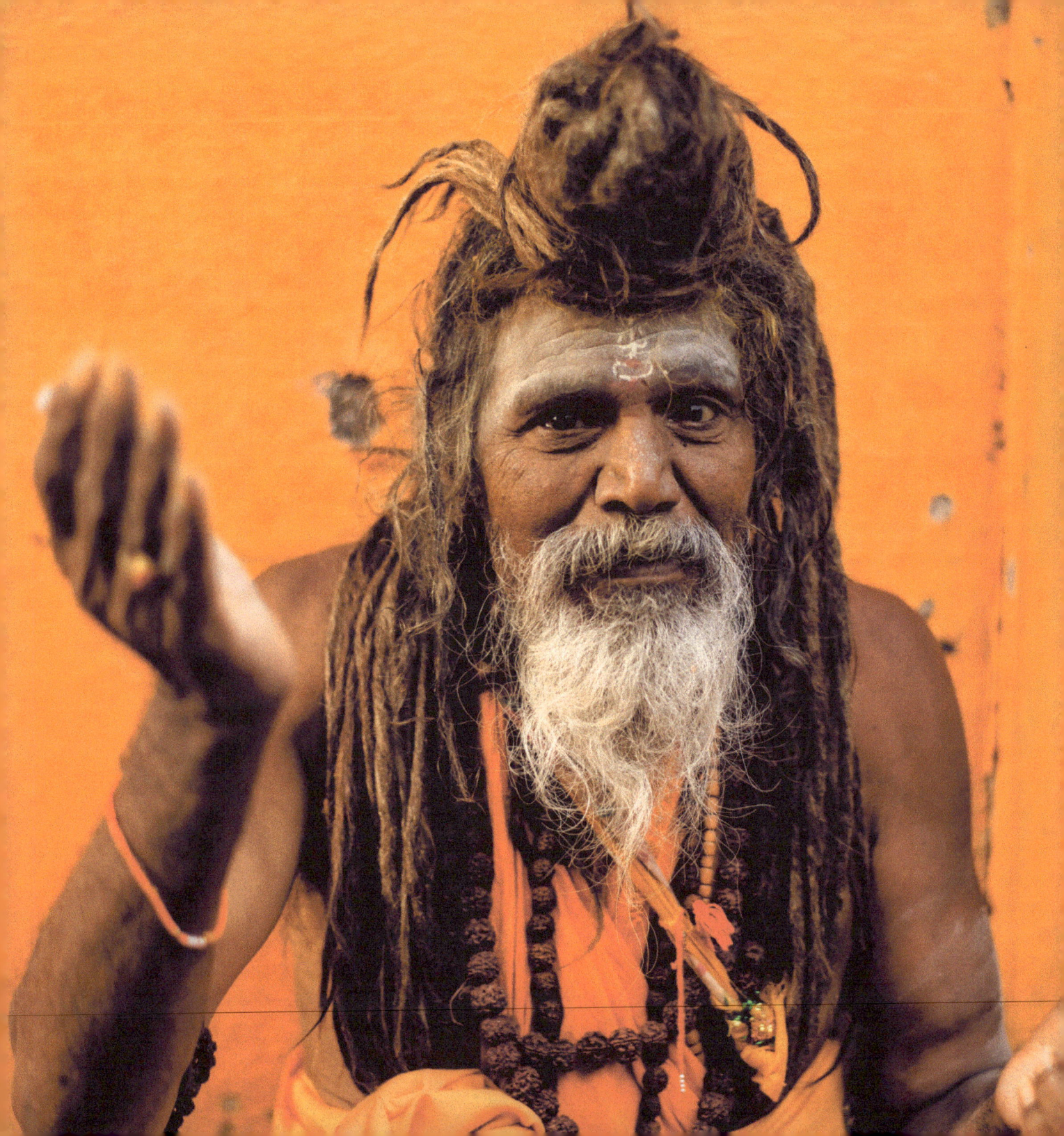

Freedom in guilt,
lightness in loss,
aliveness in pain,
love in shame.

I'm a refugee from an "-ism". I've scraped my life together from little scraps. I'm not ashamed of that. I look at this photo, this family, and I think *Ooofff!! I know THAT feeling. Happy, sad, terrified all mixed up together. Just glad I made it.* I'm not sure who to thank any more: God? Allah? Buddha? The people who have helped me along the way? Myself? I guess I'll just be thankful.

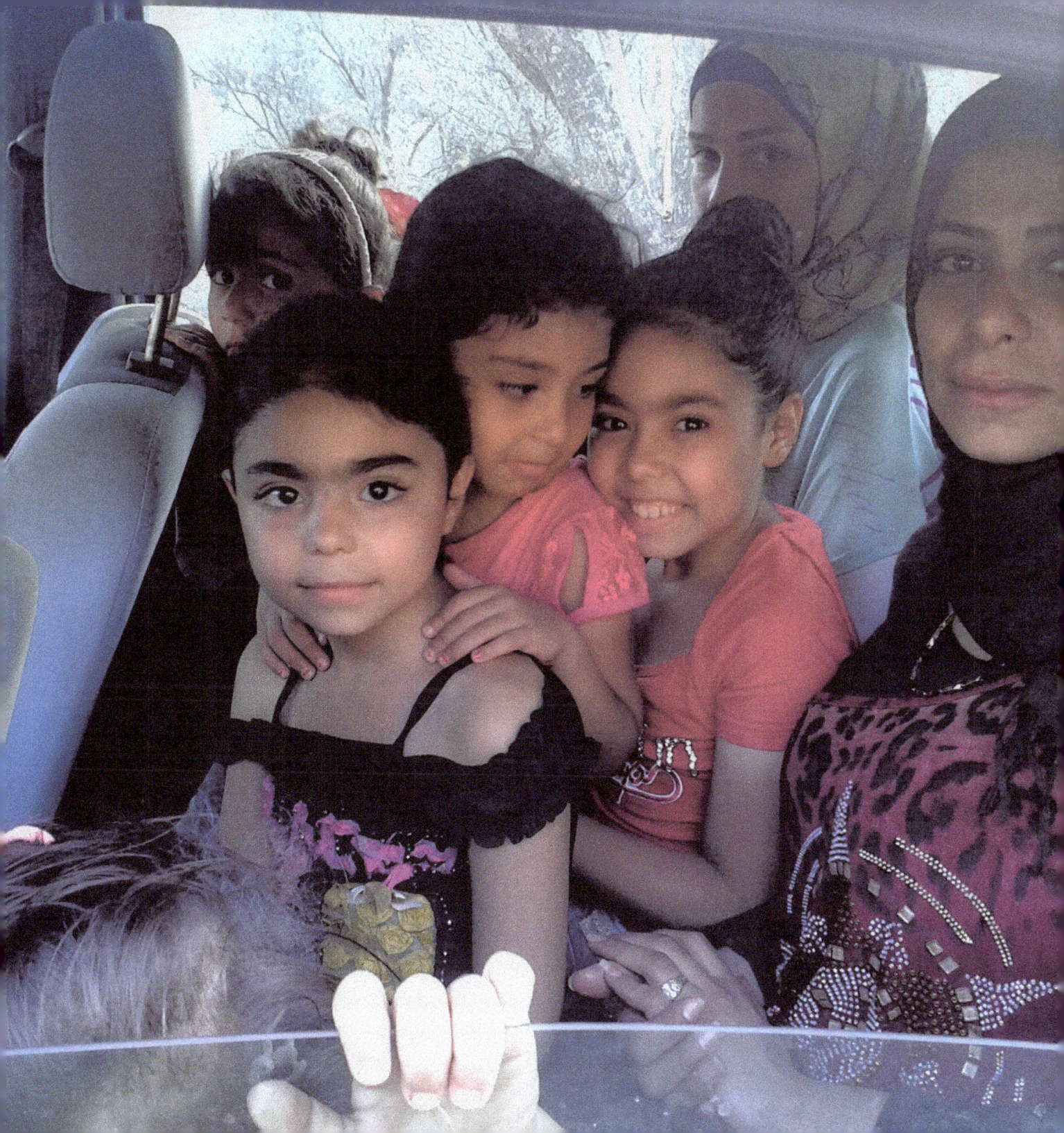

ego sum, sumus—

anomalia

There's so little
that really matters.
And so much.

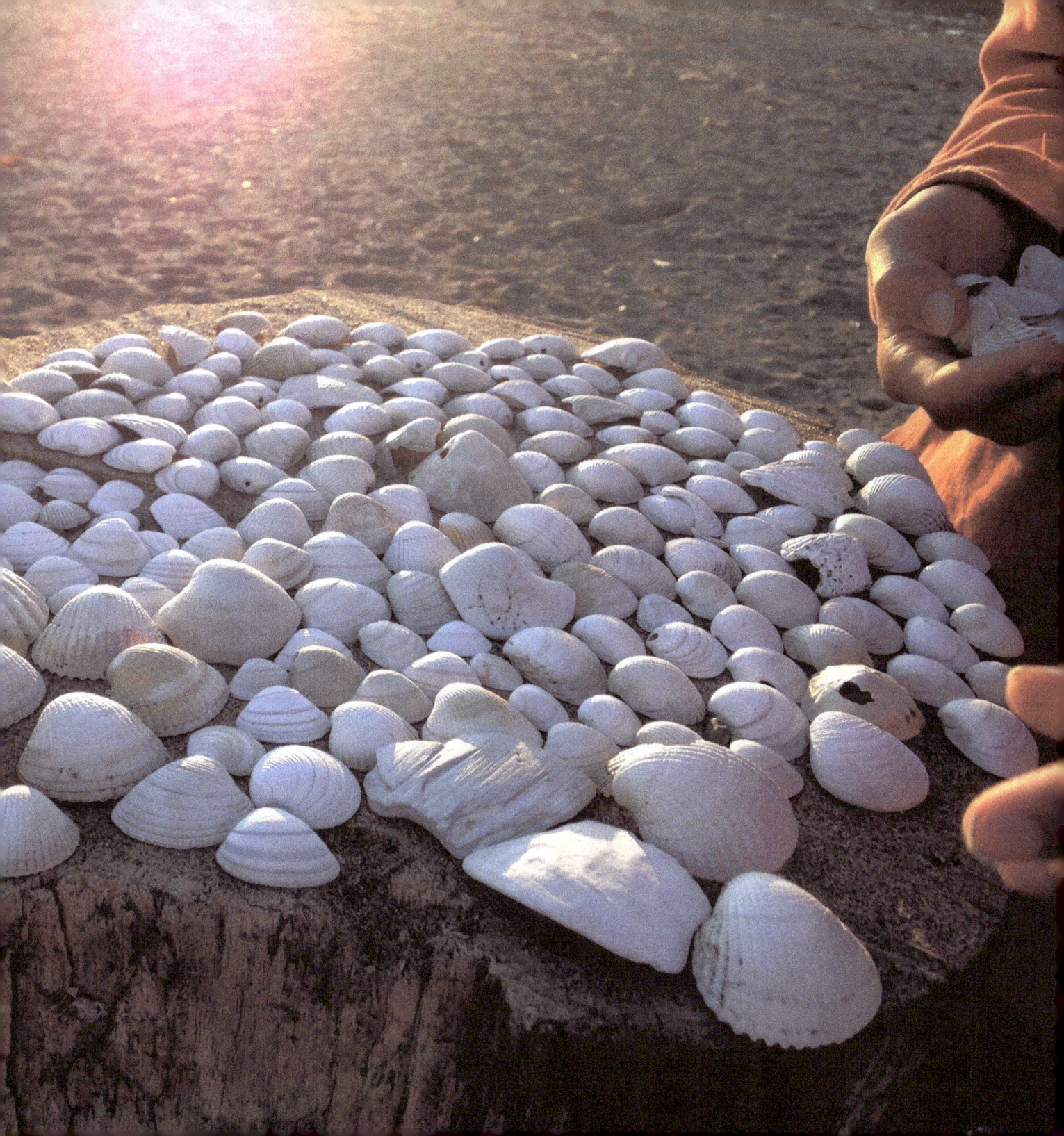

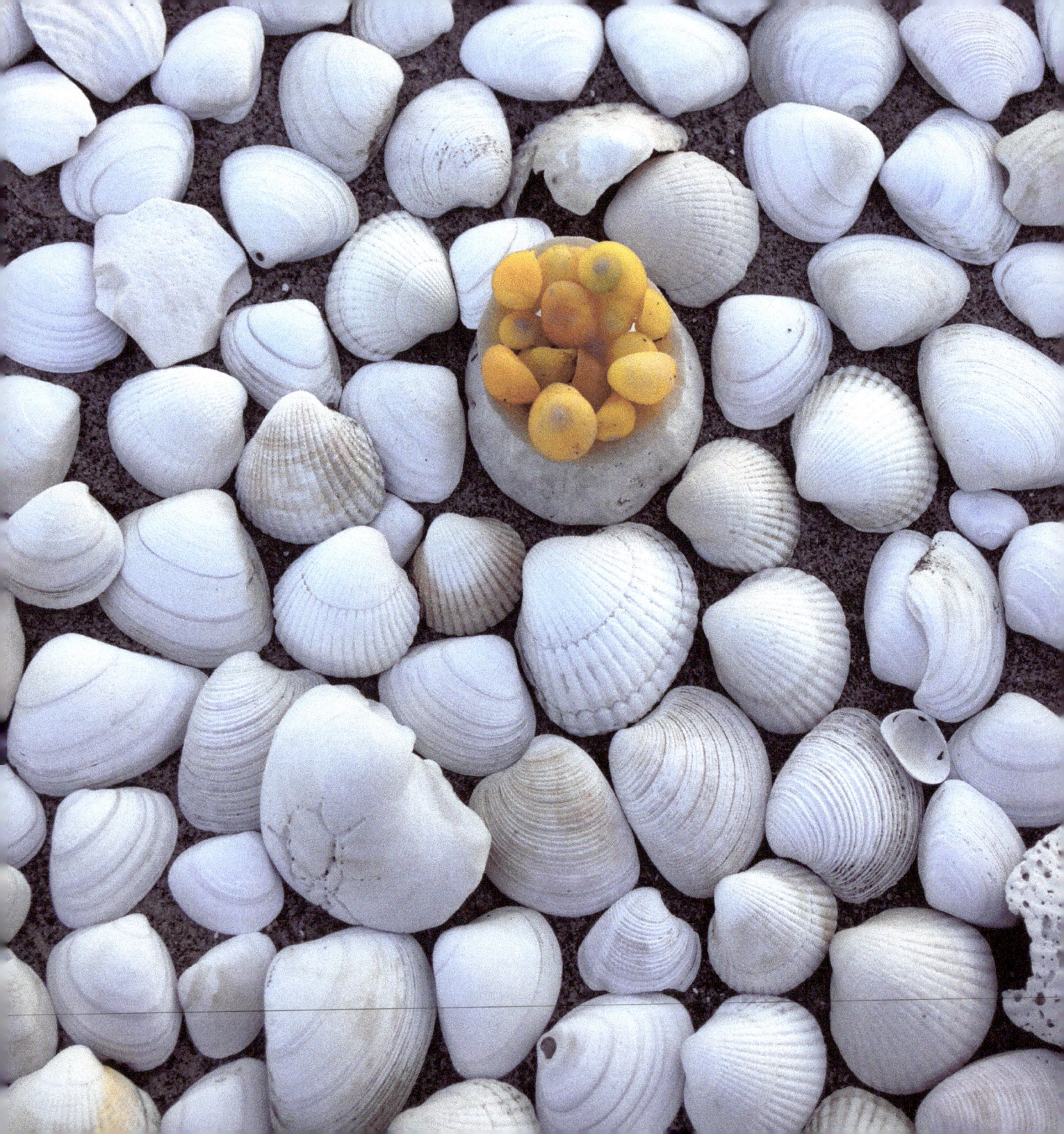

Requiescimus in lucem,
et dimitte nobis—
misertus nostri.

Vivo sunt liberandi animas suas—
sanus, sanus, sanus.

Nunc requiem—
amor exponit dolor.

Lumen ex nobis—
paradoxum.

Ego sum,
sumus—
anomalia.

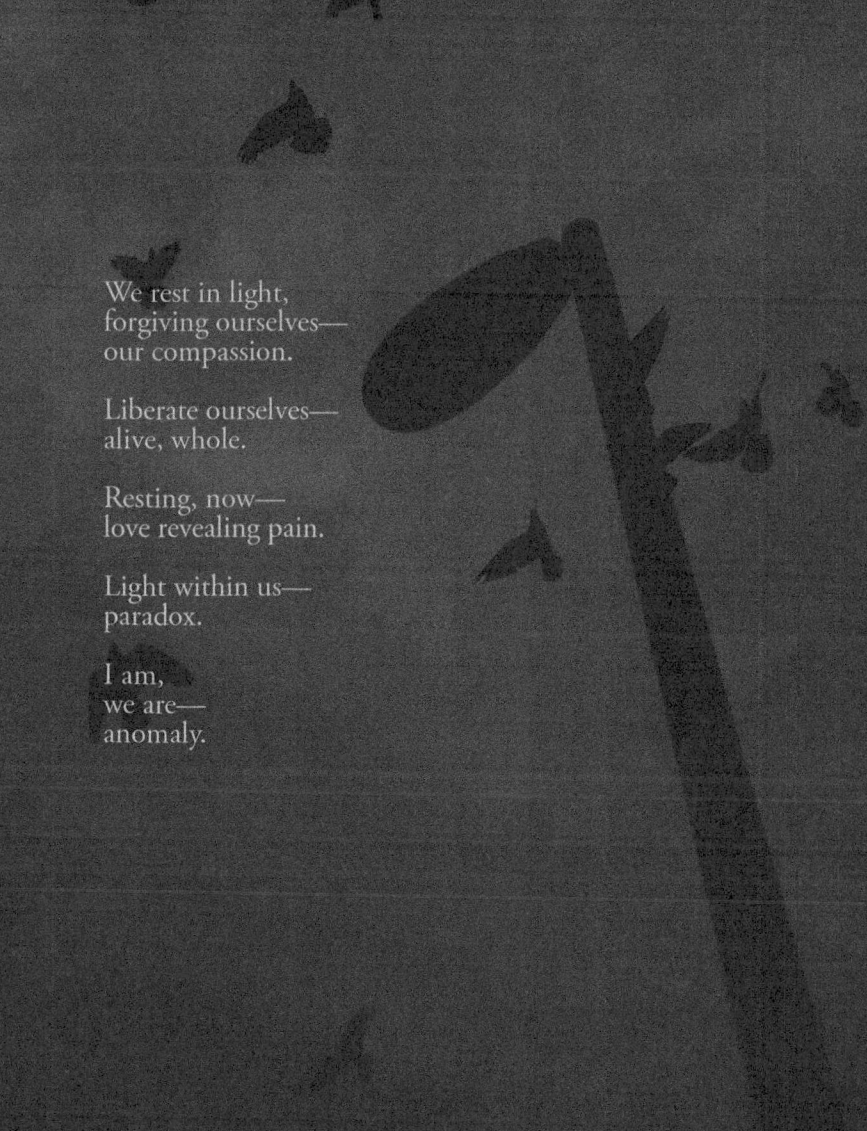

We rest in light,
forgiving ourselves—
our compassion.

Liberate ourselves—
alive, whole.

Resting, now—
love revealing pain.

Light within us—
paradox.

I am,
we are—
anomaly.

Martyn Clark and Mary F McDonough
discovered that being good, and trying to make
everyone else happy wasn't any way to live. They
decided that being Alive (with a capital A, or
maybe even ALL CAPS) is why we're all here.

Dirt is the culmination of 18 years of exploring
and letting go. Maybe it IS the letting go.

Dirt wouldn't have been possible without the support of many people.

Thanks to the Gillian Purvis Trust, for financial support; Ian Harrison, Bryony Stocker, Pascale Aebischer, Anne-Marie Monaghan, Sophie Hayley, Pauline Lindsay for their feedback on early drafts; Benjamin Clark, Dan McDonough, Villy Tentoma Zervou, Vasilis Tentomas, Stephen Smith for their photographs; Bryony Stocker, Sophie Hayley, Stephen O'Shea for proofreading.

Thanks also to the artists whose art appears in photos: Zabou (zabou.me), Yiru Feng, and Konstantinos Giotis (konstantinosgiotis.com), The Rolling People graffiti crew, among others.

www.ingramcontent.com/pod-product-compliance
Lightning Source LLC
Chambersburg PA
CBHW052143170526
45159CB00018B/3146

9780992806064